Department of the Navy
Headquarters United States Marine Corps
Washington, DC 20380-1775

17 February 2005

FOREWORD

Marine Corps Warfighting Publication (MCWP) 3-12, *Marine Corps Tank Employment*, provides Marine Corps doctrine and supporting tactics, techniques, and procedures for the employment of Marine tanks in support of the Marine air-ground task force (MAGTF). Historically, Marine tanks have played critical roles in the success of the Corps' combat operations. From World War II to Iraq, the commander's ability to effectively employ Marine tanks has provided him with a devastating direct fire capability. Today, the Marine Corps' M1A1 Abrams tanks are the most lethal direct fire and survivable weapons system within the arsenal of the ground combat element.

This publication is intended for Marine Corps combat, combat support, and combat service support unit commanders and their staffs operating with or supporting Marine tank units. It describes how the Marine Corps employs tanks throughout the range of military operations and focuses on preparing, planning, and conducting MAGTF operations with tanks.

MCWP 3-12 supersedes Fleet Marine Force Manual 9-1, *Tank Employment/Counter-mechanized Operations*, dated 1982.

BY DIRECTION OF THE COMMANDANT OF THE MARINE CORPS

J. N. MATTIS
Lieutenant General, U.S. Marine Corps
Commanding General
Marine Corps Combat Development Command

Publication Control Number: 143 000145 00

MARINE CORPS TANK EMPLOYMENT

TABLE OF CONTENTS

Chapter 3. Defensive Operations

Chapter 4. Employment with Infantry

Chapter 5. Other Tactical Operations

Chapter 7. Amphibious Operations

Chapter 8. Military Operations Other Than War

Chapter 9. Military Operations on Urbanized Terrain

Chapter 10. Scout and TOW Platoons

Appendices

Tables

Figures

Figures (Continued)

CHAPTER 1
OVERVIEW

The success of amphibious operations and subsequent operations ashore require the coordinated employment of all Marine air-ground task force (MAGTF) resources: reconnaissance, infantry, aviation, tanks, artillery, engineers, amphibious assault vehicles (AAVs) and other combat support and combat service support (CSS) units. Throughout the full range of military operations, all elements of the MAGTF are employed to achieve the effects of combined arms against enemy forces. Tank units provide the MAGTF commander the ability to attack, disrupt, and destroy enemy forces through firepower, shock effect, and maneuver in coordination with other elements of the MAGTF. The M1A1 tank offers the MAGTF a vast array of capabilities—excellent cross-country mobility, sophisticated communications, enhanced day and night target acquisition, lethal firepower to defeat most enemy mechanized platforms, highly effective armor protection—and all of its capabilities are interrelated.

Mission

The tank is designed primarily as an offensive weapon, regardless of the type of operation (defensive or offensive) conducted. Tank units, as maneuver elements, are employed throughout the full range of military operations. Therefore, the tank battalion's mission is to close with and destroy the enemy by using armor-protected firepower, shock effect, and maneuver and to provide antimechanized fire in support of the Marine division.

Employment

The tank battalion is best employed as a maneuver element without detaching units. However, the ground combat element (GCE) commander may create mechanized forces by task-organizing tank, mechanized infantry, and other combat support and CSS units based on mission, enemy, terrain and weather, troops and support available—time available (METT-T). Employment of the tank battalion must take advantage of the speed, mobility, and firepower of the organization.

To win in battle, leaders must have a clear understanding of the capabilities and limitations of their equipment in order to employ them effectively. Appendix A provides a list of the specifications, characteristics, and significant features of the M1A1 main battle tank and its supporting equipment and assists the Marine tanker and the MAGTF commander (with an attachment of tanks) in evaluating transportability, sustainment, and mobility considerations.

In extreme environments, tanks have their own unique set of employment capabilities and limitations. A detailed discussion of operating tanks in extreme environments can be found in appendix B.

Capabilities

Tanks provide five major capabilities to the MAGTF: armor-protected firepower, mobility, shock effect, extensive communications, and flexibility.

Armor-Protected Firepower

The tank is an integrated weapons system capable of defeating most targets on the battlefield. The amount and type of ammunition carried aboard the M1A1 tank allows it to engage a wide variety of targets for sustained periods of combat. The M1A1 tank's 120mm main gun is a high velocity, direct fire weapon used primarily against enemy tanks and hard targets. Along with the main gun, the M1A1 tank has one heavy machine gun (.50 cal) and two medium machine guns (7.62mm). The coaxial-mounted 7.62 machine gun is integrated into the tanks target acquisition system, which provides for extremely accurate small-arms fire.

The M1A1's armor affords protection to the tank, including its crew, from the effects of small-arms fire, shell fragments, and some direct hits depending on the type and range of the enemy weapon. Its armor also allows the tank to close with the enemy and maneuver while under either enemy fire or friendly close supporting fires with a degree of survivability that other weapons systems do not possess. The M1A1 tank also provides a significant degree of protection for the crew while operating in an environment contaminated with chemical weapons.

Mobility

Tank units are capable of conducting mobile ground combat over a broad area of operations because they can remain dispersed, yet they can mass quickly for employment at a decisive time and place. Tanks, by virtue of their full track and global positioning systems, possess a high degree of cross-country mobility that allows them to deliver firepower against several enemy locations within a short period of time. Tanks can also quickly mass the effects of their weapon systems while remaining physically dispersed in order to limit effective enemy counteraction.

Shock Effect

The shock effect on the enemy that tank units can create is both physical and psychological. Shock effect, if properly executed, can also have a favorable effect on friendly morale. Additionally, shock effect increases in proportion to the number of tanks employed. To exploit a tank's shock effect, aggressive employment of the combined-arms team is essential.

Extensive Communications

The radio is the primary means of communications for tank units. Each M1A1 tank is capable

of transmitting/receiving on one frequency while simultaneously receiving on another frequency. The use of visual signals and the single-channel ground and airborne radio system (SINCGARS) facilitates rapid and secure communication of orders and instructions.

Flexibility

Tank units are capable of responding rapidly to the everchanging environment of the battlefield. Units engaged with the enemy have the flexibility, with the proper use of supporting arms, to disengage and receive a new mission. Therefore, tanks can group, disperse, and quickly regroup again in response to changing tactical situations.

Limitations

A clear understanding of a tank's employment limitations enables commanders to both plan effectively and fully exploit the capabilities of tank units. Limitations fall into three general categories: inherent vehicle characteristics, existing obstacles, and reinforcing obstacles.

Size

The size of a tank makes it difficult to conceal in some terrain. This limitation can be overcome by positioning tanks in areas that minimize their exposure to enemy observation until they are ready to be employed.

Weight

A tank's weight prevents use of low capacity bridges and requires the use of special equipment and techniques for recovery of immobilized vehicles. Planning for the necessary support, as well as the careful selection of routes and areas of operation, reduces this limitation. Appendix A contains M1A1 weight specifications.

Noise

The noise created from the operation of a tank warns of their presence. Surprise, however, may be achieved by moving tanks forward just prior to their commitment and by advancing rapidly under the cover of supporting arms.

Visibility

Tank crews enhance visibility with vision devices; however, peripheral vision is still limited. Therefore, unless a crewmember observes the sector in which hostile actions occur, the action may go unseen. When operating in close terrain, the tank is susceptible to ambush. It is also vulnerable to mechanical damage caused by terrain (e.g., brush covered gullies) or obstacles that are hidden from view (e.g., concealed tank ditch). Conducting a detailed terrain analysis can reduce, but may not eliminate, these limitations. Infantry should accompany a tank operating in close or broken terrain and provide visual assistance in order to protect the tank from ambush.

Fuel Consumption

A tank's fuel consumption is high in comparison to a wheeled vehicle. The M1A1 tank crew can use the on board external auxiliary power unit during operational pauses to reduce the amount of fuel consumed. Careful planning and a coordinated logistic effort are required to ensure that tanks fuel requirements do not impose a logistic burden. Specifications for the refueling requirements of the M1A1 tank units can be found in chapter 6.

Maintenance

A tank's complexity requires dedicated maintenance time. Tank vehicle crews accomplish preventive maintenance during halts, rest periods, and periods of resupply without interrupting support functions. However, systematic relief of individual tanks or tank units is required to permit thorough maintenance. Failure of commanders to recognize or plan for this relief results in unnecessary and excessive tank nonavailability due to mechanical failure.

Communications

The heavy reliance upon radio communications for command, control, and coordination of a tank unit makes it vulnerable to enemy electronic warfare and/or signals intelligence efforts. The tank unit commander and tank crew must be able to operate in a hostile electronic warfare environment and employ communications security procedures to overcome this limitation.

Existing Obstacles

Of all the limiting factors that inhibit tank vehicle operations, none has a more decisive effect than terrain. The type of terrain may dictate the number of tanks that can be employed, but it will seldom prohibit their employment entirely. The full striking power of a tank is best achieved over rolling terrain that permits massing and exploitation of their cross-country mobility. Nevertheless, between the extremes of terrain—rolling terrain as opposed to impassable terrain—there is considerable ground that can still be negotiated by tanks.

In addition to obstacles created by terrain, extremes in weather can also create obstacles and reduce the efficiency of tank crews. For example, tanks may have little difficulty in snow less than 24-inches deep, but they tend to skid or slide off of embankments and are unable to negotiate slopes when the snow becomes packed or icy. Heavy rainfall usually reduces the trafficability of an area and therefore imposes restrictions on tank movements. The limiting effects of terrain and weather can be reduced by prior reconnaissance of tank routes, proper planning, and by providing for the reduction of existing obstacles that cannot be bypassed.

Reinforcing Obstacles

In past operations, the most effective reinforcing obstacle, and the one most frequently employed, was the antitank minefield. Mines, whether arranged as a barrier or planted at random, can temporarily stop the forward movement of tanks. Other reinforcing obstacles that are frequently encountered and tend to restrict the movement of tanks are tank ditches, tank traps, and roadblocks. Many of these obstacles are temporary deterrents that can be overcome by proper employment of organic weapons, equipment, and personnel. Normally, engineers can reduce difficult obstacles if given adequate time and resources.

Organization

A typical tank battalion consists of four tank companies, a headquarters and service company (H&S Co), one antitank (tube-launched, optically tracked, wire-command link guided missile [TOW]) platoon, and one scout platoon (see fig. 1-1). The tank companies are the basic tactical unit with which the battalion accomplishes its mission. The antitank platoon provides antimechanized support to the battalion. The battalion scout platoon performs reconnaissance, provides limited security, and assists in controlling movement of the battalion. Each tank battalion has 58 M1A1 tanks, 26 TOW weapons systems, 4 armored vehicle-launched bridges (AVLBs) with 8 bridges, and 6 M88A1 tank recovery vehicles.

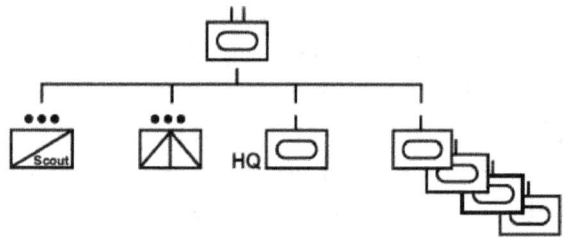

Figure 1-1. Marine Tank Battalion Organization.

Battalion Commander

The battalion commander has overall responsibility for the tank battalion. During operations, the

tank battalion commander positions himself where he can best control the battle: he may choose to be in the battalion combat operations center (COC) or he may deploy aboard the tank in order to move about the battlefield.

Executive Officer

The tank battalion's executive officer is second in command and must be prepared to assume the duties of the commander. He is the commander's principal staff assistant and advisor and directs, coordinates, and supervises the activities of the staff. The executive officer keeps the commander informed of current and developing situations, issues instructions to the staff to implement the commander's decisions, studies all situations to ensure preparedness for future operations, and represents the commander when authorized. During operations, the executive officer is normally located in the main echelon, but may also be positioned by the commander if the situation dictates. Typically, either the commander or the executive officer is present in the planning section at all times unless the executive officer is placed in command of a force organized for a specific mission or task. During displacement of the main echelon, the executive officer normally moves with and oversees the displacement to the next location unless the commander is present. However, if the commander is present, the executive officer may move with the last element to displace in order to supervise the overall effort.

S-1 (Adjutant)

The tank battalion's S-1 is the principal staff officer in matters pertaining to personnel management and administration. He monitors the administrative chain from subordinate units to higher headquarters and keeps the commander abreast of the personnel situation within the unit. The S-1 also recommends personnel policy and assists the commander in handling personnel and morale factors that influence the combat effectiveness of the unit, including supervision of legal matters and disciplinary action. During operations, the S-1 is normally located within the combat field trains and may also have the additional duty of graves registration officer.

S-2 (Intelligence)

The tank battalion's S-2 is the commander's intelligence assistant for the planning and supervision of command intelligence functions. He makes recommendations for the assignment of intelligence resources and the management and coordination of intelligence means and activities of other elements of the command. The S-2 is responsible for the production and dissemination of intelligence, counterintelligence, graphic intelligence aids, and intelligence training. During operations, the S-2 is usually in the main echelon COC and must be knowledgeable of enemy mechanized and antiarmor capabilities and work closely with the S-3 in operational planning.

S-3 (Operations)

The tank battalion's S-3 is responsible for matters pertaining to the battalion's organization, training, and tactical operations. He is responsible for planning, coordinating, and supervising the tactical employment of units; integrating fires and maneuver; planning and supervising civil-military operations; and determining priorities for allocation of personnel, weapons, equipment, and ammunition. Within the operations section are staff assistants dedicated to aviation and to nuclear, biological, and chemical (NBC) warfare defense and training. Tank battalion S-3s are usually one of the most experienced tank officers on the battalion staff and must be very familiar with all aspects of mechanized operations. Therefore, during operations, the S-3 is located in the main echelon COC and works closely with the S-4 to ensure that the tactical plan is logistically feasible.

Fire Support Coordinator

Within a tank battalion's table of organization (T/O), an artillery officer is assigned and designated as the fire support coordinator (FSC). The FSC is responsible for developing fire support plans that support the unit's scheme of maneuver and for making recommendations for priority of fire support to subordinate units. During operations, the FSC works closely with the S-3 and is usually located in the main echelon COC.

Air Officer

The air officer is the subject matter expert on matters pertaining to aviation. He is a naval aviator or naval flight officer and is under the staff cognizance of the S-3. The air officer is the officer responsible for coordinating tactical air assets and operations (e.g., close air support [CAS]) and acts as the point of contact for the two forward air controllers (FACs) assigned to the battalion. During the planning process, the air officer provides input on aviation capabilities and availability as they affect courses of action (COAs) and schemes of maneuver. The air officer has the staff responsibility for coordination of aviation support in the battalion's fire support coordination center (FSCC). The tank battalion's air officer must understand mechanized operations and the rapid and fluid nature of those operations. During operations, the air officer is usually in the main echelon COC.

NBC Officer

The NBC officer is responsible for preparing plans, annexes, and unit standing operating procedures (SOPs) on NBC defense. He develops and monitors NBC defense training of the unit and supervises and coordinates operational and technical activities essential to NBC early warning and defense. The NBC officer is under the cognizance of the S-3. During operations, the NBC officer is usually in the field train but his position depends on the nature of the NBC threat/situation. If the battalion must conduct decontamination procedures, the NBC officer will oversee those procedures. Decontamination procedures can be found in appendix C.

S-4 (Logistics)

The tank battalion's S-4 determines logistic and CSS requirements. He coordinates requirements for supply, transportation, health services, maintenance, and food services with higher headquarters. The S-4 makes recommendations for the allocation of logistic assets, prepares computation of detailed requirements for logistic support, and assists in the development of plans and orders. Within the logistic section are staff assistants for embarkation, supply, motor transport, and maintenance management. A detailed discussion regarding the personnel resident within the battalion S-4 shop is included in chapter 6.

The S-4 constantly monitors responsiveness of support. Therefore during operations, the S-4 is usually located in the field trains to ensure that the tank battalion is properly supported. However, geographic separation of units during battalion operations may require the S-4 to move throughout the area of operations to ensure that support is being maintained.

Motor Transport Officer

The tank motor transport officer (MTO) is responsible for matters concerning control of transportation and normally operates under the staff cognizance of the S-4. During operations, the MTO is usually located in the field trains. The tank battalion MTO is critical to proper logistic support and must be familiar with the demands placed on equipment during tank operations because he controls one of the largest motor transport units within the Marine division.

Maintenance Management Officer

Tank battalion maintenance management officer (MMO) has one of the largest units to maintain within the Marine division. The tank MMO is responsible to the commander, through the S-4, for the coordination and integration of all command maintenance efforts. The MMO's duties involve the management and coordination of the eight maintenance management functional areas. These functional areas are maintenance administration, personnel and training, records and reports, publications control, equipment availability, preventive maintenance checks and services and corrective maintenance, supply support, and maintenance-related programs. In order to conduct sustained mechanized operations in austere environments, the MMO's maintenance plan is critical. During operations, the MMO is usually located with the field trains.

S-6 (Communications and Electronics)

The tank S-6 is responsible for the planning and supervision of the installation, operation, and maintenance of communications systems; disseminating communications-electronics operating instructions; and managing the cryptographic material systems. The S-6 coordinates with the S-3 to ensure that communications planning and training are compatible with the overall plan. He recommends, in coordination with the S-3 and H&S Co, the location of key installations. To improve communication, the S-3 coordinates with the higher headquarters and communications officers of reinforcing, adjacent, and supporting/supported units. During operations, the tank battalion communications officer has a difficult job because of the separation of units. The distance and terrain often require the communications plan to have relay points/redundant communications to provide effective command and control (C2). In addition, the large number of radios and specialized communications equipment requires a tank battalion communications officer to have an effective preventative maintenance and training program.

Unit Command and Control

To be successful, the mechanized commander must see the battlefield and respond quickly, this can be achieved through an effective and responsive C2 system. However, the relatively large size, dispersion, and mobility of mechanized forces can pose C2 challenges for the commander. Key variables that determine how the C2 system organizes and functions include echelons of command, desires of the commander, and METT-T.

In order to see the battlefield, the commander positions himself wherever he can best influence the battle and gain as much situational awareness as possible while still being able to exercise command and control. During operations, the commander normally moves forward in order to observe and influence the course of the battle. During mechanized operations, the commander and his command group must be mounted in vehicles in order to keep up with maneuver elements.

Command Echelons

The commander establishes command echelons to assist him in the continuous collection, processing, and dissemination of combat information and orders. Control of the battle is focused through only one command echelon at a time. Command echelons must have the requisite mobility to locate where the commander wishes and should be as mobile as the rest of the unit. The echelon in which the unit or subordinate commander is located or from which the commander operates is called a command post. Depending on the situation, the commander may establish as many as three command echelons: the tactical echelon, the main echelon, and the rear echelon. Command echelons may also be split into increments to facilitate displacement and survivability.

Tactical Echelon

The commander normally collocates with the main effort during critical events and focuses on the current operations of committed forces. Therefore, the tactical echelon provides the commander freedom of movement and the information required to maintain situational awareness. The tank battalion's table of equipment includes

a section of tanks that enable the commander to establish the battalion's tactical command post or tactical air coordinator (airborne) command post. These tanks allow the commander to position himself forward, stay mobile, and maintain the communications and situational awareness necessary to command and control his unit. His survivability is directly related to their armor protection and capability to rapidly displace.

Main Echelon

The main echelon is designed, manned, and equipped to direct the actions of all organic, attached, and supporting units. The main echelon is responsible for monitoring and directing current operations and planning future operations. The main echelon includes a COC (see the Combat Operations Center paragraph on page 1-8 for more information on the COC).

When the commander is located forward of the main echelon during combat, he monitors communications between the COC and higher and subordinate units. He also might designate an individual, normally the executive officer or S-3, to act in his behalf in the event that communications with the COC are lost.

Rear Echelon

The principal function of the rear echelon is to support combat operations by providing command and control of rear area operations. The S-1 and S-4 are normally located in the rear echelon. The rear echelon must be capable of monitoring the activities of the forward units and the other two echelons. Normally, the rear echelon is collocated with, or sited near, CSS units to facilitate logistical efforts.

Increments

If a command element is split into increments, the commander organizes both increments with nearly identical structure. Typically, these increments are referred to as alpha and bravo. The alpha increment is usually composed of the S-2,

S-3, FSC, and principal fire support liaison officers. Normally, the primary function of the alpha command element is to command and control the operation that is underway. The bravo increment is usually composed of the assistants for each of the functional areas: S-2A, S-3A, assistant FSC, etc. The bravo command element monitors the current tactical situation and is immediately prepared to assume control in the event that the alpha command element becomes disabled or if operations become protracted. The bravo command may also be tasked to conduct future plans, maintain records, and submit reports. If the force is extended, the bravo command element may be used as a relay to higher and supporting units. The alpha and bravo command elements may be consolidated when required by the tactical situation. Consolidation allows full utilization of the entire staff for planning and the establishment of a single watch section and provides more time to rest personnel.

Combat Operations Center

The COC is the primary operational agency required to control the tactical operations of a command that employs ground and aviation combat, combat support, and CSS elements, or portions thereof. A COC is a unit headquarters where the commander and the staff perform their activities. The COC continually monitors, records, and supervises operations and includes all personnel and communications required to perform its mission. The COC also includes the FSCC.

Most units have established SOPs for COC operations. Well-developed SOPs and repeated rehearsals for passing command and control between increments are vital to success. When task-organized as a mechanized force, these procedures may have to be modified to maintain the ability to echelon the command element, maintain a high degree of COC mobility, and to make rapid decisions required in mechanized operations.

Typically, the tank battalion COC is comprised of an assault amphibian vehicle command model 7 (AAVC7) and an assault amphibian vehicle personnel model 7 (AAVP7) chase vehicle. The lack of space in these vehicles limits the number of personnel that can be carried on board. This arrangement often requires staff members and commanders to personally monitor radios in order to facilitate rapid decisionmaking. All staff officers operating inside the AAVC7 must maintain a high level of situational awareness. Standard message form usage within the command vehicle is imperative when the primary officers are operating on a number of radio nets. Occasionally, staff members should conduct a brief staff meeting to coordinate efforts.

The high speed, high stress, and continuous nature of mechanized operations can create a great deal of physical and mental fatigue. To provide rest and allow for continuous operations, personnel assigned to the COC should be organized into work shifts.

The AAVC7 has map boards mounted in front of the staff stations that can be removed and mounted on the outside of the vehicle for briefings. Ideally, S-2, S-3, and FSC maps/charts should be in close proximity to allow the commander and principal staff officers to view this information at one time and from a general location. However, consideration must be given to a system of maintaining and changing graphics while the vehicles are on the move.

AAVC7 can have communication problems. Many of these problems are caused by tank units operating at vast distances from one another, engine noise when moving, located in a poor position for communications, and poor preventive maintenance. Some of the following considerations may alleviate these problems:

• Utilize communications personnel to position backup radios so they do not interfere with other vehicle radios. Do not operate strap-on radios unless the primary radio is not functional.

- When moving and engine noise interferes with an important transmission, conduct a hasty and temporary halt. Sometimes reducing the speed of movement will improve the transmission.
- Communications requirements should be considered when selecting a position for a temporary or extended halt. If communications is poor, often moving to another position will greatly improve communications.
- Occasionally, in the fast-paced nature of a mechanized operation, time is not allowed for preventive maintenance. During extended halts, backup radios may be used while preventive maintenance is conducted on vehicle radios.
- Backup handsets and headsets should be maintained in each command vehicle.

During a mechanized operation there are temporary halts and extended halts. Temporary halts are relatively short term and staff personnel operate outside of the vehicle. During extended halts, chase vehicles move forward and personnel in those vehicles are employed in the COC. Consideration should be given to notifying subordinate units and all vehicles in the command group of the anticipated duration of the halt, which allows the staff to begin preparations for the COC stopping and becoming static.

Consideration should also be given to creating SOPs for immediate emplacement and displacement. These procedures might include designated teams that camouflage the vehicles, establish security, lay wire, remote antennas, and configure the COC for stationary operation. These and other procedures for emplacement and displacement should be trained and executed as drills.

Procedures that might be included in operations from a static position include the following:

- Establish a standard configuration of the COC.
- Establish standard watch sections.
- Establish standard locations for resting. A designated sleeping position for each member of the command groups will simplify finding a needed member of the group in a hurry or during periods of darkness.
- Establish a method of providing power to the vehicle radios. The AAVC7's radios can operate off the vehicle's batteries; however, they must be recharged periodically. There will be a brief disruption of all radios when the engine is started. The engine should not be started without the approval of the watch officer. While the engine is running, noise may become a problem. Another method is to slave another vehicle to the AAVC7 to provide the required power. Any vehicle with a North Atlantic Treaty Organization (NATO) slave adapter may provide the required power.
- Establish standardized force resupply system for the command group.

Tank Battalion Fire Support Coordination Center

The tank battalion FSCC is organized similarly to that of an infantry battalion. The tank battalion FSCC normally consists of an air officer, an artillery officer FSC, and the battalion S-3. While the battalion FSCC is built around this nucleus, the fire support coordination cell is augmented with personnel and equipment appropriate to the fire support coordination functions to be conducted. Augmentation sources may include Marine Corps and external sources; for example, watchstanders may require individuals with specific skills such as electronic warfare, unmanned aerial vehicles, air defense, or proficiency in fire support coordination.

During an operation, FSCC staff members are required to plan fires, conduct targeting, and integrate fires simultaneously with maneuver elements. The FSCC's coordinating responsibilities include the requirement to disseminate timely fire support information; to institute coordination measures as required; and to integrate fire support activities that affect two or more fire support agencies, subordinate elements, or adjacent units.

Fire Support Coordinator

The FSC in a tank battalion is normally an artillery captain by T/O. His responsibilities include—

- Supervising the operation of the FSCC, including organizing and training personnel.
- Advising the battalion commander on all fire support matters.
- Developing the fire support plan based on the scheme of maneuver, the intelligence estimate, requests from subordinate units, and the fire support available.
- Coordinating all fire support within the battalion zone of action.
- Processing of target information, including the shelling report.
- Ensuring the safety of friendly troops from our own fire support.

Air Officer

The air officer is a pilot or naval flight officer and is normally a captain by T/O. His responsibilities include—

- Advising the battalion commander/FSC on all air support matters.
- Developing the air fire plan based on the scheme of maneuver, the intelligence estimate, assets available, and coordination with the FSC.
- Submitting air requests.
- Coordinating the actions of FACs.

Artillery Liaison Officer

The artillery liaison officer is normally a lieutenant provided by a direct support artillery battalion. His responsibilities include—

- Advising the battalion commander/FSC on all artillery support matters.
- Developing the artillery fire plan based on the scheme of maneuver, the intelligence estimate, assets available, and coordination with the FSC.

- Passing requirements for support to the appropriate artillery fire direction center for action.
- Coordinating artillery unit requirements with the battalion commander/FSC.
- Coordinating the actions of the artillery forward observers.

Mortar Liaison Noncommissioned Officer

The mortar liaison noncommissioned officer is normally a sergeant provided by the weapons company of an infantry battalion if that unit is tasked to support a tank battalion. He is typically accompanied by two mortar forward observers who will travel with the tank companies. His responsibilities include—

- Advising the battalion commander/FSC on all mortar employment issues.
- Developing the mortar fire plan based on the scheme of maneuver, the intelligence estimate, assets available, and coordination with the FSC.
- Coordinating the actions of the mortar forward observers.
- Coordinating mortar platoon requirements with the battalion commander/FSC.

Naval Gunfire Liaison Officer

The naval gunfire liaison officer is normally a Navy lieutenant provided by the direct support artillery battalion. His responsibilities include—

- Advising the battalion commander/FSC on all naval gunfire support matters.
- Developing the naval gunfire support plan based on the scheme of maneuver, the intelligence estimate, assets available, and coordination with the FSC.
- Assisting in calling for naval gunfire support.
- Coordinating the actions of the naval gunfire spot team.
- Passing requirements for support to the appropriate naval gunfire support ship.

Target Information Officer

The target information officer is normally the battalion S-2 officer. His responsibilities concerning target intelligence include—

- Disseminating target information and intelligence to the FSCC.
- Advising the battalion commander/FSC on enemy weapons capabilities.
- Keeping appropriate records of targets.

Command Relationships

Command relationships and levels of authority, although authoritative, must be adapted to meet mission requirements. Commanders must have the flexibility to establish nonstandard relationships when required by the situation. Collectively, command relationships and levels of authority provide the flexibility necessary to organize forces to respond to all situations. Command relationships foster understanding and freedom of action and establish the basis for interaction among unit commanders.

When a Marine unit is under the command of a senior Marine unit, the subordinate Marine unit is either organic or attached. (If organic, a unit is assigned to and forms an essential part of a military organization. If attached, a unit or personnel is temporarily placed in an organization.) When a Marine unit is in a support relationship, one element or unit of the MAGTF provides a required capability to another element.

Units with tank attachments must be aware of the logistical and tactical challenges inherent with armor. Unless the attachment orders qualify the degree of control involved, attachment of a tank unit to an infantry battalion or regiment implies that the infantry battalion or regiment assumes full responsibility for the tank unit's logistics, administration, training, and operations—the tank unit is under the command of the unit to which it is attached. However, transfer and promotion responsibility normally remain with the command to which the tank unit is organic.

CHAPTER 2
OFFENSIVE OPERATIONS

When the MAGTF is involved in offensive operations, the main effort is weighted with superior combat power. Superior combat power allows the MAGTF to retain the initiative, set the tempo of operations, and achieve decisive results on the battlefield. Tank units—by their inherent speed, mobility, armor-protected firepower, and shock effect—contribute greatly to the GCE's combat power while operating in the offensive. Tank units also provide the GCE with flexibility that allows the commander to rapidly shift his main effort. The inherent flexibility of a tank unit allows the commander to maintain the momentum of attack by quickly focusing the combat power of the force at various locations on the battlefield.

SECTION I. TYPES OF OFFENSIVE OPERATIONS

There are four general types of offensive operations: movement to contact, attack, exploitation, and pursuit. See Marine Corps Warfighting Publication (MCWP) 1-0, *Marine Corps Operations*, for a detailed discussion of each type of offensive operation.

Movement to Contact

A movement to contact develops the situation and establishes or regains contact with the enemy. It is normally employed when the enemy situation is vague or not specific enough to conduct a deliberate attack. Most mechanized operations begin with a movement to contact, regardless of whether or not a deliberate attack is planned on the final objective. The movement to contact is characterized by decentralized control and rapid commitment of forces from the march. A movement to contact ends when the commander has to deploy the main body to conduct an attack or establish a defense.

A tank battalion executing a movement to contact mission is normally given a zone of action or an axis of attack and an objective. Inherent to planning a movement to contact is the assumption that enemy contact will be made and actions on contact must be immediate and successful. A properly executed movement to contact allows the tank battalion commander to make initial contact with minimum forces and to expedite the employment and concentration of the force.

Key considerations of a movement to contact using mechanized forces include:

- Focusing all efforts on finding and fixing the enemy.
- Initiating contact with the smallest element.
- Maintaining freedom of action and executing actions on contact wherever the enemy is encountered.
- Concentrating the effects of overwhelming combat power at the decisive point.

A mechanized force conducting a movement to contact normally organizes in an approach march formation with advance, flank, and rear security elements protecting the main body.

Advance Guard

The advance guard protects its main body against ground observation and surprise from the front. It prevents premature deployment of the main body and provides adequate time and space for the main body to deploy for combat. The advance guard destroys the enemy's security and combat forces and reports and breaches obstacles within its capability. It may be directed to report and bypass small enemy forces. When the advance guard comes in contact with a superior enemy force, it normally attempts to seize key terrain and conduct a hasty defense to facilitate deployment of the main body. It operates within supporting range of the main body. The advance guard prevents unnecessary delay of the main body and defers the deployment of the main body as long as possible. Reconnaissance elements normally operate to the front and flanks of the advance guard.

A tank or mechanized company usually provides the advance guard element for a tank or mechanized battalion (the main body). As the company moves along the axis of advance, it usually will have a 3 to 5 kilometer frontage if unhindered by terrain or obstacles. Advance guard responsibilities include—

- Providing security and early warning for the main body and facilitating its uninterrupted advance.
- Conducting reconnaissance to locate enemy forces along the unit's axis of advance.
- Conducting actions on contact to retain freedom of maneuver for the main body.
- Calling for indirect fires and/or close air support to impede or harass the enemy. The advance guard for a tank battalion usually has a forward observer and FAC located with the company command to help execute these missions.
- Destroying enemy reconnaissance units. Tanks are well-suited to destroy enemy mechanized reconnaissance due to their ability to acquire and kill targets at long ranges and to mass fires quickly (daylight or night).
- Finding, fixing, defeating, destroying, or containing enemy security forces in order to retain freedom of maneuver for the main body. A tank's ability to acquire and kill targets at long ranges and to mass fires quickly allows it to protect the main body and suppress the enemy.

Bypassing and reporting obstacles or acting as the tank or mechanized unit's support or breach force during breaching operations.

Flank and Rear Security

When adjacent units do not protect the flanks of a command it is necessary to provide protection by using a portion of the force to conduct flank security. Flank security missions include both guard and screen missions. The purpose of flank security is to protect the main body from observation, direct fire, and surprise attack. The mission and available combat power of the flank security element depends on METT-T. Flank security elements are subordinate to the main body. They travel on routes parallel to the main body, either by continuously marching or moving by alternating bounds. Flank security for a tank or mechanized unit must be far enough away from the main body to provide early warning and allow the main body freedom of maneuver. However, flank security should remain close enough to the main body to be responsive and provide mutual support to the main body.

The rear security element protects the rear of the main body from attack and/or observation. When properly resourced, the rear security element can be given a screen, guard, or cover mission.

Main Body

Ideally, the main body is unhindered during the movement to contact and is well positioned to conduct an attack against main enemy forces and seize the final objective. Elements from the main body may be deployed to eliminate small pockets of resistance bypassed by the advance guard. However, the main body must not be committed piecemeal. Committing tank units piecemeal diminishes their ability to mass effective fires and provides a shock effect. Tank battalions or mechanized forces normally keep the majority of its tanks within the main body and employ the main body to decisively defeat the enemy and/or secure the objective.

Maximum consideration is given to attacks upon the enemy flanks and rear before the enemy is prepared to counter these envelopments. Attacks by the main body may consist of a coordinated attack by the entire main body or an attack from a march column conducted while the remainder of the main body deploys. Piecemeal commitment is to be avoided except when rapidity of action is essential due to fleeting windows of opportunity and when local combat superiority can be achieved at a decisive point. Mechanized units use all available supporting arms to suppress the enemy forces in contact, disrupt its attacking formations, and neutralize its indirect fire assets.

Actions with Contact Imminent

The enemy situation becomes clearer as the advance guard conducts actions on contact. Key actions include developing the situation and refocusing reconnaissance, surveillance, and target acquisition (RSTA) assets. The mechanized force must remain flexible enough to rapidly exploit both intelligence and combat information. All RSTA assets are focused on determining the enemy's dispositions and ensuring the commitment of friendly forces under optimal conditions.

As contact becomes imminent, advance guards move forward on a progressively broader front. Based upon the situation, the advance guard engages in accordance with the commander's plan or seizes terrain essential to the development of its main body that affords essential observation.

Actions After Contact

Once contact with a strong enemy is made, measures are taken—hasty attack, hasty defense, report and bypass, delay and withdraw—to develop the situation and protect the deployment of the mechanized force. Knowledge of hostile dispositions, particularly enemy flank locations, is important to provide the essential information upon which the commander can base his plan of attack. When the security elements of

mechanized forces lack the strength to develop the situation fully, they may be quickly reinforced by main body elements to obtain adequate knowledge of hostile dispositions before the coordinated attack is launched.

When strong resistance is met, reconnaissance units are quickly withdrawn and replaced or reinforced by the combat elements of the advance guard. Reconnaissance units are then employed on the flanks to screen the enemy's main force, conduct further reconnaissance, or harass the hostile flanks and rear. Every effort is made to retain the initiative and to prevent the enemy from stabilizing the situation. Premature deployment of the main body is costly in terms of time, resources, and disclosure of the main effort.

While the main body is deploying for attack, the advance guard gains contact and continues to develop the enemy situation. Their mission is to determine the strength and dispositions of the enemy and the location of his flanks in order to provide the commander as complete a picture as possible before conducting an attack.

Hasty Attack

The hasty attack is characterized by rapid reconnaissance to determine the size and location of the enemy force to allow a rapid attack of the enemy by available forces.

Hasty Defense

The hasty defense is characterized by the seizure of key terrain to facilitate the deployment of the main body. The enemy reaction to such action frequently indicates both the strength and disposition of the enemy force.

Report and Bypass

Bypass criteria are established by the commander and are based on METT-T. Typically, commanders specify bypass criteria based on the size of the unit.

Delay

Units conduct delays when forces are insufficient to either attack or defend or when the design of the operation dictates maneuvering the enemy into an area for subsequent attack.

Withdraw

Withdrawal is normally the last option and only occurs when the enemy has an overwhelming superiority and the survival of the advance guard is at risk. The unit normally withdraws only after receiving permission and then only withdraws back toward the main body.

Meeting Engagement

A movement to contact often results in a meeting engagement. Meeting engagements are clashes that take place at unexpected places and times when forces are not fully prepared for battle. Such encounters often occur in small-unit operations and when reconnaissance has been ineffective. A meeting engagement may also occur when each opponent is aware of the other and both decide to attack without delay to obtain a tactical advantage. A meeting engagement may result in confusion, delay, or even in the premature employment of the main body before the commander has set conditions for decisive action. The premature employment of the main body slows the mechanized force's tempo of operations and may cause it to lose the initiative.

Attack

The purpose of an attack is to defeat, destroy, or neutralize the enemy. An attack emphasizes maximum application of combat power, coupled with bold maneuver, shock effect in the assault, and prompt exploitation of success. Principal elements in an attack include preventing effective enemy maneuver or counteraction, maneuvering to gain an advantage, delivering an overwhelming assault to destroy the enemy, and exploiting

the advantages gained. Commanders conduct various types of attacks to achieve different effects: spoiling attack, counterattack, feint, demonstration, reconnaissance in force, and raid.

The commander conducts either a hasty or a deliberate attack based on time available. A hasty attack is an attack in which preparation time is traded for speed in order to exploit an opportunity. (Joint Pub [JP] 1-02, *Department of Defense Dictionary of Military and Associated Terms*) Typically, a hasty attack is the result of a meeting engagement. The goal of a hasty attack is to destroy the enemy before he is able to concentrate or establish a defense. In order to maintain momentum or retain initiative, minimum time is devoted to preparation. Those forces readily available are committed immediately to the attack. A hasty attack seeks to take advantage of the enemy's lack of readiness and involves boldness, surprise, and speed to achieve success. A deliberate attack is characterized by preplanned coordinated employment of firepower and maneuver to close with and destroy the enemy. The deliberate attack is a fully coordinated operation that is conducted when preparation time is available for lengthy reconnaissance, precise planning, and rehearsals. Deliberate attacks normally include large volumes of supporting fires, main and supporting attacks, and deception measures. Tanks are best suited for either a hasty or deliberate attack because of their speed, mobility, and armor-protected firepower.

Spoiling Attack

A spoiling attack is a tactical maneuver employed to seriously impair a hostile attack while the enemy is in the process of forming or assembling for an attack. It is a pre-emptive, limited objective attack aimed at preventing, disrupting, or delaying the enemy's ability to launch an attack. It may be conducted like a raid with a planned withdrawal. The circumstances in which a spoiling attack is conducted normally preclude full exploitation. All or part of the reserve normally conducts a spoiling attack; therefore, it may require that another reserve force is temporarily formed.

Counterattack

Counterattacks are limited objective attacks conducted by part or all of a defensive force to prevent the enemy from attaining the objectives of his attack. It may be conducted to regain lost ground, destroy enemy advance units, and wrest the initiative from the enemy. It may also be a precursor to resuming offensive operations. The circumstances in which a counterattack is conducted normally preclude full exploitation. Normally the commander will attempt to retain his reserve to conduct a decisive counterattack once the enemy has committed his main force to the attack. All or part of the reserve normally conducts a counterattack; therefore, it may require that another reserve force is temporarily formed. Tank units counterattack by two methods: counterattack by fire and movement or counterattack by fire. The intent of the counterattack by fire and movement method is to close with and destroy the enemy. The intent of the counterattack by fire method is to use weapon standoff and/or cover to full advantage and destroy the enemy by direct fires.

When tanks counterattack by fire and movement it is also referred to as support by fire. During conduct of the counterattack by fire and movement, the tank or mechanized unit commander takes the following actions to plan and execute the attack:

- Conduct a line of sight analysis to identify advantageous positions for tanks and other weapon systems to support by fire.
- Plan to integrate both indirect and direct fires.
- Determine triggers for lifting and/or shifting direct and indirect fires.
- Plan and rehearse actions on contact, as well as maneuver to support by fire positions.
- Plan for class V expenditures depending on the mission.

- Use infantry to support mounted platforms whenever possible. They can be used to secure positions for vehicles, augment anti-tank fires with Javelins, and provide local security for vehicles.
- Continually scan the area of operations to acquire, track, and destroy any enemy threatening the movement of the attack.
- Maintain 360-degree security.
- Use the tank's main guns to destroy enemy armor while other systems engage enemy light armor or vehicles.
- Move and maneuver continually to increase survivability of the attacking force.

Counterattacking by fire is also referred to as attack by fire. The planning and execution considerations are the same as for counterattack by fire and movement; however, counterattack by fire takes advantage of long-range standoff fires inherent in tanks and other antitank systems. Counterattacking by fire most often is conducted from dominating terrain and is used when the mission or situation does not dictate occupying enemy positions.

Feint

A feint is a limited objective attack made at a place other than that of the main effort with the aim of distracting the enemy's attention away from the main effort, and it involves direct, physical contact with the enemy. A feint must be sufficiently strong to confuse the enemy as to the location of the main effort. Ideally, a feint causes the enemy to shift forces to the diversion and away from the main effort. Feints are usually shallow, limited objective attacks conducted before or during the attack of the main effort. Tanks are effective in confusing the enemy into thinking he is being attacked by the main effort when he is not. The appearance of tanks attacking can cause the enemy commander to commit his reserve forces to counter the feint; thereby leaving him no reserves when the main body attacks him from a different direction and/or place. The employment of a tank unit in a feint must be heavily weighed against the loss of combat power that is rendered unavailable to the main effort.

Demonstration

Demonstrations are operations designed to divert enemy attention, which allows MAGTF forces to execute decisive action elsewhere. A demonstration is a show of force that threatens an attack at another location but does not make contact with the enemy. The commander executes a demonstration by an actual or simulated massing of combat power, troop movements, or some other activity designed to indicate the preparations for or the beginning of attack at a point other than the main effort. The employment of a tank unit in a demonstration must be weighed with the potential loss of combat power that could be applied to the main effort.

Reconnaissance in Force

The reconnaissance in force is a deliberate attack by major forces to obtain information and to locate and test enemy dispositions, strengths, and reactions. While the primary purpose of a reconnaissance in force is to gain information, the commander must be prepared to exploit any opportunity. The protection afforded by the tank battalion can be used to protect the force; however, if the situation warrants, the tank battalion can also exploit any opportunity. A reconnaissance in force usually develops information more rapidly and in more detail than other reconnaissance methods. Since a reconnaissance in force is conducted when knowledge of the enemy is vague, combined-arms forces containing tanks are often employed because the force is capable of disengagement if superior enemy forces are encountered.

Raid

A raid is an attack, usually small-scale, involving a penetration of hostile territory for a specific purpose other than seizing and holding terrain. It ends with a planned withdrawal upon completion of the assigned mission. The organization and composition of the raid force are tailored to the mission. Raids are characterized by surprise and swift, precise, and bold action. Tanks can be employed on mechanized raids to destroy enemy installations and facilities, disrupt enemy command and control or support activities, divert enemy attention, and secure information.

Exploitation

Exploitation is an offensive operation that usually follows a successful attack and is designed to disorganize the enemy in depth. Exploitation extends the initial success of the attack by preventing the enemy from disengaging, withdrawing, and re-establishing an effective defense. The objective of the exploitation is the destruction of enemy forces to the point where they have no alternative but surrender or flight. The mechanized force is ideally suited for exploitation operations because of its inherent speed, mobility, and shock action.

The commander must be prepared to exploit every attack without delay. In the hasty attack, the force in contact normally continues the attack, transitioning to exploitation. In the deliberate attack, the commander's principal tool for exploitation is normally the reserve. The reserve is generally positioned where it can exploit the success of the main effort or supporting efforts. Typical missions for the exploitation force include cutting lines of communication, isolating and destroying enemy units, and disrupting enemy command and control. The psychological effect of an exploitation creates confusion and apprehension throughout the enemy force, reduces the enemy's capability to react, and may be decisive. Enemy forces, which cannot jeopardize the mission, are suppressed, bypassed, and reported to higher headquarters for clearing by follow-on forces.

Opportunities for exploitation occur when—

- The enemy is having difficulty maintaining his position.
- There is a significant increase in the number of prisoners captured.
- Enemy units disintegrate after initial contact.
- The enemy lacks an organized defense.
- There are confirmed reports of the capture of or absence of enemy leaders.
- There is an increase in abandoned material.
- Equipment from various units is intermixed in formations or columns.
- Enemy fire decreases in intensity and effectiveness.
- Enemy artillery, C2 facilities, and supply dumps are overrun.

Once the exploitation is begun, it is carried out to the final objective. An exploitation continues day and night, the enemy is given no relief from offensive pressure. The exploiting force retains terrain only as necessary to accomplish its mission. The exploiting force commander must be careful not to dissipate combat power in achieving minor tactical successes or in reducing small enemy forces.

Exploitation should be decentralized. The mechanized unit commander maintains sufficient control to alter the direction of the command or to prevent its overextension. He relies on his subordinates to find the fastest way to their objectives, to deploy as necessary to fight, and to seize all opportunities to destroy the enemy and accelerate the tempo of operations. The commander uses minimum control measures, but issues clear instructions concerning seizure of key terrain and the size of enemy forces, which may be bypassed. The exploitation force and the follow-on support force must maintain direct communications.

The commander must exercise aggressive and demanding leadership to keep units advancing. When fatigue, disorganization, or attrition has weakened the force or when it must hold ground

or resupply, the commander should exploit with a fresh force. Exploitation ends when the enemy loses his ability and will to fight; enemy resistance increases requiring deliberate attack; or the force conducting the exploitation can no longer be supported or sustained.

Pursuit

A pursuit often develops after a successful exploitation operation, and its purpose is the annihilation of the enemy; therefore, forces are orientated on the enemy rather than the seizure of terrain. A pursuit is an offensive operation designed to catch or cut off a hostile force attempting to escape, with the aim of destroying it. The difference between an exploitation and a pursuit is the condition of the enemy. Like exploitation, pursuit requires broad decentralized control and rapid movement; therefore, the speed and shock effect of a tank unit greatly improves the impact and effect of a pursuit.

The decision to conduct a pursuit operation is made when the enemy has lost the ability to defend or delay and begins to withdraw. Therefore, the decision to execute a pursuit must be made quickly, before the enemy can regain control or organize a defense or before the opportunity is lost.

Unlike an exploitation, in which the attacking force may or may not focus on the enemy force, the attacker in a pursuit focuses on catching and destroying the fleeing enemy force. A pursuit follows a successful attack or exploitation and is ordered when the enemy cannot conduct an organized defense and attempts to disengage. Direct pressure against the retreating forces must be combined with an enveloping or encircling maneuver to place troops across the enemy's lines of retreat. Tanks are usually assigned as the enveloping or encircling force. If it becomes apparent that enemy resistance has broken down entirely and that the enemy is fleeing the battle-field, any type of offensive operation can transition into a pursuit.

During the pursuit, commanders conduct air and ground operations to intercept, capture, or destroy the enemy. The aviation combat element can also interdict fleeing enemy forces.

Unlike exploitation, commanders are rarely able to anticipate pursuit, so they do not normally hold forces in reserve solely to accomplish this mission. Therefore, commanders must be agile enough to react when the situation presents itself. During a pursuit, the commander task-organizes the force into a direct pressure force and an encircling force.

Direct Pressure Force

The mission of the direct pressure force is to prevent enemy disengagement and subsequent reconstitution of the defense. Leading elements of the direct pressure force move rapidly, on all available routes, containing or bypassing small enemy forces that are reduced by follow-on support forces. The direct pressure force must have sufficient combat power to maintain pressure on the enemy; it attacks on a broad front and provides relentless pressure on the enemy.

Encircling Force

The mission of the encircling force is to get behind the enemy and block his escape so that he can be destroyed between the direct pressure force and the encircling force. If the encircling force cannot outrun the fleeing enemy force, it attacks the flank. The encircling force must have continuous fire support and greater mobility than the enemy, which lends it to being a mechanized force. The encircling force may seize deep blocking positions to prevent the enemy's escape. This may require that the encircling force move without flank security.

SECTION II. TANK UNIT FORMATIONS

Tank units use formations to facilitate positive command and control and to avoid confusion in combat. Formations also enhance speed and security and improve the ability to react to anticipated situations. Formations are chosen based on METT-T analysis; therefore, the commander must continuously analyze the situation and change formations as the situation changes—formations are not rigid. Subordinate commanders, down to the individual tank level, must also have the freedom to adjust to the terrain/enemy situation. The tank battalion uses formations for several purposes—

- Establish the relationship of one unit to another on the ground.
- Allow tank companies to position firepower where it is needed in support of the direct fire plan.

- Establish responsibilities for sector security among companies/platoons.
- Facilitate the execution of battle drills and directed COAs.

Formations (like movement techniques) are planned based on where enemy contact is expected and how the commander expects to react to the contact. The commander of the mechanized force must evaluate the situation and determine which formation best suits the mission and the situation. The battalion formation establishes the relationship between the battalion's companies, the actual positioning of platoons within each company is dictated by the company commanders. It is not necessary for all of the company formations to be the same within the battalion formation. It is critical, however, for company commanders to coordinate their formation with those of other elements of the tank/mechanized force. In some cases, the company may use the same formation as the battalion (for example, the companies may use the column formation within a battalion column). In other situations, however, battalion and company formations may be different as a result of METT-T factors (such as the companies moving in wedge formations within a battalion vee).

An important consideration in movement planning and execution is that formations are not rigid. Spacing requirements, as well as other METT-T considerations, will require the battalion commander and subordinate leaders to adapt the basic formations as necessary. They must be ready to adjust the distance between companies and individual platoons based on terrain, visibility, and mission requirements.

Column

The column is used when speed is critical, when the battalion is moving through restricted terrain on a specific route, and/or when enemy contact is not likely. Each company normally follows directly behind the company in front of it. If the situation dictates, however, platoons can disperse laterally to enhance security (see. fig. 2-1). The column formation has the following characteristics, advantages, and limitations:

- Provides excellent control and fires to the flanks.
- Permits only limited fires to the front and rear.
- Is easy to control.
- Provides extremely limited overall security.
- Is normally used for traveling only.

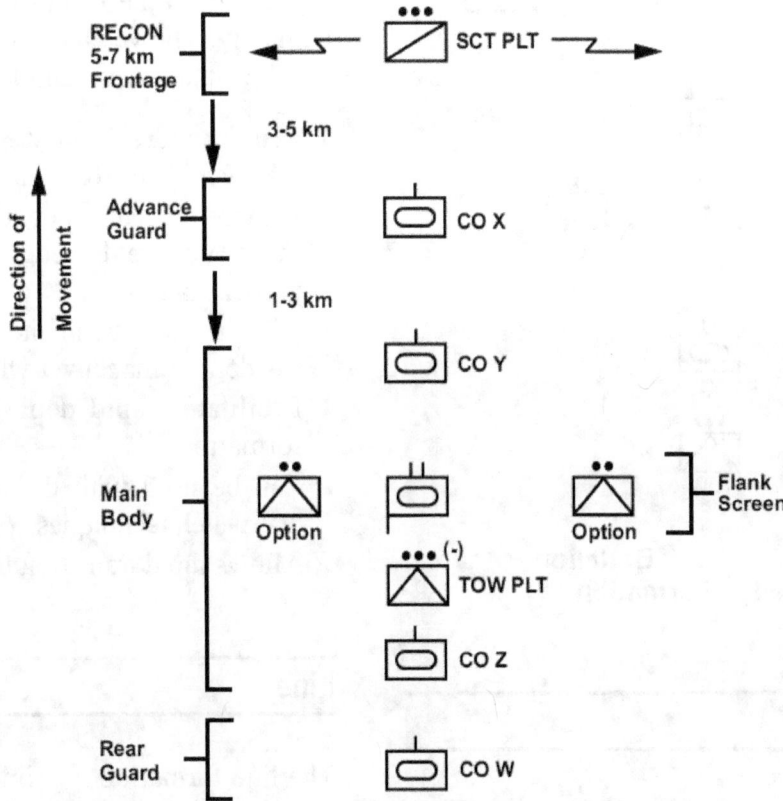

Figure 2-1. Tank Battalion in Column Formation with Dispersal for Added Security.

Wedge

The wedge formation, illustrated in figure 2-2, is often used when the enemy situation is unclear or contact is possible. In the battalion wedge, the lead company is in the center of the formation, with the remaining companies located to the rear of and outside the lead company. The wedge has the following characteristics, advantages, and limitations:

- Permits excellent fires to the front and good fires to the flanks.
- Is easy to control.
- Provides good security to the flanks.
- Can be used with the traveling and traveling overwatch techniques.
- Allows rapid transition to bounding overwatch.

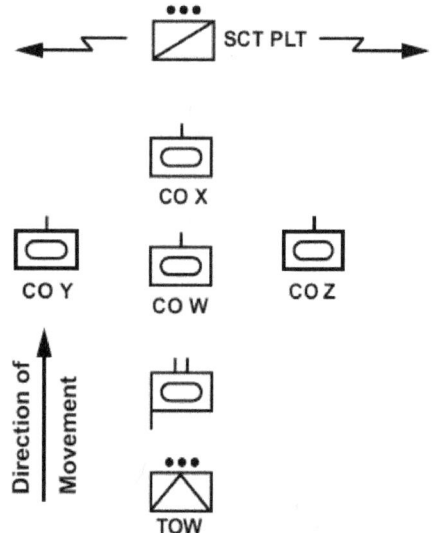

Figure 2-2. Tank Battalion in Wedge Formation.

Vee

The vee formation, illustrated in figure 2-3, is used when enemy contact is possible. In the battalion vee, the center company is located in the

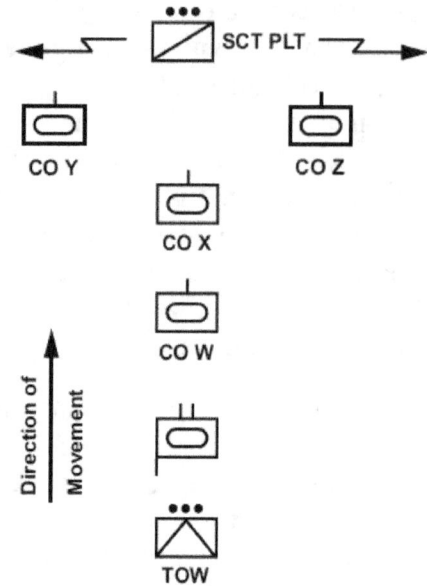

Figure 2-3. Tank Battalion in Vee Formation.

rear of the formation, while the remaining companies are to the front of and outside the center company. The vee has the following characteristics, advantages, and limitations:

- Permits more firepower to the front than the wedge and affords greater fires to the flanks.
- Is more difficult to control than the wedge and makes it more difficult for vehicles to maintain proper orientation.
- Allows one unit in the formation to maintain freedom of maneuver when contact occurs.
- Facilitates rapid deployment into any other formation.
- Can be used with the traveling and traveling overwatch techniques.
- Allows rapid transition to bounding overwatch.

Line

The line formation is primarily used when a unit or element is crossing a danger area or needs to maximize firepower to the front (see fig. 2-4). In the battalion line, companies move abreast of one

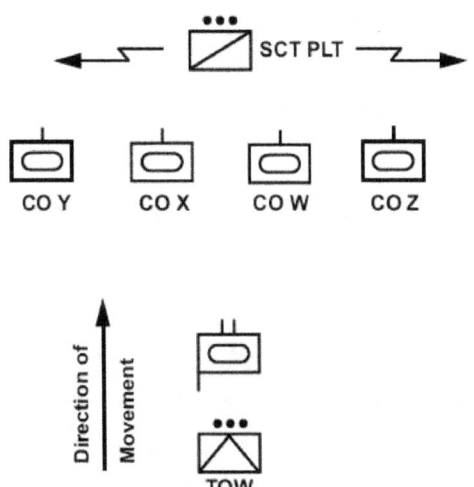

Figure 2-4. Tank Battalion in Line Formation.

another and are dispersed laterally. The line formation has the following characteristics, advantages, and limitations:

- Permits maximum fires to the front or rear, but minimum fires to the flanks.
- Is difficult to control.
- Is less secure than other formations because of the lack of depth.
- Is the most difficult formation from which to make the transition to other formations.

The line may be used in the assault to maximize the firepower and/or shock effect of the heavy company. This is normally done when there is no more intervening terrain between the unit and the enemy, when antitank systems are suppressed, and/or when the unit is exposed to artillery fire and must move rapidly.

Echelon

The echelon formation is used when the battalion wants to maintain security and/or observation of one flank and enemy contact is not likely (see fig. 2-5). The battalion echelon formation (either echelon left or echelon right) has the lead company positioned farthest from the echeloned flank, with each subsequent company located to the rear of and outside the company in front of it. The echelon formation has the following characteristics, advantages, and limitations:

- Is difficult to control.
- Affords excellent security for the higher formation in the direction of the echelon.
- Facilitates deployment to the echeloned flank.

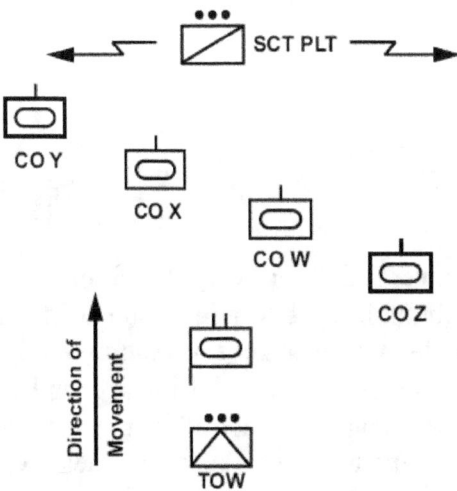

Figure 2-5. Tank Battalion in Echelon Right Formation.

Coil

The coil is a battalion or below-level formation employed when elements of the battalion are stationary and must maintain 360-degree security. See figure 2-6 on page 2-12.

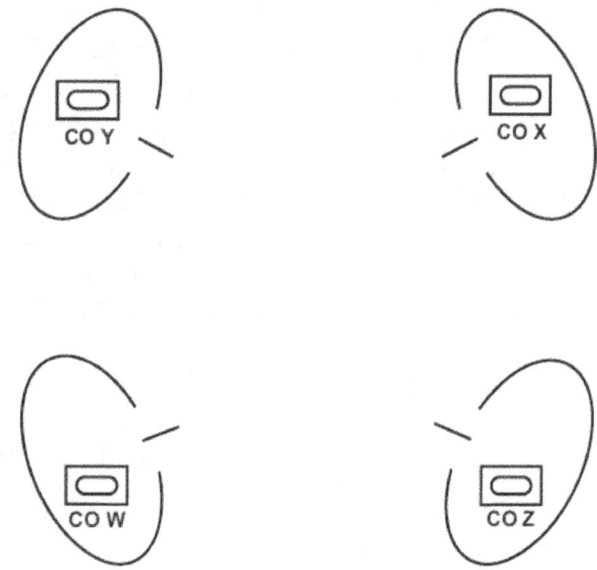

Figure 2-6. Coil Formation.

SECTION III. FORMS OF MANEUVER

Maneuver is the employment of forces on the battle-field through movement in combination with fire (or fire potential) to achieve a position of advantage in respect to the enemy in order to accomplish the mission. The basic forms of maneuver are frontal attack, envelopment, flanking attack, penetration, turning movement and infiltration.

Frontal Attack

A frontal attack is an offensive maneuver in which the main action is directed against the front of the enemy force. This is the least desirable form of maneuver for a mechanized force because it attacks into the enemy's strength and does not take full advantage of a tank's ability to maneuver. The advantages of a tank/mechanized force conducting a frontal attack are—

- Greater combat power than pure infantry forces.

- Inherent speed reduces exposure time to enemy fire.
- Vehicle armor reduces effects of enemy direct/indirect fires.

Envelopment

An offensive maneuver in which the main attacking force passes around or over the enemy's principle defensive positions to secure objectives to the enemy's rear. (JP 1-02) This is the most desirable form of maneuver for a tank/mechanized force because it utilizes maneuver and speed to avoid enemy strengths and in doing so destroys the enemy's cohesion. The advantages of a tank/mechanized force conducting an envelopment are as follows:

- Possess greater speed, which is required to surprise the enemy from an unexpected direction.

- Has the required ground mobility to rapidly seize deep objectives while providing a greater threat than a turning movement.

An envelopment is a form of offensive maneuver by which the attacker bypasses the enemy's principal defensive positions to secure objectives to the enemy's rear. An envelopment compels the defender to fight on the ground of the attacker's choosing. It requires surprise and superior mobility relative to the enemy. In mechanized tactics, an envelopment normally requires a base of fire element and a bounding element. The bounding element avoids the enemy's strength en route to the objective. The base of fire element fixes the enemy's attention to his front, forcing the enemy to fight in two or more directions simultaneously to meet the converging efforts of the attacks.

Penetration

A penetration seeks to break through the enemy's defense and disrupts the defensive system. The purpose of a penetration is to break through the enemy's main defenses, in effect creating an assailable flank where none had existed before. A penetration generally occurs in three stages: rupturing the position, widening the gap, and seizing the objective.

A penetration's main effort concentrates overwhelmingly superior combat power deep into a narrow front. A penetration is appropriate when the enemy is overextended, when his flanks are secure, or when there is no assailable flank. Because tanks can maneuver quickly and mass overwhelming fires, they are well-suited to perform this type of offensive maneuver. However, care must be taken to ensure that the enemy does not close the penetration. If this happens, it endangers the penetration forces and subjects them to being cut off from follow-on forces and possibly destroyed by an enemy counterattack.

Turning Movement

A turning movement is a form of offensive maneuver in which the attacker passes around or over the enemy's principal defensive positions to secure objectives deep in the enemy's rear. Normally, the main effort executes the turning movement as the supporting effort fixes the enemy in position. The main effort seizes objectives so deep that the enemy is forced to abandon his position and divert major forces to meet the threat. Unlike an envelopment, the main effort usually operates at such a distance from the supporting effort force that mutual support is unlikely. Therefore, the main effort must be self-sufficient and reach the objective before becoming decisively engaged. Seldom would a turning movement be executed by a MAGTF smaller than a Marine expeditionary force (MEF). Typical objectives of the main effort in a turning movement are ideally suited for mechanized forces are as follows:

- Critical logistic sites.
- C2 nodes.
- Lines of communications.

Infiltration

Infiltration is a form of maneuver in which forces move covertly through or into an enemy area to attack positions in the enemy's rear. Forces move over, through, or around enemy positions without detection to assume a position of advantage over the enemy. The commander orders an infiltration to move all or part of his force through gaps in the enemy's defense to—

- Achieve surprise.
- Attack enemy positions from the flank or rear.
- Occupy a position from which to support the main attack by fire.
- Secure key terrain.
- Conduct ambushes and raids in the enemy's rear to harass and disrupt his command and control and support activities.
- Cut off enemy forward units.

Infiltrations normally take advantage of limited visibility, rough terrain, or unoccupied or unobserved areas. Theses conditions often allow undetected movement of small elements when the movement of the entire force would present greater risks. Infiltration routes must be reconnoitered to minimize the chance that the enemy can observe or hear mechanized forces moving; therefore, it is difficult for tanks and mechanized forces to perform infiltrations due to noise, dust signatures, and the large number of vehicles usually found in mechanized units.

CHAPTER 3
DEFENSIVE OPERATIONS

The purpose of the defense is to force the attacker to reach his culminating point without achieving his objectives, to gain the initiative for friendly forces, and to create the opportunity to shift to the offense. The essence of defensive tactics is to place the enemy into a position that permits his destruction through the intelligent use of terrain and firepower, thereby creating favorable conditions for counterattack and resumption of the offense. Defensive operations achieve one or more of the following:

- Destroy the enemy.
- Weaken enemy forces as a prelude to the offense.
- Cause an enemy attack to fail.
- Gain time.
- Concentrate forces elsewhere.
- Control key or decisive terrain.
- Retain terrain.

General planning considerations include—

- Enemy's strength and mobility.
- Initial disposition, assembly areas, coordination measures, and routes or axis.
- Coordination with frontline units (key considerations include frontline unit obstacle plans and passage lanes).
- Communications/signals.
- The tank unit coordinating, reconnoitering, rehearsing, and preparing for the priority reserve missions as time allows.

Organization of the Battlespace

During defensive operations, the commander organizes his battlespace into three areas—security area, main battle area, and rear area—in which the defending force performs specific functions (see fig. 3-1.) These areas can be further divided into sectors. The size and nature of a sector depends on the situation and the factors of METT-T. A defensive sector is an area assigned to a subordinate commander in which he is provided the maximum latitude to accomplish assigned tasks in order to conduct defensive operations. Commanders of defensive sectors can assign their subordinates their own sector.

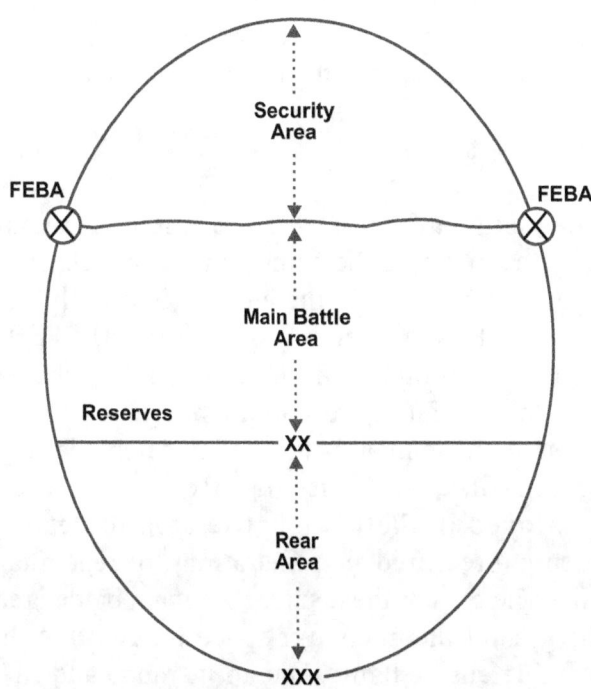

Figure 3-1. Organization of the Battlespace.

Security Area

The security area is that area that begins at the forward edge of the battle area (FEBA) and extends as far to the front and flanks as security forces are deployed, normally to the forward boundary of the area of operations. Forces in the security area conduct reconnaissance to furnish information on the enemy and delay, deceive, and disrupt the enemy. The commander adds depth to the defense by extending the security area as far forward as is tactically feasible.

Actions in the security area purposely cause the enemy to prematurely deploy into attack formations and to disrupt his plan of attack. Slowing the enemy's attack enables MAGTF forces, particularly Marine aviation, to strike the enemy's critical vulnerabilities (i.e., movement, resupply, fire support, and command and control). The utilization of tanks in the security area provides the commander with the long-range firepower necessary to engage and wear down the enemy's forward elements. The tank's speed and mobility also permits the security force to rapidly withdraw and fall back to the main defensive position.

Main Battle Area

The main battle area is that portion of the battlespace in which the commander conducts close operations to defeat the enemy. Normally, the main battle area extends rearward from the FEBA to the rear boundary of the command's subordinate units. The commander positions forces throughout the main battle area to defeat, destroy, or contain enemy assaults. Reserves may be employed in the main battle area to destroy enemy forces, reduce penetrations, or regain terrain. The greater the depth of the main battle area, the greater the maneuver space for fighting the main defensive battle. Due to its range and firepower, the tank's various weapons systems provide the commander with the capability to engage multiple targets simultaneously and accurately.

Rear Area

The rear area is that area extending forward from a command's rear boundary to the rear of the operational area of the command's subordinate units. This area is provided primarily for the performance of CSS functions. Rear area operations include those functions of security and sustainment required to maintain continuity of operations by the whole force. Rear area operations protect the sustainment effort as well as deny use of the rear area to the enemy. The rear area may not always be contiguous with the main battle area.

Organization of the Force

During defensive operations, the commander organizes his force as depicted in figure 3-2.

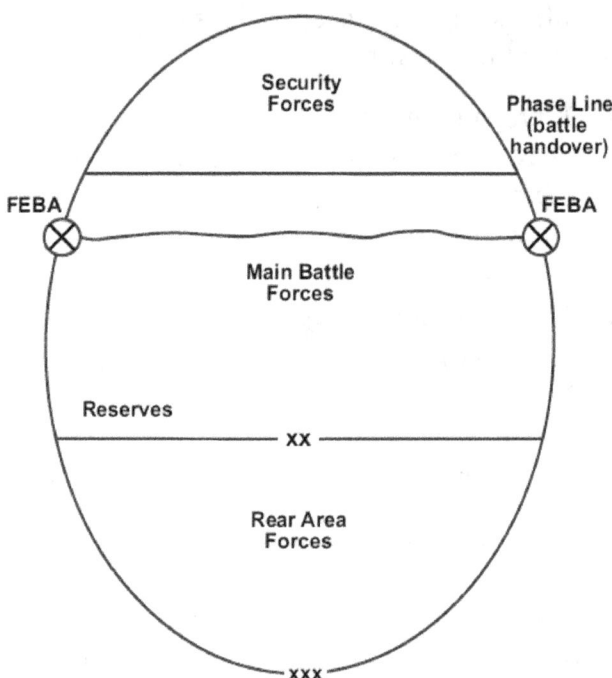

Figure 3-2. Organization of the Force.

Security Forces

The commander uses security forces forward of the main battle area to delay, disrupt, and provide early warning of the enemy's advance and to deceive the enemy as to the true location of the main battle area. Operations of security forces must be an integral part of the overall defensive plan. To ensure optimal unity of effort during security operations, a single commander is normally assigned responsibility for the conduct of operations in the security area. The element of the MAGTF assigned as the security forces depends on METT-T factors.

The commander seeks to engage the enemy as far out as possible. Suppression and obscuration fires are employed to facilitate maneuver of the security force. Maximum use may be made of all fire support assets to disrupt and destroy enemy formations as they move through the security area approaching the main battle area. Obstacles and barriers are positioned to delay or canalize the enemy and are covered by fires to destroy him while he is halted or in the process of breaching.

The commander assigns screen, guard, or cover missions to security forces:

- A security element screens a stationary force by establishing a series of positions along a designated screen line. The positions are located to provide overlapping observation. Areas that cannot be observed from these positions are normally patrolled. Screening forces report any sightings of enemy activity and engage enemy forces with fires. Maintaining contact, the screen falls back along previously reconnoitered routes to subsequent positions. Screening forces should avoid becoming decisively engaged.

- A security element guards a force by establishing a series of mutually supporting positions. The guard may establish a screen line forward of these positions. These positions immediately report any enemy contact and engage with fires at maximum range. The guard defends in place, attacks, or delays to rearward positions. Routes and subsequent positions should have been previously reconnoitered.

- Covering forces compel the enemy to deploy prematurely, confirm the direction and strength of the enemy attack, conduct counterreconnaissance, destroy the enemy advance guard, canalize the enemy advance in accordance with the commander's plan, and provide the main force

time to react. A covering force should be a self-sufficient, combined-arms force that is large enough to convince the enemy that they are the main battle force.

The security force engages the enemy first, screening, guarding, and covering as ordered. Normally, the commander designates the security force as his initial main effort. Since a tank can withdraw rapidly to the main battle area and maintain continuous long-range contact with the enemy, it can allow the security force to maintain contact with the enemy while falling back under pressure. The effectiveness and firepower of the tank's various weapon systems also facilitates the engagement and attrition of the enemy's advance guard during the withdrawal. This action impedes the enemy's momentum, forcing him to deploy his main body.

At a predetermined location, normally a phase line designated as a handover line, control of the battle is transferred to the main battle force. A handover line is a control feature; preferably following easily defined terrain features, at which the responsibility for the conduct of combat operations is passed from one force to another. The transfer of control must be carefully coordinated. The main battle force supports the disengagement of the security force as it withdraws in preparation for its subsequent mission. The commander may shift the main effort to the appropriate element of the main battle force. As the enemy's advance force approaches the main battle area, execution of the defensive battle becomes increasingly decentralized.

At some point, the defending commander must plan for the enemy force breaking through the security forces and approaching the main battle area. This requires transitioning friendly forces and control of the battle from security forces to the main battle force. Whenever the battle is transitioned, it requires coordination from the highest common commander.

Main Battle Forces

Main battle forces engage the enemy to slow, canalize, disorganize, or defeat his attack. The commander positions these forces to counter the enemy's attack along the most likely or most dangerous avenue of approach. As in offensive operations, the commander weights his main effort with enough combat power and the necessary support to ensure success. Tanks provide the commander with the fastest tactical assets available, which provide a defensive maneuver capability. Tanks also provide an effective platform for the destruction of other ground platforms (e.g., mechanized forces can successfully eliminate lightly armored enemy vehicles). Tank platoons are normally employed intact in order to properly mass their fires and still distribute the effects.

Main battle forces engage the enemy as early as possible unless fires are withheld to prevent the loss of surprise. Commanders make maximum use of fires to destroy and disrupt enemy formations as they approach the main battle area. As the enemy closes, he is subjected to an ever-increasing volume of fires from the main battle area forces and all supporting arms. Again, obstacles and barriers are used to delay or canalize the enemy so that he is continually subjected to fires.

Combat power that can be quickly concentrated, such as fires, is brought to bear while maneuver units move into position. The defender reacts to the enemy's main effort by reinforcing the threatened sector or allowing the enemy's main effort to penetrate into engagement areas within the main battle area to cut him off and destroy him by counterattack. Main battle forces maintain an offensive spirit throughout the battle, looking to exploit any advantageous situations.

A counterattack is an attack by part or all of a defending force against an attacking enemy force, for such specific purposes as regaining ground lost or cutting off and destroying enemy advance units, and with the general objective of denying to the enemy the attainment of his purpose in attacking. In many cases, the counterattack is decisive action in defensive operations. It is the commander's primary means of breaking the enemy's attack or of regaining the initiative. Once commenced, the counterattack is the main effort. Its success depends largely on surprise, speed, and boldness in execution. A separate counterattack force may be established by the commander to conduct planned counterattacks and can be made up of uncommitted or lightly engaged forces and the reserve.

The reserve is the commander's tool to influence the course of the battle at the critical time and place to exploit opportunities. It is the force that provides flexibility to the commander by allowing him to strike the enemy at the time and place of the commander's choosing. The commander uses his reserve at the decisive moment in the defense and refuses to dissipate it on local emergencies. It is a designated force, as robust and mobile as possible, that exploits success, conducts counterattacks, contains penetrations, and regains the initiative. The less that is known of the enemy or his intention, the greater the proportion of combat power that must be held in reserve. The reserve is usually located in assembly areas or forward operating bases in the main battle area. Once the reserve is committed, the commander establishes or reconstitutes a new reserve. Reserves are organized based on the factors of METT-T. The tactical mobility of mechanized and helicopterborne forces makes them well-suited for use as the reserve. Mechanized reserve forces are best employed offensively.

Timing is critical to the employment of the mechanized reserve. As the area of probable employment of the mechanized reserve becomes apparent, the commander alerts his reserve to have it more readily available for action. When he commits his reserve, the commander must make his decision promptly and with an accurate understanding of movement factors and deployment times. If committed too soon or too late, the mechanized or tank reserve may not have a decisive effect. The commander may choose to use security forces as part of or all of his reserve after completion of their security mission. He must weigh this decision against the possibility that the security forces may suffer a loss of combat power during its security mission.

Rear Area Forces

Rear area forces protect and sustain the force's combat power. They provide for freedom of action and the continuity of logistic and C2 support. Rear area forces facilitate future operations as forces are positioned and support is marshaled to enable the transition to offensive operations. When facing a threat equipped with heavy armored vehicles, the tactical combat force within the reserve area may be required to be tasked-organized with tanks. Tanks can be held in the reserve area until it can be determined where the enemy main attack is directed. Once that is determined, tanks can quickly counterattack to meet the enemies main attack and defeat it.

Preparing for the Defense

In the defense, tank units are employed to take maximum advantage of their inherent speed, mobility, armor-protected firepower, and shock effect. Tank units are ideally suited to conducting spoiling attacks and counterattacks, thereby providing offensive action during a defensive battle. They also provide long-range, direct fire capability into engagement areas and have the capability to engage both ground and air targets. Tanks have considerations that should be taken into account for both deliberate and hasty defenses and as a reserve in the defense.

Deliberate Defense

A deliberate defense is normally organized when out of contact with the enemy or when contact is not imminent and time for organization is available. A deliberate defense normally includes fortifications, strongpoints, extensive use of barriers, and fully integrated fires. The commander normally is free to make a detailed reconnaissance of his sector, select the terrain on which to defend, and decide the best distribution of forces. Tanks and/or mechanized units are given specific missions and tasks and must be integrated into the entire defensive plan to maximize each weapons platform advantages and lessen the disadvantages. Tanks and mechanized units must prioritize deliberate defensive planning and preparations according to the mission they are given and the time available to complete preparations before the enemy attacks.

Hasty Defense

A defense is normally organized while in contact with the enemy or when contact is imminent and time available for the organization is limited. It is characterized by improvement of the natural defensive strength of the terrain by utilization of emplacements and obstacles. The hasty defense normally allows for only a brief leader's reconnaissance and may entail the immediate engagement by security forces to provide time for the establishment of the defense. Because tanks have a high degree of survivability, mobility, and can engage at long ranges, they can keep enemy pressure off of other units preparing to conduct a hasty defense and buy time for friendly forces to find suitable defensive positions.

Use of the Reserve in the Defense

The reserve is the commander's tool to influence the course of the battle at the critical time and place in order to exploit opportunities. It is a designated force, as robust and mobile as possible, that exploits success, conducts counterattacks, contains penetrations, and regains the initiative. Its primary purpose is to retain flexibility through offensive action. Reserves are organized based on the factors of METT-T. The tactical mobility of mechanized forces makes them well-suited for use as the reserve.

Types of Defense

Every defense contains two complementary characteristics: a static or positional element, which anchors the defense to key terrain, and a dynamic or mobile element, which generates combat power through maneuver and concentration of forces. The positional element is characterized by use of battle positions, strongpoints, fortifications, and barriers to halt the enemy advance. The mobile element is characterized by the use of offensive action, supplementary positions, planned delaying actions, lateral shifting of forces, and commitment of the reserve. Conceptually, this results in two defensive extremes: the position defense and the mobile defense. However, neither type can be used exclusively in practice. Although these descriptions convey the general pattern of each type of defense, any defense will include both positional and mobile elements. Commanders may simultaneously conduct position and mobile defenses in order to take advantage of the strengths inherent in mechanized organizations. Mechanized forces possess the mobility required to conduct mobile-type defenses or may be tasked to be the reserve given the situation and terrain within their assigned sector.

While the positional defense is normally used to retain key terrain, the mobile defense is used to destroy the enemy force. Clearly, the positional defense weights its forces forward while the mobile defense weights its forces toward its reserve or counterattack force. The position defense normally uses its reserve to re-establish the FEBA following penetration by the enemy. In the mobile defense, the reserve or counterattack force is used to destroy the enemy. Although the mobile defense has inherent risks, it stands a greater chance of inflicting a decisive defeat and complete destruction of the enemy force than does the area defense.

Position Defense

The position defense is conducted to deny the enemy access to critical terrain for a specified period of time. It is seldom capable of achieving the outright destruction of the attacking force due to the position defense's limited mobility. However, once the attacker is dealt a tactical setback, the defender can take advantage of other opportunities to maintain the initiative. Thus, the position defense relies on other simultaneous or subsequent operations by adjacent or reinforcing forces to achieve decisive results. A position defense occurs when the bulk of the defending force is disposed in selected tactical localities where the decisive battle is to be fought. Principle reliance is placed on the ability of the forces in the defended localities to maintain their positions and to control the terrain between them.

The tank battalion is typically used as the reserve in a positional defense. As a reserve, tank units are normally employed to add depth, block penetrations, or restore the battle position by counterattack.

Mobile Defense

A mobile defense is an area or position in which maneuver is used together with fire and terrain to seize initiative from the enemy. It requires depth and focuses on the destruction of the enemy by permitting him to advance into a position that exposes him to counterattack by a strong mobile reserve. Tank units will not normally conduct a mobile defense as a separate maneuver element; they are usually employed as part of a mechanized force within a MAGTF mobile defense. Mechanized pure units are normally assigned to the main battle area while units task-organized with tanks (teams or task forces) are often assigned reserve roles.

Defensive Maneuver

Mechanized units can be given the mission to defend in sector, from battle positions or from a strong point. Regardless of the defensive mission, tanks must carefully choose their positions to properly engage the enemy using engagement areas to defeat him.

Sectors

Sectors are areas designated by boundaries within which a unit operates and for which it is responsible. Assignment of a defensive sector provides tank units with maximum latitude to accomplish assigned tasks. It is the most common method of defending with a mechanized force and prevents the enemy from concentrating overwhelming firepower on the bulk of the defending force at one time. The strength of this defense comes from its flexibility and focus on the enemy, rather than terrain. Its depth must come from the initial positioning of units throughout the sector and a viable reserve/counterattack force. The extent of the sector is METT-T dependent. Forces deployed in depth must confront the enemy with effective fires from multiple, mutually supporting locations as the enemy tries to maneuver. The sector is organized around many dispersed, small units, which attack the enemy throughout the depth of his formations.

Battle Position

A battle position is a defensive location oriented on the most likely avenue of approach from which a unit may defend. Battle positions should be positioned to achieve depth, surprise, mutual support, and to allow for maneuver. They effectively concentrate combat power into an engagement area, while preventing the enemy from isolating any one part of the unit. Units of platoon to battalion size may be assigned a battle position. The use of on-order battle positions adds flexibility and depth to the defensive plan. Tanks units are normally tasked to provide security outside of a battle position, overwatch a battle position, or serve as a spoiling attack or counterattack force.

Strongpoints

Strongpoints are heavily fortified battle positions that are tied to a natural or reinforcing obstacle to create an anchor for the defense or to block a key piece of restricted terrain; therefore, they are typically located on key or decisive terrain. The tank's survivability makes it an effective addition to a strongpoint. They also retain the capacity to carry enough ammunition for a sustained engagement should resupply efforts become difficult.

The strongpoint requires significant engineer support. Positions are prepared for all weapons systems, vehicles, Marines, and supplies. Positions are prepared for all-around defense when they anticipate being surrounded. Once isolated, unit movement will be restricted within the confines of the strongpoint position.

Alternate and Supplementary Positions

The alternate position is a position given to a weapon, unit, or individual to be occupied when the primary position becomes untenable or unsuitable for carrying out its task. Alternate positions provide additional lines of sight into the same engagement area or sector of fire and are sited to fulfill the original task. Alternate and supplementary positions should be designated and prepared as time permits. They increase the survivability of a weapons system by enabling it to engage the enemy from multiple positions. Supplementary positions provide the means to accomplish a task that cannot be accomplished from the primary or alternate positions. They allow a unit or weapons system to engage enemy forces approaching from another direction such as the rear or flank.

When considering primary and alternate positions, the commander must ensure that the fires from these positions support his obstacle array in the engagement area. The alternate position may be slightly to the front, flank, or rear of the primary position. These positions must provide excellent observation and fields of fire covering the area where the commander desires to engage the enemy, and should also have covered and concealed routes into and out of the positions. These positions must enable the tanks to identify all designated target reference points (TRPs) in the tank units sector so that the tank unit can adequately cover its sector with mutually supporting and overlapping fires.

Tanks do not have an organic capability to dig their own positions when needed and must rely on engineer assets to perform this task. Normally, engineer armored combat earthmover vehicles or dozers dig these positions. Each tank position should be constructed to provide both a level hull-defilade firing position and a level turret-defilade observation position. Hull-defilade allows the tank to engage targets with its main gun and machine guns. The turret-defilade allows the tank commander to observe the engagement area without exposing the tank to enemy fire. Figure 3-3 illustrates a correctly prepared tank defensive position.

Digging positions for tanks and vehicles can take a considerable amount of time. Time to dig tank positions is determined by how many digging assets are available to the unit, other tasks assigned to engineer digging assets, and the composition of the terrain being excavated (i.e., hard rocky soil takes longer than soft clay). Therefore,

to avoid having to dig a position for each tank, the tank/mechanized unit commander should take advantage of the natural terrain when selecting tank positions. Specific Marines in the tank unit should be given the task of marking tank positions for the engineers and ensuring that the positions are dug correctly (i.e., they are large enough and oriented correctly into the engagement area).

Engagement Areas

The engagement area is where the tank/mechanized unit commander intends to trap and destroy the enemy force using the massed fires of all available weapons. The success of the engagement depends on how effectively the commander can integrate the obstacle plan, the indirect fire plan, and the direct fires plan within the engagement area to achieve the unit's tactical purpose. Therefore, effective planning is critical to the commander's success. At the tank/mechanized company level, the following areas must be considered when properly developing an effective engagement area.

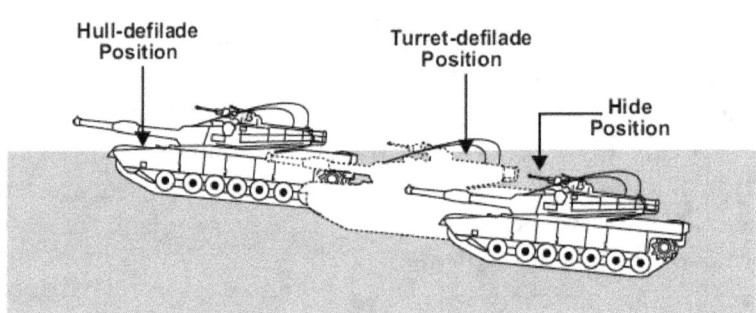

Berms attract attention. Dig down, not up.

Do not put spoil to the front, sides, or rear of the firing position. Reduce spoil so that it blends into existing terrain.

Tie down all antennas and keep reflective surfaces covered.

Make sure the firing position has a covered exit route and a covered route to the next firing position.

Construct overhead cover and add camouflage to create a hide position if time and materials are available.

Figure 3-3. Correct Hull-defilade and Turret-defilade Defensive Tank Positions.

Identify Likely Enemy Avenues of Approach

Reconnaissance must be performed to identify all likely enemy avenues of approach. If possible, this should be done from the enemy's perspective (direction). During reconnaissance, key land or terrain that affords positions over the enemy as well as natural obstacles/chokepoints that restrict forward movement of the enemy are identified. After reconnaissance, planners determine which of the avenues afford the enemy the greatest cover and concealment while allowing him to maintain his attack tempo and evaluate lateral routes adjoining each enemy avenue of approach.

Determine Likely Enemy Schemes of Maneuver

To determine the enemy's most likely scheme of maneuver, the commander should again view the engagement area from the enemy's perspective in order to determine how the enemy will most likely be structured for the attack and how he will use his reconnaissance assets. Planners then determine how the enemy will change formations and/or establish firing positions within the engagement area. For example, if the enemy is a mechanized company, when will he most likely shift from a company wedge formation to a company vee formation just prior to assaulting on line?

Determine Where to Kill the Enemy

Determining where to kill the enemy starts by identifying TRPs that match the enemy's most likely scheme of maneuver in the engagement area. Each TRP is then identified and recorded by grid. TRPs should also be marked for tank thermal identification. Next, the commander determines how many tanks and/or weapons systems will fire on each TRP to achieve the desired end state. The commander may also determine which subordinate units will fire on each TRP. Once the TRPs are established, the outside boundaries of the engagement area can be determined. Finally, planners develop the direct fire plan.

Plan and Integrate Obstacles to Support Mechanized Unit Weapons Systems

Once TRPs are identified, the next step is to plan and integrate obstacles into the engagement area. Initially, planners must determine the desired intent of the obstacles with the engineer commander and ensure that the obstacle plan meets the intent of the engagement area commander. With the engineers, planners identify, site, and mark the obstacles within the obstacle group and integrate protective obstacle types and locations within the unit's defensive plan. All obstacles need to be covered by direct fire and responsibility for guides to open and close obstacle lanes must be assigned. The engagement area commander must also work with the engineer commander to ensure that everyone understands disengagement criteria, actions on contact, and security requirements. Effective tank engagement obstacles force the enemy to slow or halt his attack or force the enemy to expose his vehicles' flanks, which present easier targets for tank gunners to acquire and kill.

Emplace Weapons Systems for Maximum Effect

The emplacement of weapons systems maximizes each weapons platform's ability to support the mission. The commander selects tentative battle positions within and/or overseeing the engagement area and confirms that the battle positions are tactically advantageous. The battle positions are marked after ensuring that they do not conflict with those of adjacent units and have mutually overlapping fires with other battle positions. Once the battle position is established, primary, alternate, and supplementary positions are established for tanks, vehicles, and other weapon systems. Each position should support firing on TRPs that are the responsibility of that battle position.

Once the positions are chosen, commanders proof the positions to ensure that they are correct. The battle positions utilizing tanks must consider the M1A1 tank gun's standoff ranges: optimal engagement ranges are from 2,300 to 2,700 meters for main gun engagements but the guns are capable of engagements over 3,000 meters. In addition, tanks can be used for closer engagements of enemy infantry or antitank guided missile (ATGM) teams using their machine guns and/or main gun. Tanks should also have their combat trains close by the battle position (usually one terrain feature behind their battle position) in case they need to rearm and/or resupply. Antiarmor weapons (i.e., TOWs and Javelins) are usually placed in depth along the flanks of the engagement area in battle positions for longer range flanking fires into the engagement area.

Plan and Integrate Available Indirect Fires

Planners must plan and integrate indirect fires based on the purpose of the fire and where that purpose will best be achieved in the engagement area. Planners establish an observation plan with redundancy for each target, determine firing triggers based on enemy movement rates, and obtain accurate target locations using global positioning system devices. Target locations are then refined to ensure coverage of obstacles and artillery and mortar targets are adjusted. Final protective fires are planned. All no-fire areas are identified and requested for the engagement area. Indirect fires should also be planned for all dead space in the engagement area that cannot be covered by direct fire systems.

Plan and Integrate Available CAS

Planning for CAS requires knowing what CAS is available on station during the expected time of the enemy attack or knowing how long it will take for CAS to be on station to support the defense. Marine attack helicopters should be used to engage and attrite the enemy deep in the engagement area and/or even before the enemy enters the engagement area. Attack helicopters are able to engage enemy tanks and vehicles with ATGMs and chain guns and to provide the engagement area commander with enemy locations and actions. Attack helicopters may also act as an airborne forward observer for deep indirect fires or as a FAC for other fixed-wing aircraft delivering munitions. Tank fires combined with attack helicopters are very effective in slowing or stopping enemy mechanized attacks.

Rehearse the Execution of Operations

One of the most important engagement area preparation steps is to conduct a rehearsal. The rehearsal ensures that every Marine understands the defensive plan and knows what to do and when to do it. One effective rehearsal technique is to have vehicles drive through the engagement area from the attackers avenue of approach and simulate engaging the vehicles within the engagement area. A rehearsal should include the following when required:

- Rearward passage of lines.
- Closure of lanes.
- Movements from hide positions into the battle positions.
- Fire commands, triggers, and/or maximum engagement lines to initiate fires.
- Shifting and redistributing fires.
- Preparation and transmission of critical reports.
- Assessment of effects of enemy weapons systems.
- Disengagement and/or displacement of units to their alternate or supplemental positions or to subsequent battle positions.
- Resupply of the battle positions.
- Evacuation of casualties.

Figure 3-4 illustrates what an engagement area might look like for a mechanized company with tanks and a section of TOWs.

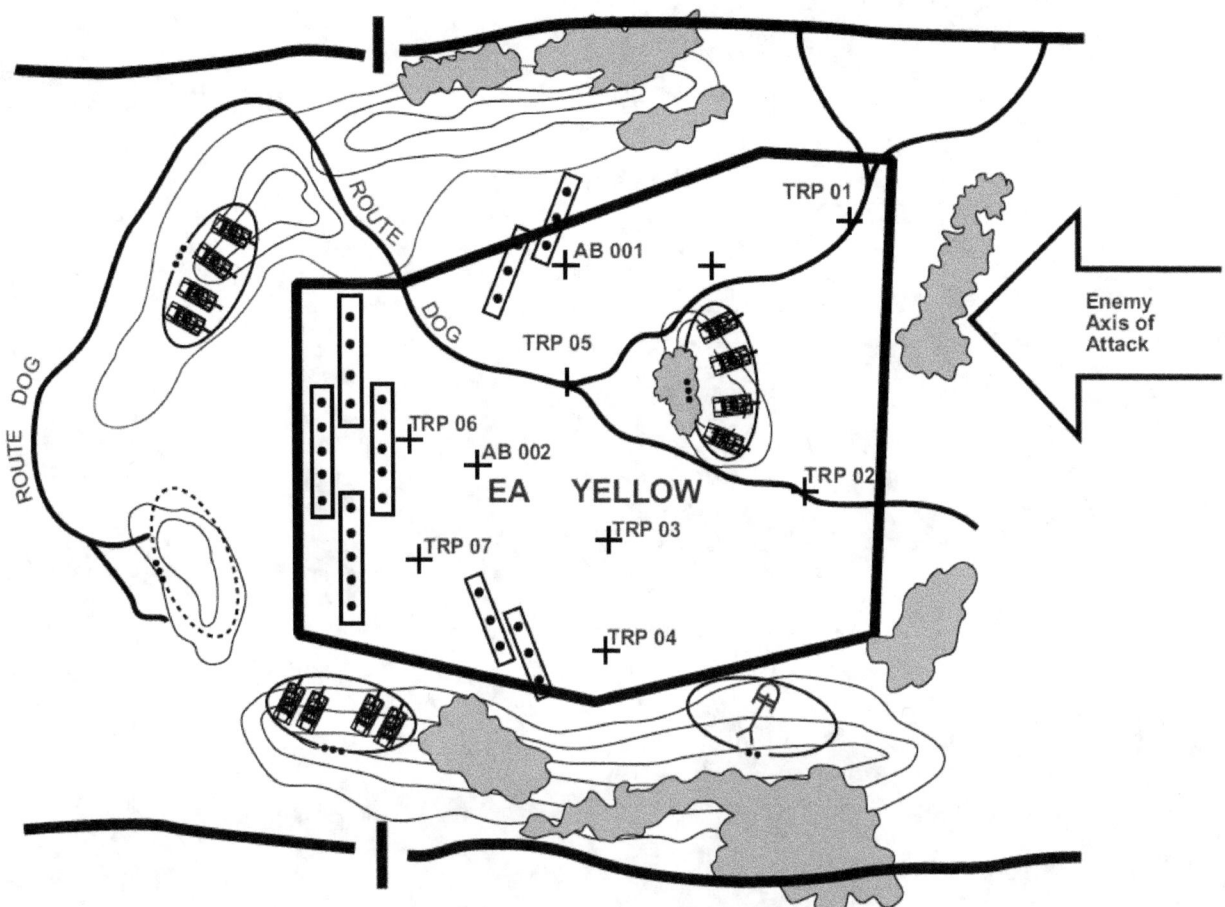

Figure 3-4. Example of Tank Company Engagement Area.

CHAPTER 4
EMPLOYMENT WITH INFANTRY

Marine tank units rarely fight alone. Typically, tank units fight as part of a MAGTF where they are task-organized with other MAGTF elements to achieve a combined-arms effect. Combined arms integrate the effects of various arms—infantry, tank, artillery, and aviation—to achieve the greatest possible effect against the enemy. The strengths of various arms complement and offset each other, while the weaknesses and vulnerabilities of each arm are protected and offset by the capabilities of others.

Mechanized operations are tactical operations designed to maximize the ground mobility, protection, shock action, and firepower of combat vehicles in order to concentrate combat power rapidly against the enemy. Combat power is generated by the massed employment of tanks and by enhancing the mobility of infantry through the use of AAVs and other ground mobility means.

Unrestricted terrain (e.g., flat countryside, desert, plains) is conducive to the conduct of mechanized operations characterized by the employment of massed armor formations. In such terrain, infantry supports the forward movement of the tank units by providing local security, retaining key terrain, clearing dug-in enemy positions, and enhancing direct fires with organic small-arms and antitank fires. Restrictive terrain (e.g., urban areas, forests, jungles) increases the vulnerability of tank units by reducing the speed, mobility, and firepower advantages of the tank. In such terrain, it is necessary for tanks to work closely with dismounted infantry.

When infantry and tanks move together, the infantry moves using one of three methods: dismounted, truck-mounted, or AAV-mounted. This chapter examines how a tank unit is employed to support the advance of infantry.

Task Organization

The Marine Corps does not maintain permanent, mechanized infantry units; instead, it maintains well-trained, general-purpose infantry units capable of task organizing to execute a myriad of ground combat missions. In Marine mechanized operations, mechanized infantry refers to a task-organized force of Marine infantry mounted in AAVs.

Note: Outside the Marine Corps, mechanized operations used in conjunction with infantry (friendly or enemy) operations traditionally refers to the personnel riding in an armored personnel carrier or infantry fighting vehicle that are organic to infantry units.

A Marine mechanized force is a task-organized, ground combat force of combined arms built around an infantry or tank unit and reinforced with substantial assault amphibian assets. A Marine mechanized force is normally supported by air, artillery, light armor, antitank, engineer, reconnaissance, motor transport, combat support, and CSS units. Commanders at every level of command determine their best organization for combat; typically, by cross-attaching units. Cross attachment is the exchange of subordinate units with other units for a temporary period. For example, a tank battalion detaches a tank company that is subsequently attached to an infantry battalion mechanized in AAVs, and the infantry battalion mechanized in AAVs detaches a company to the tank battalion to create two battalion-sized task forces. Mechanized forces are task-organized into mechanized task forces at the regimental and battalion level and company teams at the company level.

Mechanized Task Force

Mechanized task forces are organized as follows:

- A tank-heavy force has more subordinate tank than infantry units. The headquarters of a tank-heavy task force is usually that of a tank battalion.
- A mechanized-heavy force has more subordinate infantry units mounted in tracked vehicles than subordinate tank units. The headquarters of a mechanized-heavy task force is usually that of an infantry battalion or regiment.
- A balanced task force is organized with an equal number of subordinate tank and infantry units. The headquarters for a balanced task force can be either that of a tank battalion or infantry battalion/regiment.
- A pure tank/infantry task force has either tank or infantry units, but not both.

Company Team

A company team is organized by the cross attachment of one or more tank platoons and/or mounted or dismounted infantry platoons. Based on METT-T, an infantry or tank battalion commander who is receiving tank or mechanized infantry companies may increase the effectiveness of his units by forming company teams. This is done by cross-attaching tank platoons and mechanized infantry platoons. Company teams are organized as follows:

- Tank-heavy teams.
- Mechanized-heavy teams.
- Balanced teams.

The tank company is normally the smallest task-organized mechanized element. The tank platoon is normally the smallest unit that is attached/detached. When tanks are task-organized at the company team level, logistic support is normally obtained from the infantry battalion S-4. If the platoon's parent company is in the vicinity, it may be able to coordinate some assistance through the parent unit. Habitual assignment is the routine task organization of one unit to another; although it may not always be practical, it is highly desirable for the following reasons:

- Attached units become familiar with unit SOPs of the units to which they are attached.
- Teamwork is built between units, which is key to achieving unity of effort.
- Unit commanders joining an attached unit become familiar with unit capabilities.

Coordination

Mechanized operations demand effective coordination between the tank unit and the infantry unit it is supporting. The tank platoon/company commander must have a thorough tactical and technical knowledge of his tank's systems and logistical needs in order to advise the infantry unit commander and/or the S-3 with respect to tank employment. Plans should maximize use of a tank's lethal firepower, enhanced target acquisition (including thermal sights), and effective armor protection capabilities. In addition to understanding a tank's capabilities and limitations, the tank unit leader must also understand the disparate capabilities of the mechanized force. For example, infantry mounted in AAVs has less firepower and armor protection and normally moves slower than tanks over certain types of terrain. Another specific example is that sabot ammunition cannot be fired over the heads or flanks of unprotected infantry because of the danger created by the discarding sabot petals and the concussion of the main gun.

Mutual Support

Based on METT-T, the mechanized force's combination of tanks, AAVs, and infantry provides the commander with several options:

- Mounted maneuver with tanks.
- Mounted maneuver with AAVs.

- Mounted maneuver with tanks and AAVs.
- Dismounted maneuver alone.
- Dismounted maneuver combined with any of the mounted maneuver options.

To best exploit the mechanized force's offensive capabilities, tanks and mechanized infantry must work together in pursuit of a common goal. Each element of the mechanized force provides a degree of mutual support to the other element. Tanks support mechanized infantry by—

- Providing mobile protected firepower.
- Neutralizing or destroying hostile weapons by fire and movement.
- Clearing paths for dismounted infantry through obstacles.
- Neutralizing fortified positions with direct fire.
- Supporting dismounted infantry by direct fire.
- Assisting in the consolidation of the objective

Mechanized infantry assists tanks and AAVs by—

- Breaching or removing antiarmor obstacles.
- Assisting in the neutralization or destruction of enemy antiarmor weapons.
- Designating targets for tanks and AAVs.
- Protecting tanks and AAVs from enemy infantry and antiarmor weapons.
- Clearing bridges and fording areas.
- Clearing restrictive terrain such as urban, swamp, or woodland areas.
- Conducting dismounted security patrols.

Employment Methods

There are two general methods to employ tanks and mechanized infantry together in an attack:

- Tank and mechanized infantry (mounted in AAVs or dismounted) attack together.
- Tanks and AAVs support by fire only.

Based on METT-T, a combination of the two methods (called a multiaxis attack) may also be employed.

Tanks and Mechanized Infantry Attack Together

This method of attack allows tanks and mechanized infantry to advance together within mutually supporting distances of each other. Tanks normally lead the formation. Ideally, the infantry remains mounted in AAVs to close with the enemy. However, the infantry remains mounted in AAVs only when the enemy presents a low antiarmor threat. Advantages of tanks and infantry attacking together are as follows:

- Exploits the complete mobility, speed, armor protected firepower, and shock action of the mechanized force.
- Reduces enemy reaction time.
- Disorganizes the enemy's defense since his positions have been breached before the infantry dismounts.
- Conserves the energy of the mechanized infantry since they are carried by AAVs to dismount points short of, on, or behind the objective.
- Reduces the amount of time that the infantry is exposed to enemy fires.

Disadvantages of tanks and infantry attacking together are as follows:

- Greater potential for casualties among elements of the mechanized force if enemy antiarmor fires cannot be bypassed or effectively reduced by suppressive fires.
- AAVs with light armor protection are vulnerable to antiarmor weapons and may be destroyed if employed like a tank. AAV armor can provide protection against hand grenades, shell fragments, and some small-arms fire. However, even when enhanced appliqué armor kits are installed, the AAV can be vulnerable to the fires of tank and antitank guns, ATGMs, and rockets.

- The entire mechanized force can become vulnerable to enemy fires if obstacles are not breached quickly or bypassed.

Tanks and AAVs Support by Fire Only

During planning, the commander of the mechanized force may decide to attack using the tanks and AAVs support by fire only method. However, if during a mounted assault, surprise antiarmor fire is received in such volume that it cannot be suppressed by all immediately available fire support resources, and to continue would result in unacceptable casualties, the infantry dismounts in defilade locations if possible. Tanks and AAVs then adopt the tanks and AAVs support by fire only method. Therefore, commanders must develop plans that provide multiple COAs. Specifically, a plan that incorporates the tanks and mechanized infantry attack together method should also have the flexibility to incorporate the tanks and AAVs support by fire only method if the situation changes unexpectedly. The following are examples of situations in which the infantry should plan to dismount from the AAVs and use the tanks and AAVs support by fire only method:

- Obstacles prevent mounted movement and cannot be quickly breached or bypassed.
- Enemy antiarmor capability poses significant threat to both tanks and AAVs.
- Terrain canalizes mounted movement into likely enemy ambush sites and minefields (e.g., close terrain such as urban or woodland, restrictive terrain such as defiles).
- Visibility is limited.

Key considerations are as follows:

- Prior planning to ensure communications can be maintained between the base of fire element(s) and dismounted infantry during the attack (e.g., prepositioned retransmission sites and preplanned radio relay procedures that can overcome a potential loss of communications during the attack).

- The scheme of maneuver and fire support plan (direct fire, indirect fire, and aviation delivered fires) are developed concurrently and understood by all elements of the mechanized force. Fires are primarily used to engage targets on the objective. Fires are also planned to isolate the objective by engaging targets on adjacent positions or likely enemy avenues of approach. Illumination and obscuration fires are planned regardless or not the mechanized forces intend to employ these fires in the attack.
- Positive control of supporting fires between the dismounted infantry and base of fire element(s) must be maintained throughout the attack.
- Radio communications, pre-arranged visual signals (e.g., pyrotechnic), and/or messengers are used by the infantry to designate targets and coordinate supporting fires.
- AAVs, tanks, and other available direct fire support assets normally displace forward to new support by fire positions as they become available.
- A sustained, heavy volume of fires helps the dismounted infantry maintain the momentum of the attack. Suppressive fire helps compensate for the infantry's lack of armor protection and decreased mobility. Long-range accurate fires (e.g. TOWs) are employed against enemy vehicles, protected antitank guns and ATGMs, and other priority hard targets.
- Ideally, the base of fire element supports from covered and concealed positions. Units comprising the base of fire element should regularly reposition themselves to avoid presenting the enemy with easily acquired stationary targets.
- Dismounted infantry advances on a route that provides cover and concealment and prevents or minimizes masking of the fires of the base of fire element. If available, engineers accompany the dismounted infantry to breach obstacles and destroy fortified positions.

A disadvantage of the tanks and AAVs support by fire only method is that the infantry loses the mobility, shock action, and close support of the tanks and

AAVs. The infantry is unsupported on the objective when the tanks and AAVs shift or cease fires. Also, tanks and AAVs are not initially available on the objective to cover the consolidation.

Multiaxis Attack

A multiaxis attack is a combination of the two employment methods: tanks and mechanized infantry attack together and tanks and AAVs support by fire only. The adoption of this method is based on METT-T. A primary consideration in choosing to use a multi-axis attack is the availability of suitable avenues of approach for tanks, AAVs, and the infantry. The multiaxis attack is used to exploit the amphibious capability of the AAV in crossing streams, rivers, lakes, and marshes. Another application is when a single avenue of approach is too narrow to accommodate the entire mechanized force and tanks follow the more open terrain, while the infantry advance follows an axis offering cover and concealment. Tanks initially support the infantry advance by fire and join the infantry as soon as practicable. Tank movement is normally timed so that the tanks assault the objective slightly in advance of the infantry to take maximum advantage of their shock effect. The greatest challenge to employing this method is to achieve proper timing among the various elements and the coordination of fires during the attack.

Mechanized Movement

Tanks normally lead the mechanized formation due to the tanks relative advantage over the AAV in terms of armor protection and main gun firepower. When the situation permits, AAVs can support the mechanized force by following the tanks close enough to fire around the tanks and deliver suppressive fire against enemy infantry and antiarmor weapons encountered on exposed flanks. Movement of tanks with AAVs is generally based on the following criteria:

- Tanks lead in open areas or when faced with a significant armor threat.
- Mechanized infantry leads mounted only if enemy infantry is pure with no antiarmor reinforcements or capabilities.

The desired distance between tanks and AAVs should be determined before starting the attack. This distance is based on METT-T.

Maneuver Considerations

The critical decision of whether the infantry attacks mounted or dismounted is based on the following considerations.

- Tanks lead and infantry remains mounted when—
  - Enemy antiarmor fires can be effectively bypassed or suppressed by fire.
  - Terrain is relatively open or manmade and natural obstacles can be easily overcome.
  - Terrain and weather affords good trafficability and visibility.
- Infantry leads dismounted when—
  - Terrain and vegetation are restrictive. For example, when terrain and vegetation canalizes movement into likely enemy ambush sites and minefields (e.g., urban areas and woodland terrain).
  - Visibility is limited.
  - Antiarmor fire cannot be bypassed or suppressed by fire.
  - Significant obstacles or fortified positions are encountered that may prevent mounted movement and cannot be bypassed.

Dismounting

Note: The decision to dismount must be made prior to committing the force to the final assault.

Once the commander of the mechanized force decides to dismount his infantry, he chooses when and where (the dismount point) to dismount the infantry. Commanders normally stay well forward to personally judge the situation and make an appropriate decision of whether or not to change the dismount point. Timing is critical because dismounting too early slows the force's momentum and unnecessarily exposes the infantry to hostile fire. The commander should also take into account that speed can provide for the security of a mechanized force already committed to the final assault. Ideally, the infantry is dismounted after forward defensive positions have been breached. The following are some dismount point considerations:

- The dismount point should provide good cover and concealment, yet be as near to the objective as possible to reduce the amount of time that the dismounted infantry is exposed to fires while closing with the enemy.
- Rapid dismount and good vehicle dispersion reduces the mechanized force's vulnerability to enemy fires.

Dismount points may be short of the objective, on the objective, or after passing through the objective.

Dismount Short of the Objective

Tactical conditions may require seeking a dismount point short of the objective. Infantry dismounted short of the objective is usually not within range of small-arms and handheld antiarmor weapons. Ideally, the dismount point should be located on easily recognizable terrain that provides cover from enemy direct fires. Advantages of dismounting short of the objective include—

- Dismounted infantry are protected from small-arms and observed indirect fires while dismounting.
- Infantry can be oriented as they approach the objective.

- Control can be established in the dismount point.
- Organic and supporting fires can suppress the enemy while the infantry is dismounting.

Disadvantages of dismounting short of the objective include—

- Dismounted infantry are exposed longer to enemy small-arms and indirect fire as they move forward in the assault.
- Suitable dismount points that are forward of enemy positions may be targeted by enemy direct and indirect fires.

Dismount on the Objective

Dismount on the objective is a technique used when the mechanized force has achieved surprise or when the enemy's antiarmor defense is weak. The following are advantages of dismounting on the objective:

- Greater speed and shock effect.
- Mechanized infantry remains protected by AAV light armor longer from the fires of enemy small arms.
- Supporting fires can continue while the mechanized force approaches its objective since mounted infantry have greater protection against shell fragments and other small projectiles.

Disadvantages of dismounting on the objective include—

- Difficulty orienting mechanized infantry to specific objectives.
- Difficulty establishing control at the dismount point due to potentially close enemy fires.
- Difficulty in directing supporting fires against enemy positions in close proximity to friendly dismounted infantry.
- Vulnerability of AAVs to short-range antiarmor weapons.
- High volume of suppressive fire is required to support dismounted infantry.

Dismount After Passing Through the Objective

Dismounting after passing through the objective is employed when a mounted attack is more effective. The capabilities of the enemy antiarmor defense dictate if this is feasible. Advantages of dismounting after passing through the objective include—

- Dismounted infantry fights from an area and direction unexpected from the enemy.
- Control is usually more easily established when not on the objective.
- Shock effect on the enemy caused by a mechanized force moving through its position is likely to be considerable.

Disadvantages of dismounting after passing through the objective are as follows:

- This method may run afoul of enemy positions in depth.
- Enemy indirect and direct fires might still target suitable dismount points.
- Facing the AAV toward the objective before dismounting is desirable from the viewpoint of limited armored protection and the AAV crew employment of the upgunned weapons station. However, the act of turning AAVs around in close proximity to enemy fires can make the AAVs more vulnerable to flank shots. Also, turning AAVs and dismounting infantry may reverse the relative positions of the tanks, AAVs, and infantry. The dismounted infantry may initially mask direct fires from AAVs and tanks until the AAVs and tanks can maneuver around the infantry to new support by fire positions.

Base of Fire and Maneuver Elements

To facilitate fire and maneuver, mechanized forces normally organize into a maneuver element and base of fire element. Fires are primarily employed to suppress, neutralize, destroy, and demoralize enemy forces. Maneuver, which is movement supported by fire, brings firepower into positions from which it extends and completes the destruction of the enemy force. The composition of base of fire and maneuver element is determined by the commander's task organization of the mechanized force.

The base of fire element covers the maneuver element's advance toward the enemy position by engaging all known or suspected targets. Upon opening fire, the base of fire seeks to gain fire superiority over the enemy. Fire superiority is gained by subjecting the enemy to fire of such accuracy and volume that the enemy fire ceases or becomes ineffective.

The mission of the maneuver element is to close with and destroy or capture the enemy. It advances and assaults under covering fire of the base of fire element. The maneuver element uses available cover and concealment to the maximum. Fire superiority is maintained throughout the attack in order to ensure the success of any maneuver.

When mechanized units conduct attacks, they will utilize one or more of the following techniques:

- Fire and maneuver is the process of one or more elements establishing a base of fire to engage the enemy, while the other element(s) maneuvers to an advantageous position from which to close with and destroy or capture the enemy. Supporting fires may consist of direct, indirect, and aviation-delivered fires, which are integrated to achieve the effects of combined arms. Supporting fires should be followed closely by the maneuver element so that the shock effect of fire upon the enemy is not lost.
- Fire and movement is employed once the maneuver element meets enemy opposition and can no longer advance under the cover of the base of fire. It allows forward movement to a position from which units can continue to assault the enemy position. Fire and movement is primarily used in the assault wherein a unit or element advances by bounds or rushes, with subelements alternately moving and providing

covering fire for other moving subelements. Fire and movement may be done by individuals (personnel or vehicles) or units. Usually, fire and movement is used only when under effective fire from the enemy because it is relatively slow and difficult to control.

There are situations when maneuvering to close range of the enemy is not required. Attack by fire is fires employed to destroy the enemy from a distance. This task is usually given to the supporting element during offensive operations and as a counterattack option for the reserve during defensive operations. An attack by fire is not done in conjunction with a maneuvering force. When assigning this task, the commander of the mechanized force specifies the intent of fires—either to destroy, fix, or suppress.

Assault on the Objective

The purpose of the assault is to place violent and intensive firepower on the objective and move rapidly across it to destroy or capture the enemy as quickly as possible. The term assault refers only to that phase of an attack when the attacking force actually closes with the enemy. Mechanized forces assault the objective either mounted or dismounted.

Mounted Assault

The decision to make a mounted assault is based upon METT-T. A mounted assault is best used when the enemy is occupying a hasty fighting position, antiarmor fires can be suppressed, and when the terrain in the vicinity of the objective allows for rapid movement onto and across the objective. The assault must be carried out rapidly. Normally, tanks lead and are followed closely by AAVs. As the assault force approaches the objective, the AAVs should move closer to the tanks for added protection from enemy, short-range antiarmor weapons.

Movement across the objective must be fast and continuous. A heavy volume of suppressive fires is maintained to keep enemy soldiers down in their positions. Stabilized turrets allow tanks to continue moving while conducting fire and movement. AAVs normally stay as close to the tanks as possible to provide protection to the flanks and rear of the tank.

Once the tanks and AAVs reach the far side of the objective, they occupy hull-down positions (if possible). From support by fire positions, the tanks and AAVs can engage any retreating enemy forces, continue the attack, or defend against counterattack. If it is necessary to seize the objective, the dismounted infantry is used to clear remaining pockets of enemy resistance and to secure prisoners.

A mechanized pure force assaults mounted without tanks in essentially the same way it assaults with them.

Dismounted Assault

If the enemy is in well-prepared, defensive positions, antiarmor fires cannot be suppressed, or the terrain restricts vehicle movement onto the objective then the assault is normally conducted dismounted. If the attack starts as mounted, the infantry should be dismounted in a covered and concealed position that is as close to the objective as possible. The base of fire element delivers supporting fires while the dismounted infantry deploys. Dismounted infantry uses radios, prearranged visual signals (e.g., pyrotechnic), and/or messengers to direct the base of fire element to shift and cease supporting fires. The dismounted infantry then employs fire and movement through the objective. Elements of the base of fire element normally displace to subsequent support by fire positions just before their fires are masked by the dismount element. When the tanks and AAVs from the base of fire element rejoin the dismounted infantry, the infantry—

- Suppresses any remaining enemy position as the tanks and AAVs move to the objective.

- Reconnoiters initial support by fire positions and guides tanks and AAVs into the positions when necessary.
- Provides flank and rear security for the AAVs and tanks.

Based on METT-T, the tanks may be employed to continue through the objective, engage resistance, and pursue by fire until the infantry has consolidated the position.

Consolidation and Reorganization

The mechanized force consolidates and reorganizes as soon as it takes the objective. This is done so the force can either repel a counterattack or continue the attack. The mechanized force consolidates the objective by—

- Tanks and AAVs are positioned in support by fire positions and assigned sectors of fire while antiarmor weapons are being positioned. Tanks and AAVs are normally positioned on terrain that both provides cover and concealment and permits the vehicles to overwatch the infantry in the event of enemy counterattack. If possible, tanks and AAVs are placed in hull-down positions.
- All elements of the mechanized force establish local security and mutual support between units.
- The dismounted infantry eliminates any remaining pockets of enemy resistance and secures prisoners of war. Dismounted infantry

normally designates targets for the overwatching vehicles and uses organic and supporting fires to destroy any enemy resistance.

- After consolidation, the infantry either remounts the AAVs to continue the attack or sets up a hasty or deliberate defense.

Reorganization consists of the following:

- Replacing key leaders who became casualties.
- Redistributing ammunition.
- Arranging for medical evacuation of casualties.
- Safeguarding prisoners of war to collection points or to the rear.

During mechanized operations in unrestricted terrain, tanks should always lead in offensive movement formations. Speed, mobility, firepower, and survivability are otherwise reduced. The survivability, superior target acquisition, range of weapon systems, and lethality of tank units provide the unit commander with time to develop the situation and choose an appropriate COA.

Transporting Infantry

On very rare occasions, the platoon leader may be required to transport infantrymen on tanks (see fig. 4-1 on page 4-10). This occurs only when contact is not expected. If the platoon is moving as part of a larger force and is tasked to provide security, the lead section or element should not carry infantry.

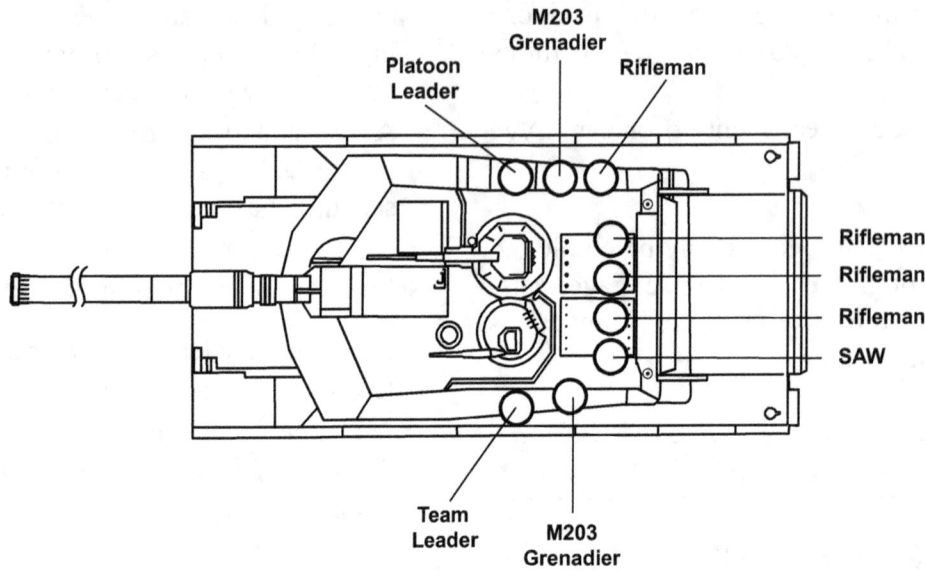

Figure 4-1. Notional Positions for Infantry Riding on a Tank.

CHAPTER 5
OTHER TACTICAL OPERATIONS

SECTION I. SECURITY OPERATIONS

Security operations are designed to provide reaction time, maneuver space, and protection for the force as a whole. The primary mission of the security force is the protection of the main body as opposed to a terrain or enemy objective.

At the tactical level, security forces protect against surprise attack and observation by hostile air and ground forces by ensuring the enemy is not able to see or engage the main force. They maintain freedom of maneuver for the main force by providing reaction time and maneuver space. Forces conducting security missions focus their movements on the main force or facility that they are assigned to secure.

Security forces may operate at varying distances from the main body based on conditions of METT-T. They employ the minimum combat power necessary to cover extended frontages in order to provide the main body commander early warning. This allows the commander to retain the bulk of his combat power to be committed at the decisive place and time to engage the enemy.

Security forces report enemy activities to the main body commander and to other affected security forces. The main body commander ensures that the security force commander has access to all pertinent intelligence and combat information obtained by the main body to supplement the security force's capabilities. Through the continuous exchange of information, both the security force and main body commander have the time to choose a COA suitable to the situation. When tanks are employed as a security force, they are usually augmented with other forces that help provide intelligence and quick analysis in order to develop the situation as quickly as possible once contact is made. Tank units usually focus on avenues of approach large enough for enemy mechanized units to utilize since they can be the largest threat to a mechanized main force.

To help tank units conduct security operations, aviation assets work in concert with ground security forces to create a synergism that facilitates rapid mission execution. Aviation assets can alert tanks of the approaching enemy, and they may also help to attrite the enemy forces before engagement with ground security forces.

Tank units conducting security operations must also take into account that the enemy may have assets that are employed to detect them. Careful planning before the security mission should be done to determine the enemy's ability to employ its air and RSTA assets, likely enemy locations and/or routes, enemy surveillance devices, indirect fire capabilities, and both mounted and dismounted antitank platform capabilities.

Regardless of the type of security mission, a tank's ability to perform a successful security operation depends on the proper application of the following fundamentals:

- *Providing early warning and reaction time.* The security force provides early warning by detecting the enemy force quickly and alerting the main body. It provides reaction time for the main body by taking actions within its capability and mission constraints to delay the enemy's advance.

- *Orienting on the force to secure.* The security force orients all its actions to protect and provide early warning to the force that it is to secure. It aggressively seeks out the enemy and only occupies terrain in order to enhance its ability to protect the main body.
- *Performing continuous reconnaissance.* The security force conducts its operations by aggressively seeking out the enemy and reconnoitering key terrain. Security forces continuously employ a combination of observation posts, mounted/dismounted patrols, sensors, and defensive positions.
- *Maintaining enemy contact.* The security force commander arrays his available assets to ensure continuous contact with the enemy. At the same time, the security force must not become decisively engaged and fixed in place. It must retain its flexibility to stay in front of the enemy and ability to report. Contact with the enemy is maintained both physically and with technical assets.

There are three types of security operations: cover, guard, and screen. Each type of operation provides an increased measure of security and reaction time to the force; however, the more combat power allocated to the security force, the less will be available for the main effort. A cover allocates considerable combat power to engage an enemy force at a considerable distance from the main force if provided the maximum early warning and reaction time. A guard contains sufficient combat power to defeat or contain lead elements of an enemy force. A screen allocates minimal combat power to cover an extended flank, yet only provides early warning.

Covering Force

Typically, a covering force operates forward of the main force; however, it may operate to the rear or on either flank. Although a covering force aggressively develops the situation independent of the main force, its main role is to prevent the surprise and untimely engagement of the main force.

A covering force differs from a screening or guarding force in that it is normally a self-sufficient, combined-arms force equipped with enough combat power to develop a situation at a considerable distance away from the main force. While the covering force provides the most security to the main force, it generally requires a considerable amount of dedicated logistic support. Therefore, a commander only assigns a covering force mission whenever the enemy possesses a strong mobile force that is capable of rapid and decisive action and there are sufficient assets to resource both the covering force and the main force. A rear covering force normally protects a force moving away from the enemy. The covering force deploys behind the forward maneuver units of the main force, accepts battle handover and passes the main force through it, and then defends or delays. Alternatively, the covering force may conduct a relief in place as part of a deception plan or to take advantage of the best defensive terrain. The covering force establishes passage points and assists the rearward passage of the main force if necessary. As the main force moves, the covering force displaces to subsequent phase lines in depth.

Offensive Cover

During offensive operations, a covering force may operate to the front or flanks of the main body. An offensive covering force may accomplish the following:

- Perform reconnaissance along the main body's axis of advance.
- Deny the enemy information about the size, strength, composition, and objective of the main body.

- Destroy or repel enemy reconnaissance and security zone forces.
- Penetrate enemy defense in order to develop the situation to determine enemy strengths, weaknesses, and dispositions.
- Defeat, repel, or fix enemy forces as directed by the higher commander.
- Exploit opportunities.

The covering force should clear the zone of enemy security and small combat elements and penetrate the leading elements of the enemy's defensive positions. When it can advance no further, it prepares for the main body to conduct a forward passage of lines. It continues to perform close reconnaissance of enemy positions to locate gaps or vulnerable flanks. A good covering force allows the commander of the main force the ability to attack the enemy's weak point at the time of his choosing with previously uncommitted forces.

Defensive Cover

A defensive covering force operates to the front, flanks, or rear of a main force. The primary mission of a defensive covering force is to strip away enemy reconnaissance, force the enemy to reveal his main effort, disrupt his attack, and deny him the initiative. Defensive covering forces—

- Maintain continuous surveillance of high-speed avenues of approach.
- Destroy or repel enemy reconnaissance and security forces.
- Determine the size, strength, composition, and direction of the enemy's main effort.
- Defeat the lead enemy echelons if possible.
- Force the enemy to deploy repeatedly in order to fight through the covering force and commit his reserve or follow-on forces to sustain momentum.
- Create ambiguity as to location and disposition of the main force.

The covering force screens, defends, delays, and counterattacks to execute a defensive cover. If the covering force area is not yet occupied, the covering force may have to reconnoiter and clear the area or route. As in offensive operations, aerial reconnaissance is critical to extending the battlespace. It can screen less threatened sectors and rapidly reinforce fires when other elements of the covering force are heavily engaged. During defensive operations, the commander of the main force designates the forward and rear boundaries of the security force with phase lines. The lateral boundaries of the security area are normally extensions of main body boundaries. The rear boundary of the covering force area is the FEBA.

Guard Force

A guard force protects the main force by preventing the enemy from being able to engage main forces with direct fire weapons. The guard force accomplishes its task by reconnoitering, attacking, defending, and delaying enemy forces in order to provide time for the main force to counter enemy actions.

A guard differs from a screening force in that it contains greater combat power and is employed to engage enemy forces within its capability as opposed to a screen that only provides early warning and destroys enemy reconnaissance. A screening mission may transition to a guard mission upon the approach of a sizable enemy force. For example, a tank company conducting a screen may be reinforced with the remaining tank battalion if it is determined that a sizeable enemy mechanized force is approaching and may need to be destroyed before reaching follow-on forces.

A guard force is normally task-organized from elements of the main force; therefore, it operates within supporting range of the main body. If units need both protection and early warning, the commander of the main force assigns a guard mission to subordinate units when there are little or no other security forces between the main force and probable enemy forces. The commander may use a guard to the front of his main forces (advance guard), to the rear (rear guard) especially during retrograde operations, or to the flank (flank guard) when there is a threat of significant enemy contact.

The commander may designate a tank unit as a guard force for protection from enemy ground observation, direct fire, and surprise attack for a given period of time. A guard force allows the commander to extend the defense in time and space to prevent interruption of the organization of the main battle area.

Advance Guard

The advance guard is the lead element of an advancing formation or column. The advance guard's mission is to clear the axis or zone of enemy elements and to allow the unimpeded movement of the main force. If an advance guard operates behind the security force of a higher echelon, then the higher echelon security force initially develops the situation. The advance guard may then reinforce the higher echelon security force or expand the area of contact with the enemy force.

Flank Guard

The flank guard has the responsibility to clear the area between the main force and the flank guard's position. Typically, the flank guard operates on a smaller frontage than a screen. The commander of the flank guard considers the axis taken by the main force, enemy's capabilities, and avenues of approach in order to determine his initial dispositions. Sectors should be sufficiently deep to provide early warning and reaction time, yet remain within supporting range of the main force.

Should an enemy attack appear imminent from the flank, the flank guard normally occupies preplanned or hasty defensive positions. Should the enemy prove too strong for the flank guard, the flank guard will normally delay in sector. Flank guard operations can be employed while the main force is stationary or moving. Whichever technique is used, the flank guard must remain in contact with the leading elements of the main body.

A stationary flank guard reconnoiters out to its initial security positions. This allows the flank guard to clear the zone and become familiar with the terrain that may subsequently be defended. Upon reaching its initial positions, the flank guard establishes a defense. The commander plans the defense or delay in depth from the initial positions. The following critical tasks apply during a stationary flank guard mission:

- Maintain continuous surveillance of enemy avenues of approach.
- Maintain contact with the main body.
- Provide early warning and defeat, repel, or fix enemy ground forces, within capabilities, before they can engage the main body with direct fire.

The techniques for movement and establishment of a moving flank guard force are similar the to techniques used during flank screening operations. Whichever technique is used, the flank guard must remain in contact with the leading elements of the main body.

Based on the speed of the main body, the likelihood of the enemy attack, and the distance to the objective, the guard force uses one or a combination of the following movement techniques:

- Successive bounds is used when the enemy action against the flank is light and the movement of the main force is expected to include frequent short halts.
- Alternate bounds is used when strong enemy action is anticipated against the flank, this technique requires slow movement by the main force. Alternate bounds are the most secure, yet the slowest technique.
- Continuous movement is used when enemy activity on the flank is unlikely and the main force is moving with all possible speed. Traveling in column with an on-order defensive mission is the quickest but least secure technique.

Rear Guard

The rear guard protects the exposed rear of the main force during offensive operations or retrograde operations. Rear guards are normally established during a withdrawal, during a retirement, or when conducting deep maneuver forward of the forward line of own troops when there is significant enemy threat to the rear of the main force.

Establishing a rear guard during a retrograde operation may be done in two ways. The rear guard may relieve other units in place along the forward line of own troops as they move to the rear. Alternatively, the rear guard may establish a position in depth behind the main force and pass those forces through.

The rear guard employs both sector and battle positions while executing its mission. The commander of the main force prescribes the distance that the rear guard must maintain between itself and the main force. The rear guard for a moving force displaces to successive, in-depth battle positions as the main force moves. The nature of enemy contact determines the method of displacement.

Screening Force

A screening force primarily provides early warning. It observes, identifies, and reports information. It generally fights only in self-defense, but does engage enemy reconnaissance elements within its capabilities. Commanders generally establish screens on an extended flank, to the rear, or to the front of a stationary force. A screen is often executed as a series of observation posts with patrolling between them.

The GCE commander may establish a screening force utilizing tank units to gain and maintain contact with the enemy, to observe enemy activity, to identify the enemy main effort, and to report information. In most situations, the minimum security force, normally organized by the GCE, is a screening force. Normally, the screening force only fights in self-defense, but it may be tasked to—

- Repel enemy reconnaissance units as part of the GCE's counterreconnaissance effort.
- Prevent enemy artillery from acquiring terrain that enables a front line unit to be engaged.
- Provide early warning.
- Attack the enemy with supporting arms.

A screen is not conducted forward of a moving force. The security element forward of a moving force must conduct either a guard or cover. The senior commander determines the general location at which he wants the screening force to operate. Screens for a moving force must remain physically tied into the main force. The initial screen line must be within supporting range of the main force, yet far enough away to provide sufficient early warning. Normally, there is little or no depth along the screen, except along high-speed avenues of approach. This depth allows commanders to maintain continuous contact while observation posts along the initial screen line are displacing.

The screening force commander controls movement in sector by designating subsequent screen lines. Subsequent screen lines are essentially phase lines. Displacement to a subsequent screen line is event driven. The approach of an enemy force, relief of a friendly unit, or movement of the protected force dictate screen movements.

A screening force provides security for a main force that is either stationary or moving. The terms stationary and moving describe the actions of the protected force, not the screening force.

Stationary Screen

A security force conducts a screen to the front, flank, and rear of a stationary force in a similar manner. The tasks associated with a stationary screen normally consist of movement to the initial screen line, establishment of the screen, and displacement to subsequent screen lines. Additionally, the screening force commander coordinates battle handover lines (BHLs) and passage of lines with the main force commander.

Moving Screen

A screen is maintained along the flanks and/or the rear of the main force. Responsibilities for a moving flank screen begin at the front of the lead combat element in the main force and end at the rear of the protected force.

A moving screen may be placed to the rear of the main force conducting an attack or a retrograde operation. In this situation, the screen line displaces to a subsequent screen line based on movements of the main body or enemy force. Movement along the screen line is determined by the speed of the main force, the distance to the objective, and the enemy situation. There are four basic methods of controlling movement along the screen line:

- Alternate bound by individual observation posts from rear to front.
- Alternate bound by subordinate units from rear to front.
- Successive bound by units along the screen line.
- Continuous march along the route of advance.

The movement of the screen is keyed to the movement of the main force. There are three techniques of performing this type of screen:

- Screening force crosses the line of departure separate from the main force when the main force is moving quickly or the line of departure is uncontested. This is the fastest but least secure technique.
- Screening force's lead element reconnoiters the zone when the main force is moving slow or

the line of departure is uncontested. This technique is slower than the previous technique, but provides better security.
- Screening force crosses line of departure with the main force when the main force is moving slowly, the line of departure is also the line of contact, or the enemy situation is vague. This technique provides security for the screening force and the main force, but it is the most time consuming.

Screening Operations During Limited Visibility

Limited visibility caused by weather conditions often affects the screening force's ground and air observation capabilities. While technical intelligence assets can be employed to offset limited visibility, the screening force should adjust its techniques and procedures (e.g., observation posts should be adjusted; night and thermal observation devices employed; electronic surveillance devices, trip flares, and observation posts placed along dismounted avenues of approach). Depth in the screen can facilitate acquisition of enemy forces that may elude forward elements. Patrols are closely coordinated to prevent misidentification and engagement by friendly elements. Indirect illumination is planned and used as necessary.

Integration of Intelligence Systems

In addition to aviation, technical assets can greatly expand the area covered by screening forces. Remote sensors, unmanned aerial vehicles, and downlinks from theater and national assets can all greatly expand the area covered by a screening force, thereby providing the main force and the screening force commanders time to adjust to situations if necessary.

Section II. Retrograde Operations

Retrograde operations are organized movements to the rear or away from the enemy. The enemy may force these operations or a commander may execute them voluntarily. Retrograde operations are transitional operations, and they are not considered in isolation. They are conducted either before or after defensive or offensive operations. They are part of a larger scheme of maneuver to regain the initiative and defeat the enemy. In any retrograde, consideration must be given to possible refugee traffic that will both clog high-speed avenues of approach and also require displacement assistance/humanitarian aid, which will be exacerbated in the highly populated regions of the world. Commanders execute retrogrades to—

- Wear down the enemy, trading space for time in situations that do not favor a defense.
- Disengage from combat.
- Avoid combat under undesirable conditions such as continuing an operation that no longer promises success.
- Draw the enemy into an unfavorable situation.
- Place forces in a more favorable position.
- Allow the use of a portion or all of the force elsewhere.
- Conform to the movement of other forces.

The forms of retrograde include delay, withdrawal, and retirement operations.

Delay

In the delay, the destruction of the enemy force is secondary to slowing his advance in order to gain time for friendly forces. Mechanized units are ideally suited for delay operations because their long-range weapons and mobility allow the enemy advance to be slowed and/or attrited while forces conduct the delay and gain time. Delays are conducted—

- When the force's strength is insufficient to defend or attack.
- To reduce the enemy's offensive capability by inflicting casualties.
- To gain time by forcing the enemy to deploy.
- To determine the strength and location of the enemy's main effort.
- When the enemy intent is not clear and the commander desires intelligence.
- To protect and provide early warning for the main battle area forces.
- To allow time to re-establish the defense.

The delay succeeds by forcing the enemy to repeatedly concentrate his forces to fight through delay positions. Delaying forces displace once the enemy concentrates sufficient resources to decisively engage and defeat friendly forces.

Tanks are well-suited for delay operations due to their high rate of fire, armor protection against enemy artillery, and mobility. Tanks may also be retained in a reserve to extricate forces that have been decisively engaged or to conduct counterattacks.

Techniques of Delay Operations

There are two main techniques of delay operations: delay from alternate positions and delay from successive positions. In the execution of either technique, it is crucial that the delay force maintains contact with the enemy between delay positions.

Alternate Positions

Delay from alternate positions involves two or more units in a single sector that occupy delaying positions in depth. As the first unit engages the enemy, the second occupies the next position in depth and prepares to assume responsibility for the operation. The first force disengages and passes around the second. It then prepares to re-engage the enemy from a position in greater depth, while the second force takes up the fight.

Delay from alternate positions is useful on particularly dangerous avenues of approach because it offers greater security than delay from successive positions. However, it requires more forces and continuous maneuver coordination. Additionally, there is the risk of losing contact with the enemy between delay positions.

Successive Positions

Delaying from successive positions occurs when the sector is so wide that available forces cannot occupy more than a single tier of positions. Delaying units are positioned forward in a single echelon. Maneuver units delay continuously on and between positions throughout their sectors. As a result, this technique is simpler to coordinate than the delay from alternate positions.

Delaying from successive positions is easier to penetrate than a delay from alternate positions because the force has less depth and less time to occupy subsequent positions. To facilitate the rapid occupation of positions, units normally perform reconnaissance on subsequent positions before occupation and post guides on one or two subsequent positions.

In restrictive terrain, where infantry conducts the primary action, successive positions may be close together. In more open terrain, delay positions are often further apart. In the selection of positions, commanders consider the location of natural and artificial obstacles, particularly when the enemy possesses sufficient armored combat systems.

Organization of Forces

As in defensive operations, commanders assign their delaying force a sector with flank and rear boundaries and the commander selects delay positions on key terrain astride likely enemy avenues of approach. Delay positions are normally battle positions that commanders plan throughout the depth of the delay sector. Phase lines are designated along identifiable terrain features to control the displacement of friendly forces. Selected phase lines may be designated as delay lines. Delay lines require the delaying force to prevent the enemy from crossing the line until a specified time or the occurrence of an event.

Coordination is critical during a delay. To ensure coordination, commanders designate contact points at the boundaries along delay lines to ensure units coordinate each series of delay positions.

In the delay, reconnaissance and surveillance assets are focused on named and target areas of interest. It is essential that the delaying commander identify the enemy's advance early enough to adjust his scheme of maneuver and concentrate sufficient combat power to effectively delay the enemy.

Commanders normally retain a reserve to contain enemy penetrations between delay positions, reinforce fires into an engagement area, or help a unit disengaging from the enemy. The size of the reserve depends on the situation and forces available.

Execution of the Delay

A mechanized force will normally be assigned sectors in which to delay and the initial delay positions. Phase lines may be employed to control the timing of the delay. The tank should be employed as the primary weapon to engage enemy tanks.

Rear Operations

Rear operations in a delay are similar to rear operations in the defense. However, the echeloning of CSS organizations required to maintain continuous support during the delay, coupled with the additional dispersion inherent to the delay, complicates the conduct of these operations. Critical to the success of the delay is the ability of the rear to provide class III and V to the force.

Concluding the Delay

A delay operation terminates when one of the following three conditions exist:

- The advancing enemy force reaches a culmination point. The delaying force then has three choices: they maintain contact in current positions, they withdraw, or the delaying force transitions to the offense.
- The delaying force passes through another force. Typically, the delaying force will conduct a rearward passage of lines, which may be under enemy pressure, at the BHL and move into the assembly areas. Smooth transfer requires coordinating passage points, establishing recognition signals, and determining supporting fires and routes through the defended position. The BHL should be in front of the FEBA. It is preferable to pass delaying units to the rear in sectors not under direct attack.
- The delaying force reaches defensible terrain and transitions to the defense.

Withdrawal

A withdrawal occurs when a force in contact disengages from an enemy force. It is a type of retrograde operation in which a force in contact plans to disengage from the enemy and moves away from the enemy. The tank battalion's mobility makes it ideally suited to perform rear guard duties for a withdrawing force. Withdraws may be executed at any time and during any type of operation. Units undertake a withdrawal for the following reasons:

- If the unit achieves its objective and there is no further requirement to maintain contact.
- To avoid baffle under unfavorable tactical conditions (e.g., if a force cannot achieve the object of its operation and defeat threatens the force).
- To draw the enemy into an unfavorable position.
- To extend the enemy's lines of communication.
- To conform to the movements of adjacent friendly forces.
- As an economy of force measure that allows the use of the force or parts of the force elsewhere.
- As a prelude to a retirement operation.
- For logistical reasons.

Withdrawals are inherently dangerous since they involve moving units to the rear away from what is usually a stronger enemy force. An aggressive enemy will attempt to prevent or delay a unit's withdrawal. In all withdrawals, the commander should attempt to conceal from the enemy the force's intention to withdraw. Since the force is the most vulnerable if the enemy attacks, commander's plan for a withdrawal under pressure. Commanders then develop contingencies for a withdrawal without pressure. In both cases, the commander's primary concerns will be to:

- Break contact with the enemy.
- Displace the main body rapidly, free of enemy interference.
- Safeguard the withdrawal routes.
- Retain sufficient combat, combat support, and CSS capabilities throughout the operation.

A withdrawal normally occurs in three overlapping phases. The preparatory phase occurs when all nonessential personnel, including combat trains, are relocated to the rear. Next, the disengagement phase has units begin sequenced movement to the rear. When contact is broken, a tactical march is conducted to an assembly area. During the security phase, a detachment left in contact assists disengagement of other elements, it assumes responsibility for the battalion sector, deceives the enemy, and protects the movement of disengaging elements with maneuver and fires. This phase is completed when the detachment left in contact breaks contact with the enemy and completes its movement to the rear.

Types of Withdrawals

Withdrawal Under Enemy Pressure

A withdrawal under enemy pressure depends on maneuver and firepower to break contact as the enemy attacks the withdrawing unit. The goal is to preserve the unit and prevent the enemy from forcing the withdrawal into a disorganized retreat. In a withdrawal under pressure, you conduct fire and movement to disengage from the enemy. The withdrawal begins with the withdrawing unit (not the security force) engaging the enemy along all avenues of approach. The withdrawing unit disengages, conducts a rearward passage through the security force, assembles, and moves to the next position. The security force assumes the fight from the forward elements. This includes delaying the enemy advance while the bulk of the withdrawing unit conducts a movement to the rear. On order or when predetermined criteria are met, the security force disengages itself and moves to the rear as a rearguard. The rearguard may be required to maintain contact with the enemy throughout the operation.

Withdrawal Not Under Enemy Pressure

If the unit is not under actual attack, the withdrawal is not under pressure. A withdrawal not under pressure depends on deception and speed of execution. The enemy must not be aware that the withdrawal is taking place. Deception and operations security are essential to the success of the operation. Two things can be done to deceive the enemy: leave a detachment left in contact (DLIC) to make the enemy believe that forces are still in position or use limited visibility to cover the withdrawal. If a tank battalion must form its own DLIC, it is normally organized from elements of each tank company in contact with the enemy. The DLIC would normally be commanded by the battalion executive officer or operations officer. The company DLICs would normally be commanded by the company executive officers. Another option is for the tank battalion commander to leave a single company as the DLIC. If enemy contact is just in one company's sector, this approach is preferred. The DLIC should be able to engage the enemy on all avenues of approach with both direct and indirect fire. The main body and combat support elements displace using stealth along designated routes to a new assembly area. Reserve forces may be positioned along the withdrawal routes and be given on-order missions to defend, delay, or counterattack during the withdrawal.

Assisted Withdrawal

In an assisted withdrawal, the assisting force may provide:

- The security force through which the withdrawing force will pass.
- Reconnaissance of withdrawal routes.
- Forces to secure chokepoints or key terrain along withdrawal routes.
- Elements to assist in movement control such as the establishment of traffic control points.
- Required combat, combat support, and CSS. This can involve conducting a counterattack to assist the withdrawing unit disengage from the enemy.

Unassisted Withdrawal

In an unassisted withdrawal, the withdrawing unit must do everything by itself. It must establish its own security force, perform reconnaissance and secure routes to the rear, and disengage from the enemy.

Organization of Forces

Units avoid changing their task organization, unless they have sufficient planning time. However, circumstances may dictate rapid task organization changes immediately before the withdrawal. A commander typically organizes his force into security forces, a main body, and a reserve.

Security Forces

If the security force cannot prevent the enemy from closing on the main body, it must either be reinforced by the reserve or the overall commander must commit some or all of the main body to restore the situation. The greater the stand-off advantage that the security force has, the easier it will be for the security force to successfully cover the main body's withdrawal. The security force maintains contact with the enemy until ordered to disengage or until another force takes over this task.

When a security zone exists between the two main opposing forces, the existing security forces can transition on order to a rear guard. They then conduct delay operations until ordered to disengage and break contact with the enemy.

Sometimes the withdrawing force is in close contact with an enemy and a security zone does not exist. Withdrawals under these conditions require different techniques by security forces. If a security zone is not possible, a DLIC provides the means to sequentially break contact with the enemy. The DLICs attempt to deceive the enemy by giving the impression that the original defending unit continues to hold the position in strength. The detachments left in contact simulate, as nearly as possible, continued presence of the main body until it is too late for the enemy to react. This force must have specific instructions about what to do when the enemy attacks, and when and under what circumstances to withdraw. If required, these detachments receive additional recovery, evacuation, and transportation assets for use after disengagement to speed up their rearward movement.

Often when a detachment is left in contact, additional security forces set up behind the existing main defensive positions to assist the withdrawal process. These additional forces can be part of the withdrawing unit or an assisting unit may provide them. The DLIC can then delay back on these additional security forces and join them. Alternatively the detachment delays back to the additional security force, conducts battle handover, and conducts a rearward passage of lines. In either case, the security force then becomes the rear guard.

Main Body Forces

On order, the main body moves rapidly on multiple routes to reconnoitered positions (having previously dispatched quartering parties). It may occupy a series of intermediate positions before completing the withdrawal. Usually CSS and combat support units (with their convoy escorts) precede combat units in the withdrawal movement formation. The main body itself delays or defends if the security force fails to slow the enemy. If the enemy blocks movement to the rear, the main force shifts to alternate routes to bypass the interdicted area or the main force can choose to attack through the enemy.

Reserve

When the complete formation withdraws under pressure, the task of the reserve may be to take limited offensive action, such as spoiling attacks, to disorganize, disrupt, and delay the enemy. It can counter penetrations between delay positions, reinforce threatened areas, and protect withdrawal routes. Reserves may also extricate encircled or heavily engaged forces.

Retirement

A retirement is a retrograde operation in which a force, out of contact with the enemy, moves away from the enemy (usually to the rear). Retiring units organize for combat, but do not anticipate interference by enemy ground forces. Typically, another unit's security force covers the movement of one formation as it conducts a retirement. Mobile enemy forces, unconventional forces, air strikes, air assaults, or long-range fires may attempt to interdict the retiring unit and commanders must plan accordingly. A unit conducts a retirement to:

- Extend the distance from the enemy.
- Reduce the support distance from other friendly forces.
- Secure more favorable terrain.
- Conform to the dispositions of the larger command.
- Allow its employment in another area.

When a withdrawal from action precedes a retirement, the actual retirement begins upon completion of the organization of march formations.

In a retirement there will normally be designated security elements and the main body. The initial action is to move logistical and administrative units and supplies to the rear. The formation and number of columns employed by the retiring unit depends upon the number of available routes and potential enemy interference. If there is a threat of enemy interference, the column may designate an advance guard that is augmented with engineers.

At the designated time, troops execute a withdrawal from action, move into assembly areas (if necessary), and form into march formation. During the initial phase, the force retires in multiple small columns. As the distance from the enemy increases, smaller columns consolidate into larger ones. Road nets and the potential for hostile interference influence the time and manner in which this occurs.

The commander designates flank security responsibilities to guard against potential enemy interference against the retiring force and a surprise flanking attack against the retirement's extended columns. Flank guard responsibilities may be designated to subordinate march units. Flank guards must be mobile. Light armor reconnaissance, mechanized infantry, armor, artillery, and engineer forces usually form part of the flank and rear guards.

Terrain and the enemy threat dictate if the retiring force establishes a single rear guard or if each column forms a separate rear guard. The rear guard is normally the principal security element of each retiring column. It protects the column from surprise, harassment, and attack by any pursuing enemy force. Its size and composition depend upon the strength and imminence of the enemy threat. The rear guard generally remains in march columns unless there is a potential for enemy interference. Should the enemy establish contact, the rear guard conducts a delay.

The main body organizes in a manner inverse to that for an approach march. The movement of CSS and combat support units should precede the movement of combat forces. When necessary, elements of the main body can reinforce the rear guard or any other security element. Fire support and attack helicopter elements of the main body are usually the first elements tasked for this mission because they are capable of rapid respond. If the retiring formation can resource a reserve, it performs the same functions as discussed in the withdrawal.

SECTION III. RECONNAISSANCE OPERATIONS

Reconnaissance is continuous and intrinsic to all Marine operations. Reconnaissance is a directed effort to collect information about the enemy and the friendly commander's operational area. Reconnaissance information includes information relating to the activities and resources of an enemy, or about the meteorological, hydrographic, or geographic characteristics of the particular area of operation. Reconnaissance is a focused collection effort, accomplished by observation or mechanical detection method. There are five forms of reconnaissance operations: route, zone, area, force-oriented, and reconnaissance in force. Tank units are rarely assigned reconnaissance operations but the tank battalion can utilize its scout and TOW platoons to conduct limited reconnaissance operations for its own tactical missions. For a more detailed discussion on the capabilities of the scout and TOW platoons refer to chapter 10.

Route Reconnaissance

The route reconnaissance effort occurs along a specific line of communications, such as a road, railway, or waterway. It provides new or updated information on route conditions and activities along a specific route.

Zone Reconnaissance

A zone reconnaissance is a directed effort to obtain detailed information within a zone defined by boundaries. A zone reconnaissance provides data concerning all routes, obstacles (to include chemical or radiological contamination), terrain, and enemy forces within the zone of action.

Area Reconnaissance

An area reconnaissance provides detailed information concerning the terrain or enemy activity within a prescribed area, such as a town, ridgeline, woods, or other feature critical to operations. Areas are smaller than zones, and a zone reconnaissance may include several areas. At its most basic level, an area reconnaissance could be made of a single point, such as a bridge or an installation.

Force-Oriented Reconnaissance

Force-oriented reconnaissance differs significantly from the previous forms of reconnaissance. The objective of force-oriented reconnaissance is to quickly find a specific enemy force and stay with it wherever it moves on the battlefield. Units performing this mission provide timely, accurate, first-hand information on the enemy force's disposition and its depth. Units conducting force-oriented reconnaissance may sift through the enemy to reconnoiter in depth. They may also guide attacking friendly forces to the preferred point of attack. Very little time is spent on detailed terrain reconnaissance and terrain-related reports and terrain-oriented control measures are minimal.

Reconnaissance in Force

Reconnaissance in force is a limited purpose form of reconnaissance conducted by a considerable force to obtain information and test enemy dispositions, strengths, and reactions. It is conducted by reconnaissance and general-purpose forces to aggressively develop the situation. The size and strength of the force must be sufficient to cause the enemy to respond in some manner, and it must able to protect itself.

SECTION IV. RIVER CROSSING OPERATIONS

The purpose of a river crossing, whether in the offensive or in a retrograde operation, is to project combat power across a water obstacle in order to accomplish a mission. River crossings require specific procedures for success because the water obstacle prevents normal ground maneuver. Inherent within the tank battalion T/O is four AVLBs and their compliment of six bridges. Typically organized as a bridging platoon within the tank battalion, the AVLB enables the tank battalion to traverse 40-foot water obstacles without the assistance of MEF bridging assets. Refer to appendix A for vehicle characteristics of the AVLB.

There are three basic river crossing types: hasty, deliberate, and retrograde. For a more in-depth discussion on river crossing operations refer to MCWP 3-17.1, *River-Crossing Operations*.

Hasty River Crossing

A hasty river crossing is a task conducted as part of a larger operation, typically an attack, with no intentional pause at the water line to prepare. It capitalizes on speed while suppressing the enemy. A hasty crossing is possible with appropriately equipped forces when the enemy is not defending the river line in strength at the crossing and the characteristics of the river do not exceed the capabilities of the engineer systems accompanying the force. A hasty crossing is the preferred option. Characteristics of a hasty river crossing include: speed and surprise, minimum loss of momentum at the river, minimal concentration of forces, and well-understood unit SOPs and detailed prior planning.

The hasty crossing uses all possible organic, existing, or expedient means to get across the obstacle in stride. Clearance of enemy forces from the near bank is not a prerequisite to a hasty river crossing. Air assault and airborne forces can simplify the crossing of a river line by use of vertical envelopment. Most combat systems organic to armor and mechanized infantry units cannot swim. Therefore, these units must rely on accompanying engineers for the means to conduct the hasty river crossing. Although success of a hasty crossing is not predicated on the seizure of intact bridges, a rapid advance to the river may allow seizure of bridges before the enemy can destroy them. A force crossing a river should prepare to take maximum advantage of any bridges seized.

Deliberate River Crossing

When a hasty river crossing is not feasible, a hasty crossing attempt fails, or friendly offensive operations resume at a river line after a pause, the force conducts a deliberate river crossing operation. The deliberate river crossing requires unique planning, control, and specialized support measures. Detailed planning, deliberate buildup and preparation, deception, and clearance of enemy forces from the near bank characterize this type of crossing. Commanders conduct extensive reconnaissance, full-scale rehearsals, and ensure all necessary logistic preparations.

Retrograde River Crossing

A retrograde crossing is a movement to the rear across a water obstacle while in contact with the enemy. The retrograding force may re-establish its defense.

Section V. Linkup Operations

Linkup operations are conducted to join two forces. Linkup operations may occur in a variety of circumstances. They are most often conducted:

- To join two forces regardless of where they are on the battlefield.
- To join an attacking force with a force inserted into the enemy's rear; e.g., a helicopterborne force or an infiltration force.
- To complete the encirclement of an enemy force.
- To assist the breakout or come to the relief of an encircled friendly force.

The headquarters ordering the linkup establishes the command relationship between the forces and the responsibilities of each. It should also establish control measures, such as contact points and boundaries between converging forces, restrictive fire lines, and other measures to control maneuver and fires. Such control measures may be adjusted during the operation to provide for freedom of action as well as positive control.

A linkup involves a stationary force and a moving force. If both units are moving, one is designated the stationary force and should occupy the linkup point at least temporarily to effect the linkup. The commanders involved must coordinate their schemes of maneuver. They agree on primary and alternate linkup points where physical contact between the advance elements of the two units will occur. Linkup points must be easily recognizable to both units and are located where the routes of the moving force intersect the security elements of the stationary force. Whenever possible, joining forces exchange as much information as possible prior to the operation.

There are two methods of linkup: linkup when one unit is stationary and linkup between two moving units.

Linkup When One Unit is Stationary

Linkup when one unit is stationary is the preferred linkup method when the moving force(s) has an assigned limit of advance near the other force. When one of the units involved is stationary, linkup points are usually located near the limit of advance. It is also near the stationary force's security elements. Alternate linkup points are also designated since enemy action may interfere with linkup at primary points. Stationary forces assist in the linkup by opening lanes in minefields, breaching or removing selected obstacles, furnishing guides, and designating assembly areas. A restrictive fire line is established between the two forces and a restrictive fire area may be established around one or both forces linking up. A fire support coordination line is established beyond the area where the two forces are linking up. When a moving force is coming to relieve an encircled force, it brings the additional logistical assets required to restore the encircled unit's combat effectiveness to the desired level.

Linkup Between Two Moving Units

Linkup between two moving units is used during highly fluid, mobile operations when an enemy force is escaping from a potential encirclement or when one of the forces affecting the linkup is at risk and requires reinforcement immediately. In this method, the moving force or forces continue to move and conduct long-range recognition via radios or other communications means, stopping only when they make physical contact.

Linkup between two moving or converging units is one of the most difficult operations. Limits of advance are established to prevent fratricide. Primary and alternate linkup points for two moving forces are established in the vicinity of the limit of advance. Fire support considerations are similar to when a stationary and moving force linkup. Leading elements of each force should exchange liaison teams and be on a common radio net.

SECTION VI. PASSAGE OF LINES

A passage of lines is an operation in which a force moves forward or rearward through another force's combat position with the intention of moving into or out of contact with the enemy. It is always conducted in conjunction with another mission, such as to begin an attack or to conduct an exploitation or security force mission. Passage of lines operations are conducted to—

- Sustain the tempo of an offensive operation with fresh forces.
- Maintain the viability of the defense by introducing fresh forces.
- Free a unit for another mission, reconstitution, routine rest, resupply, refresher/specialized training, or maintenance.

The conduct of a passage of lines involves two forces: the stationary force and the moving force. In the offense, the moving force is normally the attacking force and is organized to assume its assigned mission after the passage. The stationary force facilitates the passage and provides maximum support to the moving force. Normally, the plans and requirements of the moving force have priority. The time or circumstances at which responsibility for the zone of action transfers from the stationary force to the moving force must be agreed upon by the two commanders or specified by higher authority. Normally, the attacking commander assumes responsibility at or before the time of attack. Responsibility may be transferred before the time of attack to allow the attacking commander to control any preparation fires. In this latter case, elements of the stationary force that are in contact at the time of the transfer must be placed under the operational control of the attacking commander. Liaison between the forces involved should be established as early as possible.

SECTION VII. RELIEF IN PLACE

A relief in place is an operation where one unit with a tactical mission is replaced by another. It is conducted as part of a larger operation primarily to maintain the combat effectiveness of committed units. The higher headquarters directs when and where to conduct the relief and establishes the appropriate control measures. The directing authority transfers responsibility for the mission and the assigned sector or zone of operations of the replaced unit to the incoming unit. Normally, the unit relieved is defending. However, a relief may set the stage for a resumption of offensive operations. A relief during an offensive operation will most likely occur during an operational pause. Otherwise, during an offense, the two forces concerned in the relief conduct a forward passage of lines. A relief may also serve to free the relieved unit for decontamination, reconstitution, routine rest, resupply, maintenance, specialized training, or another mission.

There are two types of reliefs: a deliberate and a hasty relief in place. The major differences between them are the depth and detail of the planning and, potentially, the execution time. In a deliberate relief, units exchange plans and liaison personnel, conduct briefings, perform detailed reconnaissance, and publish orders with detailed instructions. In a hasty relief, commanders use an abbreviated planning process and direct the execution using oral or fragmentary orders. In both cases, the relieved unit designates liaison personnel from its combat, combat support, and CSS elements that remain with the relieving unit until completion of the necessary plans.

SECTION VIII. BREAKOUT FROM ENCIRCLEMENT

Units normally attempt to conduct breakout operations when—

- They are specifically directed by the senior commander or if it falls within commander's intent.
- They do not have sufficient, relative combat power to defend themselves if encircled.
- There is not adequate defensible terrain available.
- They are not able to sustain themselves for a sufficient period of time.

Generally, the best opportunity for a breakout attempt comes in the early stages of enemy encirclement because the enemy does not have sufficient combat power to encircle the friendly force in strength and weak points exist in the enemy force.

An encircled force may be operating under adverse conditions and may not have all of its technical intelligence systems operating. The commander may be forced to operate with low levels of intelligence concerning enemy strengths, weaknesses, and intentions. Within this environment, aggressive reconnaissance is required in order to ascertain information on the enemy. The commander should also obtain information from available reconnaissance and surveillance assets. If the enemy is in close contact, the commander may be forced to conduct reconnaissance in force to ascertain information on enemy strengths.

The unit must re-organize to conduct the breakout based on available resources. Without resupply, tank and mechanized infantry units may not be able to move all their vehicles in the breakout attack. Priority of support may be limited to the rupture force and rear guard, with the remainder of the force keeping only sufficient transportation assets to move them. The breakout plan should outline destruction criteria, identify all vehicles and equipment that cannot be moved, and destroy unmovable items as soon as possible.

Organization of Forces

The encircled force normally conducts a breakout by task-organizing with a rupture force, a main body, and a rear guard. If the commander has enough forces, he may organize separate reserve, diversionary, and supporting elements. The forces may consist of aviation or ground combat units (one or both as individual elements or as task-organized, combined-arms teams) and appropriate CSS organizations based on METT-T.

Rupture Force

The encircled forces attack as soon as possible by employing one or more rupture forces to penetrate the enemy defensive positions. The commander must produce overwhelming combat power at the breakout point. The rupture force, which may vary in size from one-third to two-thirds of the total encircled force, is assigned the mission of penetrating the enemy-encircling position, widening the gap, and holding the shoulder of the gap until all other encircled forces can move through. The rupture force must be of sufficient strength to penetrate the enemy line. A favorable combat power ratio must be achieved at the point of attack by means of surprise, troop strength, mobility, and firepower.

Initially, the rupture force is the main effort. The rupture force commander will probably have additional assets attached to his unit. These assets might include air defense or additional engineer personnel from any encircled engineer unit. The commander should integrate these assets properly for maximum combat power to achieve the rupture.

Tanks are well-suited to be all or part of the rupture force because their speed and mobility allow them to quickly engage targets and clear a gap through the enemy for other follow-on forces to exploit.

Reserve Force

The reserve follows the rupture attack in order to maintain the attack's momentum and secure objectives past the rupture. After the rupture force secures the gap, the reserve normally becomes the lead element. When a unit receives the reserve force mission, the commander must coordinate closely with the rupture force commander on the gap's location, the enemy situation at the rupture, and the enemy situation (if known) along the direction of attack past the rupture point.

Initially, the reserve passes through the gap created by the rupture force. It is essential that the reserve continue a rapid movement from the encircled area toward the final objective (probably a linkup). If the reserve makes secondary attacks, it is important that it does not become bogged down. Artillery preparation may assist the reserve force in maintaining momentum out of the encircled area.

Main Body

The main body consists of the main command post, the bulk of the CSS, and some combat support assets. It contains those combat forces not required for other missions and should contain sufficient combat power to protect itself. It moves rapidly as a single group on multiple routes immediately behind the reserve. Security elements protect the flanks of the main body during movement. One commander should have sole command of this element to ensure orderly movement.

Rear Guard

The rear guard consists of the personnel and equipment left on the perimeter to provide protection for the rupture and diversionary attacks (if a diversionary attack force exists). Forces left in contact must fight a vigorous delaying action on the perimeter so that no portion of the force is cut off. Under a single commander, the rear guard acts as a covering force to protect the main body from attack while it is moving from the area. In addition to providing security, it deceives the enemy as to the encircled force's intentions. It simulates the activities of the encircled force until they clear the gap. Once the breakout commences, the rear guard and any diversionary forces disengage or delay toward the rupture. Perimeter forces integrate smoothly into the rear of the breakout column. Upon achieving the breakout, priority of fires may be shifted to the rear guard action. Above all else, the force must maintain the momentum of the attack or the force will be more vulnerable to destruction than it was prior to the breakout.

As other units support or follow the breakout, the rear guard commander must spread his forces over an extended area. This requires flexibility and mobility on the part of the rear guard. The rear guard must also ensure that the perimeter withstands enemy pressure.

Diversionary or Supporting Force

The encircled force should divert enemy attention from the location of the rupture. A supporting or diversionary attack can assist the breakout attack by diverting enemy attention and resources away from the rupture effort. The forces conducting a supporting or diversionary effort may be from either inside or outside the encirclement area. The commander should direct their efforts to a point where the enemy might expect a breakout or where a relief effort might occur. The forces participating in these efforts are as mobile as available vehicles and trafficability will allow. Mobile, self-propelled weapons systems ideally suit the needs of a diversionary or supporting force.

Success of the diversionary force is important to the success of any breakout operation. If the force fails to deceive the enemy of the encircled force's intentions, the full combat power of the enemy could be directed at the rupture point. On the other hand, the diversionary force may rupture the enemy's lines. If a rupture occurs, the diversionary force commander must know the commander's intent. He may exploit this success, or he may have to disengage and follow and support the reserve force.

Conduct of the Breakout

Detailed planning for a breakout attack may not be possible because the attack must be initiated so quickly after a friendly force is encircled. Units will conduct aggressive reconnaissance to confirm the enemy disposition. If the enemy-encircling force occupies strong positions in close proximity, the encircled unit may be required to conduct a reconnaissance in force at selected locations to ascertain enemy strengths and reactions. The unit initiates its breakout attack as soon as it develops sufficient intelligence concerning enemy dispositions. Its attack exploits conditions of limited visibility and gaps or weaknesses in the enemy's positions. If friendly forces enjoy air superiority, the breakout attack may be initiated during daylight hours to fully exploit the capabilities of close air support. Additionally, the probability of a successful breakout increases measurably if another friendly force attacks toward the encircled force as it attempts to breakout.

The unit takes all possible precautions to deceive the enemy as to the location of the main attack. The rupture force minimizes occupation of attack positions prior to the main attack. A supporting attack may be required to assist the rupture force in penetrating enemy positions and expanding the shoulders. Feints and demonstrations may also be employed to deceive the enemy as to the main attack. However, diversionary attacks need not always occur first.

The commander organizes and controls his rupture force as he would a deliberate attack or movement to contact. The rupture force generates overwhelming combat power at the point of the main attack and attempts to rapidly penetrate enemy positions and expand the penetration. If the commander is hard-pressed to generate sufficient combat power with the rupture force and still maintain the perimeter defense, he may have to initiate a withdrawal in certain sectors, prior to the main attack, to generate combat power. If enemy forces are in strength at the point of penetration, the rupture force will likely hold the shoulders. If the enemy is not in strength, the commander may have the rupture force continue its attack as the main effort. If there are no identified enemy formations beyond the penetration, the rupture force may transition to a movement to contact. The follow and assume force is prepared to assume the main effort if the rupture force becomes decisively engaged short of its objectives.

The reserve moves in the approach march formation and is prepared to react to enemy counterattacks or exploit the success of the rupture force. The main body follows the reserve. It moves on multiple routes in either the approach or road march formation. It contains sufficient combat power to protect itself and reinforce the flank or rear security forces should they come under attack. Typically, flank security forces conduct a screen or guard mission.

Initially, the rear guard conducts a withdrawal to break contact with enemy forces around the perimeter and then diminish the perimeter as it delays back behind the main body. If the enemy closely pursues the breakout force, the rear guard may become the main effort. The reserve should then be positioned where it can also support the rear guard.

The priority for fire support is initially with the rupture force. Fire support assets must also move with the main body and rear guard so that security forces have adequate fires.

Engineers with the rupture force focus on mobility operations. Engineers with a follow and assume force or reserve improve routes and replace AVLBs with other bridging assets. Engineers are also task-organized with the flank security elements whose focus is countermobility operations. The rear guard must also have adequate engineers to conduct countermobility operations.

Air defense assets are prioritized to protect the rupture force, rear guard, and then the main body. Sufficient medium- and short-range air defense systems must be dedicated to cover all critical points through which the encircled force will pass.

All units and vehicles will carry the maximum supplies possible, with emphasis on classes III and V. The encircled force will only take those vehicles it can support. It may be possible for the encircled force's higher headquarters to establish an intermediate support base as the breakout attack moves toward a linkup.

Exfiltration

If success of a breakout attack appears questionable and a relief operation is not planned, one way to preserve a portion of the force might be through organized exfiltration. Exfiltration is the act of passing stealthily out of enemy-held territory. An exfiltration effort is preferable to capture and can distract the enemy from his main effort. It may produce intelligence for the main force. Exfiltration by the encircled force is employed only as a last resort by the encircled force after destroying or incapacitating all equipment (less medical) not accompanying the breakout force. Casualties may have to be left in place by exfiltrating forces with supplies and medical attendants.

Exfiltration is most feasible over rough or difficult terrain, through areas unoccupied by the enemy, or through areas not covered by enemy observation and fire. These conditions often allow undetected movement of small elements when movement of the entire force would present more risk. It is unlikely that the entire force will be able to exfiltrate since there may be a requirement to create a diversion.

Based on reconnaissance, the exfiltrating unit subdivides into small groups and exfiltrates during periods of limited visibility by passing through and around enemy defensive positions. If detected, they seek to bypass. Units use preparatory fires to cover their movement as well as to get rid of stockpiled ammunition. Rally points, routes, and linkup plans all must be coordinated.

Exfiltration may be more difficult to accomplish in tanks and/or mechanized vehicles. This is due to the limitations they impose upon exfiltration routes and the increased noise involved in their operation that makes their detection by the enemy more likely.

Attacking Deeper

A COA that the enemy is not likely to expect from an encircled force is that the force attacks deeper. This involves great risk, but may offer the only feasible COA under some circumstances. It is only feasible if a unit can sustain itself while isolated. When the enemy is attacking, attacking deeper into the enemy rear may disrupt the enemy's offense and provide an opportunity for linkup from another direction. If the enemy is defending and the attacking force finds itself isolated through its own offensive action, it may continue the attack toward its assigned objective.

Logistical shortfalls can be relieved somewhat by aerial resupply, external forces establishing intermediate support bases, and possibly by using captured supplies. Close air support will have greater difficulty in providing support due to the enemy situation around the encircled force.

SECTION IX. ROAD MARCH AND ASSEMBLY AREAS

Tactical Road March

A tactical road march is a tactical movement used to relocate units within the combat zone in order to prepare for combat operations. Typically, mechanized units travel long distances, via a road march, in order to position themselves to perform their next assigned mission. The primary consideration of the march is rapid movement, but security is also required even though contact with enemy ground forces in not expected. During tactical road marches, the commander is always prepared to execute maneuver. A mechanized unit, when executing its tactical mission, moves across the terrain using the formations and techniques of movement appropriate to the situation.

Prior to the execution of the road march, the tank battalion plans and issues a march order that includes the following:

- Routes to the release point and start point.
- Route strip map.
- Order of march.
- Start point and reference point locations and times.
- Maximum catch-up speed.
- Designation of quartering parties.
- Intervals between vehicles and march units.
- How routes will be marked and by whom.
- Road restrictions.
- Actions on enemy contact.
- Actions at halt or for disabled vehicles.
- Actions in assembly area.
- Resupply, maintenance, and feeding procedures.
- Scheduled halts.
- Fire support plan.

The tank battalion scout platoon conducts a route reconnaissance that identifies the following:

- Availability and conditions of routes.
- Start point/release point confirmation.
- Location of critical points.

- Location and suitability of holding/assembly area and areas for maintenance/refueling.
- Distances between critical points and total distance between start point and release point.
- Location of obstacles.
- NBC monitoring of assemble area.
- Information on the enemy positioned along the routes.
- Alternate routes, if required.

The tank battalion conducts the road march ensuring that it maintains security during the march. Designated security elements eliminate enemy elements, allowing uninterrupted movement of the main body.

Assembly Area

An assembly area is an area in which a command assembles in order to prepare for further action. The tank battalion's assembly area typically requires a minimum of a four square kilometer area. In the assembly area, the tank unit reviews and issues orders, services and repairs vehicles, receives and issues supplies, and feeds personnel. The assembly area, when used to prepare for an attack, is usually well forward. If possible, it should be out of range of enemy artillery.

The tank battalion selects an assembly area with the following characteristics: cover from direct fire, good exits and entrances, adequate internal roads, and space for dispersion of vehicles and equipment. Overhead concealment is important if the unit is to remain in the area for any length of time. Vehicles, equipment, entrances, and exits should be camouflaged to keep the enemy from detecting the location of the unit.

As the battalion occupies the assembly area, the main body moves into position without halting or blocking routes. Security is established immediately and radio listening silence or minimum radio transmissions is maintained. All units are resupplied and operation orders (OPORDs) are issued.

CHAPTER 6
TACTICAL LOGISTICS

Logistics is the science of planning and carrying out the movement and maintenance of forces. Logistics provides the resources of combat power and limits what tank units can do on the battlefield. Marine tank units strive to use precision logistics that seeks to maximize its logistic asset capabilities. To improve efficiency, precision logistics applies a "just-in-time" inventory management mindset, which ensures that the right logistics are forecasted for and delivered on the battlefield in an effective and efficient manner.

During operations and training, tank units typically consume tremendous amounts of resources. Therefore, it is imperative that thorough logistical planning be conducted in order to sustain tank units. The tank battalion is capable of self-administration, organic supply support, food service support, and medical services that provide routine and emergency medical care. The battalion has significant, organic logistic capabilities for short-term self-sufficiency, but it requires extensive CSS (especially fuel and ammunition) for sustained operations. The battalion's tank companies conduct first and second echelon maintenance of all organic equipment. The battalion provides second echelon maintenance on motor transport equipment and third echelon maintenance on tanks, tank-mounted weapons, and TOW systems.

Distribution procedures of logistical resources generally fall into one of two categories: demand pull or supply push. In the pull method, the supported unit directly controls the orders for resupply and other support services. The push method relies on precalculated logistic requirements to position/deliver resources when and where they are likely to be needed. Marine logistics traditionally employ a combination of both methods. Routine support, such as resupply of food, water, and fuel, are planned on a standard schedule, or pushed, based on consumption rates and employment. The pull method means the supported unit requests specific kinds of resupply (such as maintenance, medical support, and ammunition) on an as-required basis.

Trains

A train is a means of internally task-organizing and employing the organic CSS assets of the tactical unit. They are the link between the forward/subordinate elements of the tactical units and the supporting combat service support element (CSSE). The organization and capabilities of the trains vary with the mission and the tactical situation. Trains predominately provide supply, evacuation, and maintenance services. At tank battalion and company levels, trains increase responsiveness to the tactical situation.

Unit trains centralize CSS assets of the supported unit at a single location under the control of the unit commander. Unit trains are most appropriate in either the defense or during periods of low operational tempo. The commander uses this option when the tactical situation dictates self-contained train operations or when the terrain may require this configuration. Unit trains provide simplicity, economy, and survivability against ground attack.

The most important criterion for trains is responsiveness. However, seldom will the commander find a site that provides all the desired characteristics to provide maximum responsiveness. Therefore, the commander must prioritize and weigh the characteristics based on METT-T and the associated risk. Good train locations should have—

- Defensible terrain that allows the best use of limited personnel.

- Enough space to permit dispersion of both vehicles and activities.
- Concealment from hostile ground and air observation.
- Firm ground to support materials handling; heavy equipment operations; and ammunition and petroleum, oils, and lubricants (POL) activities.
- A helicopter landing site for helicopter resupply and medical evacuation.
- An adequate road network between the train and forward elements and between the train and the CSSE supporting the tank battalion.
- Good communications with forward elements and the supporting CSSE.
- A source of water.
- No terrain features that are obstacles to CSS operations or that give the enemy targeting sources.

Built-up areas are often good locations for trains because they provide cover and concealment for vehicles and sheltered areas for maintenance at night. When located in built-up areas, trains normally occupy buildings near the edge of the area for better security and to reduce the chances of being cut off and trapped.

Proper positioning of trains minimizes displacements and increases the quantity and quality of CSS. The tactical situation determines the method of displacement. Trains may be displaced in their entirety concurrently with the maneuver of the tank unit or by echelon.

To increase responsiveness of CSS assets, the tank battalion will often task-organize and echelon its CSS assets into combat trains and field trains. Echelonment of the trains provides immediate responsive support, flexibility in usage, and may increase survivability of assets. When trains are echeloned into combat and field trains, the S-4 normally controls the combat trains and designates the commander of the field trains.

Combat Trains

Combat trains are organic elements that provide critical CSS in forward areas, and they are tailored for the tactical situation. They normally contain POL; ammunition and other ordnance items; maintenance contact teams with a recovery and limited repair capability; and medical support. However, their exact composition depends on METT-T. The combat trains area must not take up space needed by the forward units, and supply and maintenance vehicle traffic must not impede the freedom of movement of combat and combat support units. Combat trains at the tank battalion level normally include the battalion aid station.

Field Trains

Field trains consist of the remaining organic and attached CSS elements that are located further to the rear. The commander selects this option to improve responsiveness, flexibility, and survivability against air attack. This option is preferable when the unit is in the offense.

Organic Capabilities

The nature of mechanized warfare demands that tank units be self-sufficient to a certain degree. In order to maximize the tank unit's organic logistical capabilities, the unit must identify critical requirements, enhance its organic logistics through other sources when possible, and ensure its logistics are safeguarded.

Identify Critical Requirements

Many logistic requirements cannot be predicted with satisfactory accuracy. High-use repair items can be identified and stockpiled prior to a deliberate operation. The CSSE of the MAGTF builds and maintains a class IX repair parts block based on empirical data. Repair items that are low-demand, but critical, may not have been planned for by the CSSE so the tank unit should always plan for alternative sources when possible (e.g., Army logistic units operating close by). The class IX block should be reviewed by the tank unit commander, or his representative, to identify any combat deadlining components that may be overlooked. Critical logistic requirements should be forecasted to the CSSE.

Enhance Organic Capability

Mechanized forces tend to operate over great distances throughout the battlespace. The mobility of the M1A1 tank provides for a nonlinear array of forces with considerable separation between units, including CSSE units. Tank units should enhance their organic CSS capability whenever possible. For instance, qualifying several crewmen as helicopter support teams allows for greater flexibility in vertical resupply.

Safeguard Resources

Tank units require certain organic CSS capabilities. These organic capabilities are vital to the success of most tank operations and need to be protected. Protection of these resources is normally afforded by locating them at safe distances from direct combat, which reduces responsiveness, or by allocating sufficient forces for defense, which reduces forces available for other operations. However, these safeguards are necessary because failure to protect the tank unit combat trains from enemy destruction could quickly render the tanks ineffective in combat, hinder or halt the operational tempo, and make the tanks vulnerable to a mechanized counter attack.

Outside Agency Support

Because tanks require such a large degree of logistics, they will usually have to interface with outside agencies if operations are of a lengthy duration. To ensure that tank logistic operations are carried out correctly with outside agencies, requirements must be prioritized, resupply must be responsive, a redundant request policy is used, and key personnel should be collocated.

Prioritize Requirements

Resupply requests must be prioritized. The establishment of priorities and the allocation of resources in accordance with those priorities is a function of command, not logistics. The priorities are determined by the commander.

Rapid Response

Anticipated future resupply, not identified as preplanned support, must be prepared for immediate shipment. Resupply items identified but not carried by the maneuver forces should be packaged for rapid resupply.

Redundant Requests

Requests for logistic resupply should be concurrently routed through higher headquarters to the supporting unit and to the supported unit. Current communications systems, such as the data automated communications terminal, support redundant and immediate requests. Preformatted messages allow users to quickly compose and transmit logistic requests to higher headquarters and the supporting unit.

Collocation of Key Personnel

Positioning key personnel, where they can be most effective in the relay and transfer of information, can be tremendously beneficial. For instance, a maintenance representative from the GCE cross-decked to the operations section of the CSSE would be able to interpret and forecast maintenance requirements.

Logistic Responsibilities of Tank Battalion Personnel

Battalion S-4

The battalion S-4 is responsible to the commanding officer for the battalion's CSS. When trains are echeloned into combat and field trains, the S-4 normally controls the combat trains and designates a commander for the field trains. The battalion S-4 is responsible for the immediate logistical needs of the supported units and the logistical needs of the field trains for future resupply. The S-4 must keep abreast of the tactical situation at all times in order to anticipate the battalion's needs. He also keeps the S-4A informed of the current situation and coordinates any special logistical requirements with him.

Battalion S-4 Assistant (S-4A)

The S-4A is positioned by the S-4. He must work in unison with the S-4 to deconflict logistical requirements, ensuring that logistic requests have not been duplicated by mistake and that logistics are consolidated for transport whenever possible. He works with the H&S Co for security requirements, the supply officer for resupply, and the MTO for delivery of logistics packages (LOGPACs). He is responsible to the S-4 for organizing and directing resupply forward from the field trains to the combat trains. The S-4A directs the formation of LOGPACs for any special or nightly resupply. He works closely with the MTO in forming the composition of the LOGPACs. He keeps the S-4 informed of the current situation and anticipates any special logistical requirements that may exist.

Headquarters and Service Company Commander

The H&S Co commander normally serves as the headquarters commandant in the field. In addition to his duties in planning for the security and displacement of the COC, the H&S Co commander has responsibility for the layout, physical security, and movement of the battalion's trains. He works closely with the S-4A and advises him of all security matters. He is also responsible for coordinating fire support with the FSC for the field trains. Additionally, he normally leads the quartering party to locate new sites prior to displacement of the COC and trains or acts at the convoy commander when moving the COC and/or battalion trains.

Motor Transport Officer

The MTO is normally positioned in the field trains. During the planning stages of the operation, the MTO is tasked with consolidating all wheeled vehicle requirements and organizing convoys. The MTO must be aware of what supplies and equipment will be sent forward so that an adequate number of vehicles are available. He assembles any special LOGPACs and the nightly LOGPAC as directed by the S-4A. The MTO will work closely with the S-4A to ensure all convoys are prepared to move in a timely manner. The MTO may lead delivery of the LOGPACs forward personally or task one of his subordinate. When the field trains must move, the MTO assists the H&S Co in preparing all movement orders and may become the convoy commander when moving. Once at the new field trains location, the MTO assists in the initial layout of the field trains.

Battalion Maintenance Platoon Commander

The battalion maintenance platoon commander is normally positioned in the field trains with the tank maintenance platoon. He advises the S-4A as to what maintenance assets should be sent to the combat trains when needed. The battalion maintenance platoon commander coordinates with the H&S Co commander concerning security and is responsible for the security of his assigned sector within the field trains perimeter. He establishes maintenance operations and makes liaison with CSSE maintenance elements for requested support.

Tank Maintenance Officer

The tank maintenance officer (TMO) is normally positioned in the combat trains and coordinates the forward maintenance and evacuation effort. The TMO acts as the officer in charge of the maintenance contact teams located in the combat trains. When called forward to assist the company/team, the TMO, in conjunction with company personnel, decides whether the tank can be fixed in place, taken to the unit maintenance collection point (UMCP), or evacuated to the field trains.

Battalion Supply Officer

The battalion supply officer is located in the field trains. He is responsible for the requisition, receipt, maintenance, and disposition of supplies necessary to the operation. The battalion supply officer is normally the officer in charge and is responsible for logistics operations center operations and setting up a logistics operations center watch. He is the primary point of contact with the CSSE for classes I, III, and V resupply.

Battalion Maintenance Management Officer

The battalion MMO serves as the battalion liaison officer at the CSSE. He is the primary point of contact for the coordination of logistical support for all elements, including detachments and attachments. The MMO monitors the CSS nets, and he is linked, by wire, to the field trains when possible. If the MMO is not with the force service support group, he is responsible to the H&S Co for the security of his assigned sector within the field trains perimeter.

Battalion Motor Transport Officer

The battalion MTO is normally located in the field trains. He normally works under the supervision of the battalion MTO and coordinates repair/recovery/evacuation of all wheeled assets.

Battalion Communications Maintenance Officer

The battalion communications maintenance officer is normally located in the field trains. He normally works under the supervision of the battalion communications officer and coordinates repair/evacuation of communications assets.

Battalion S-4 Chief

The battalion S-4 chief is normally located in the combat trains and assists the S-4 with the operation and movement of the combat trains. He assists the battalion S-1 (located with the S-4) with security for the combat trains and personnel accountability. Additionally, the battalion S-4 chief is responsible to the H&S Co for the security of his assigned sector within the field trains perimeter.

Headquarters and Service Company Gunnery Sergeant

The H&S Co gunnery sergeant assists the H&S Co commander with his duties. He normally works in the logistics operations center and assists the H&S Co commander with security. He also provides logistical support for all personnel in the field trains.

Company Maintenance Chief

The maintenance chiefs of the tank companies organize and supervise company mechanics. They supervise engine running onload/offload preparation, distribute class IX supplies, and coordinate with platoon sergeants on platoon maintenance status and recovery of vehicles to the UMCP.

Tank Leader

Tank leaders normally receive LOGPACs and guide service support elements to and from their tank company positions.

Company Supply Sergeant

The company supply sergeant is normally located in the field trains. During the day, he coordinates the company resupply needs and ensures that all items are placed in the company LOGPAC for the night resupply. At night, the company supply sergeant usually accompanies the resupply convoy forward to the combat trains and checks in with the S-4, and/or the tank leader, and leads the appointed vehicles to their respective resupply. Once resupply has taken place, the supply sergeant returns to the combat trains that are en route to the field trains.

Resupply Operations

The Marine tank unit uses three methods while conducting supply operations: prepositioning, routine resupply, and emergency resupply. The method to be used is determined after an analysis of METT-T factors.

Prepositioning

Prepositioning of supplies may be required in some defensive operations. Normally, only class V items are prepositioned, but class I and class III supplies may be included. The location and amount of prepositioned assets must be carefully planned and then verified through reconnaissance and rehearsals. Each tank commander must be informed of prepositioning locations. The following considerations influence selection of prepositioned sites and execution of the resupply operation:

- Availability of overhead cover for the prestock location.
- Cover and concealment of the location and routes used by vehicles.
- Security procedures required to safeguard the resupply operation.
- Procedures for protecting friendly personnel and vehicles in the event prestocked ammunition is ignited.

There are several techniques for accomplishing prepositioned resupply in the defense. Normally, class V (ammunition) is positioned next to or within a vehicle's fighting position, enabling the tank crew to resupply during an engagement without displacing. Another technique is to locate class V supplies en route to or within a subsequent battle position. Use of this method requires consideration of security procedures to safeguard the prepositioned assets. Resupply of class III (specifically fuel) is usually accomplished behind a unit's current battle position or en route to a subsequent battle position. In the defense, the tank unit may rotate vehicles or sections through prestock positions based on the enemy situation and shortages within the unit.

Routine Resupply

Routine resupply operations include regular resupply of items in classes I, III, V, and IX and of any other items requested by the tank unit. Routine resupply is planned at the battalion level and occurs whenever possible. The company LOGPAC is a mixture of company and battalion assets that transport supplies to the company.

LOGPACs are normally assembled in the battalion field trains area under the supervision of the S-4 (or designated representatives) and the tank company commander (or designated representatives). Replacements and hospital returnees normally travel to company/platoon locations on LOGPAC vehicles as required. Once the LOGPAC is prepared for movement, the tank leader moves the vehicles forward from the field trains as part of the task force resupply convoy to the logistic release point (LRP). The company first sergeant or his representative meets the LOGPAC and guides it to the company resupply point. The company then executes tailgate or service station.

Emergency Resupply

Emergency resupply, normally involving classes III and V, is executed when the tank unit has such an urgent need for resupply that it cannot wait for the routine LOGPAC. Emergency resupply procedures start with immediate redistribution of ammunition in individual vehicles, followed by cross leveling of ammunition. Once requested through the commander, first sergeant, or tank leader, the battalion brings emergency supplies forward. The tank unit may have to conduct resupply while in contact with the enemy. To resupply the unit in contact:

- Limited supplies are brought forward to the closest concealed position, where the tailgate technique of resupply is used.
- Individual vehicles or sections disengage and move to a resupply point, obtain their supplies, and then return to the fight. This is a version of the service station technique.

Techniques of Resupply

The tactical situation dictates which technique of resupply the tank unit will use: tailgate, service station, a variation of one type, or a combination of both types. The situation also dictates when to resupply. Generally, the unit should attempt to avoid resupply during the execution of offensive operations and resupply should be done during mission transition. Resupply is unavoidable during defensive missions of long duration.

Tailgate Resupply

In the tailgate technique, fuel and ammunition are brought to individual tanks by the tank leader or his assistant (see fig. 6-1). This technique is used when routes leading to vehicle positions are available and the unit is not under direct enemy

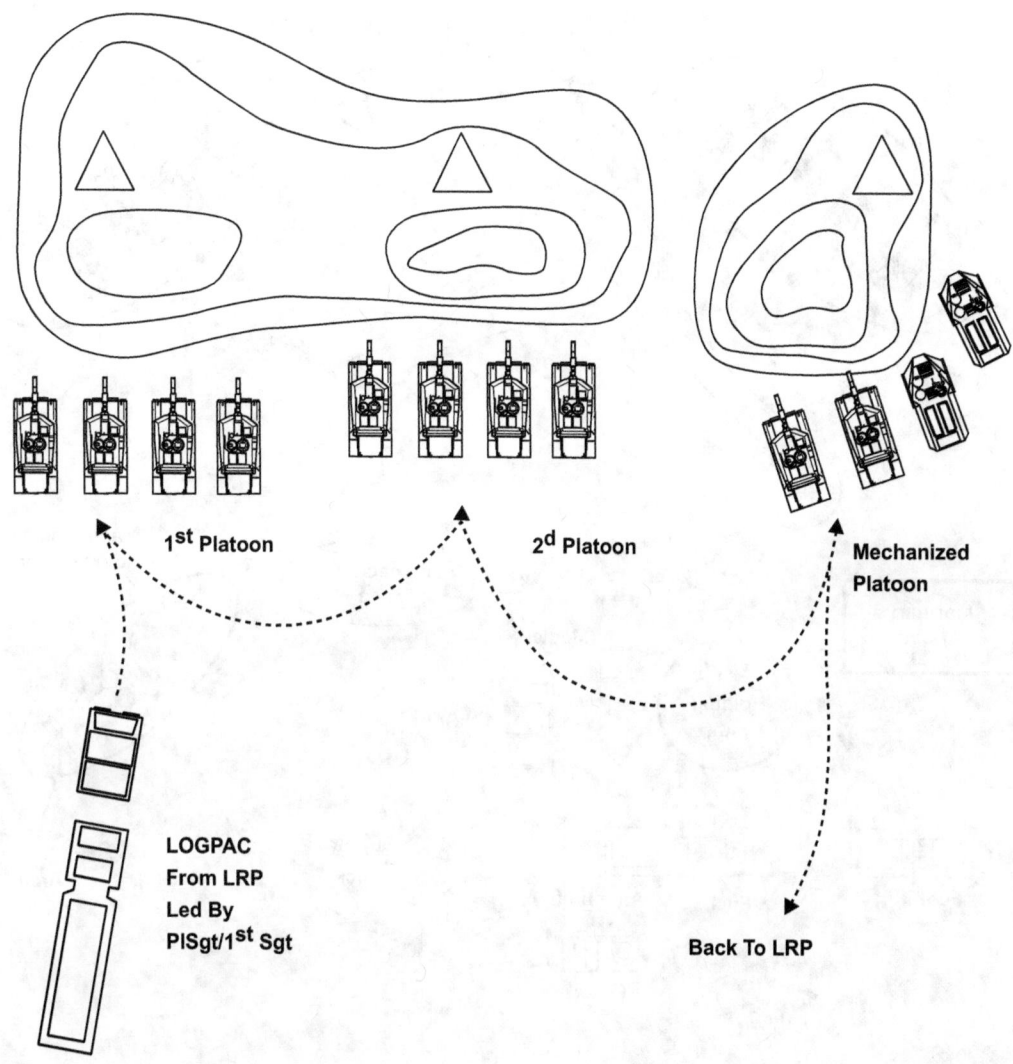

1st Platoon

2d Platoon

Mechanized Platoon

LOGPAC From LRP Led By PlSgt/1st Sgt

Back To LRP

Figure 6-1. Tailgate Resupply Technique.

observation and fire. It is time-consuming, but it is useful in maintaining stealth during defensive missions because tanks do not have to move.

Service Station Resupply

In the service station technique, vehicles move to a centrally-located point for re-arming and refueling, either by section or as an entire platoon (see fig. 6-2). Service station resupply is inherently faster than tailgate resupply because vehicles must move and concentrate; however, it can create security problems. During defensive missions, the platoon must be careful not to compromise the location of fighting posi-tions. A company being resupplied using this technique can maintain security by having only one platoon move at a time; a platoon can do the same by moving a section to the resupply point at a time.

Combination Resupply

A platoon leader can use the two basic tech-niques in combination. For example, during a defensive mission, a platoon leader may use the tailgate technique for a mounted forward obser-vation post and the service station method for the remainder of the platoon located in hide positions (see fig. 6-3).

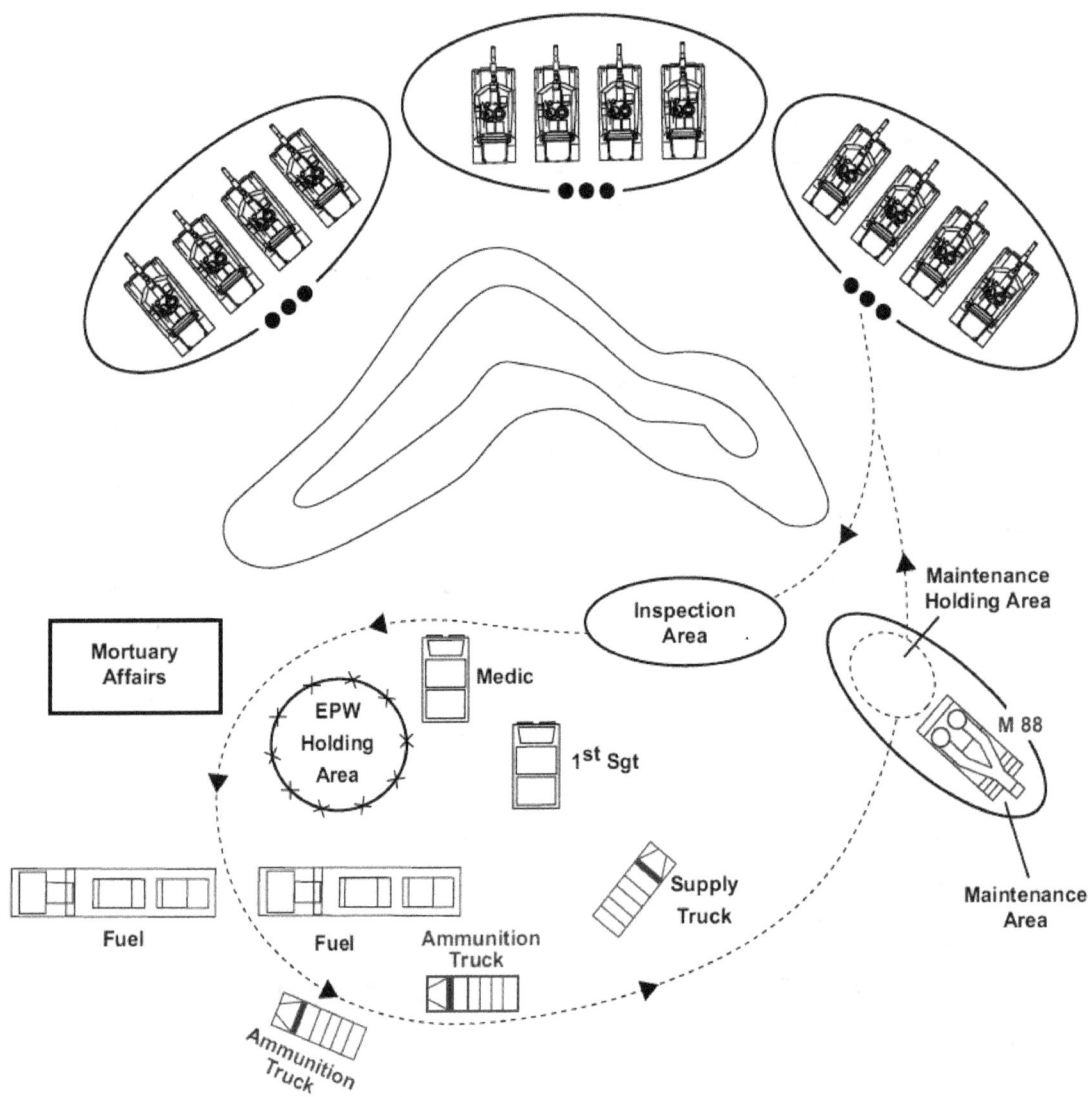

Figure 6-2. Service Station Resupply Technique.

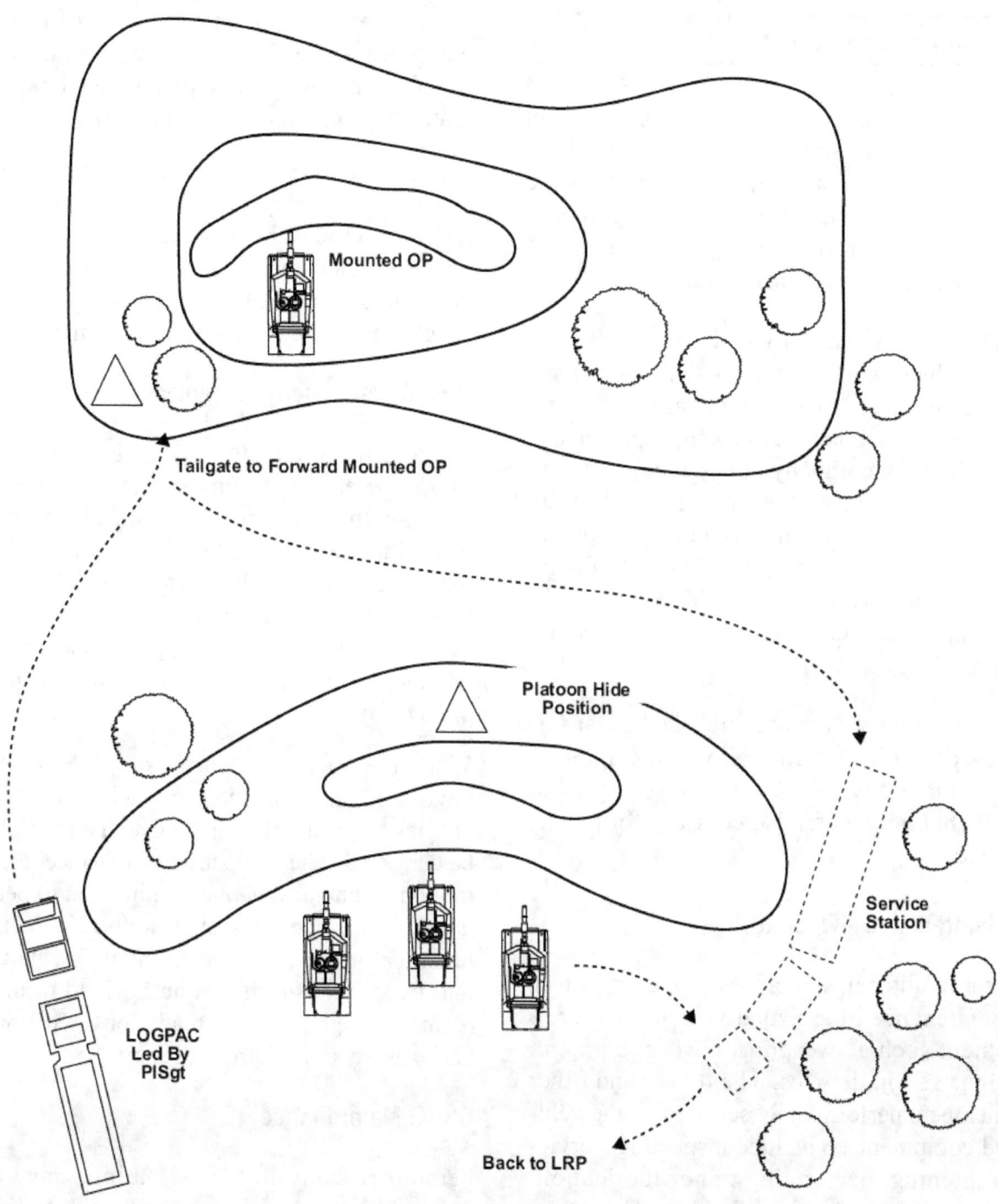

Figure 6-3. Combination of Resupply Techniques.

Maintenance Operations

Proper maintenance keeps equipment and materiel in serviceable condition. It includes preventive maintenance checks and services, as well as the functions of inspecting, testing, servicing, repairing, requisitioning, recovering, and evacuating equipment and materiel whenever necessary.

Maintenance tasks are divided into levels: unit (which includes both operator and organizational maintenance), combat service support group (CSSG) (direct support and general support), and depot. The tank company commander and tank platoon leader are concerned primarily with supervising operator maintenance, ensuring scheduled services are performed as part of organizational maintenance, and providing support for direct support maintenance elements when equipment must be evacuated.

Repair and recovery are accomplished as far forward as possible. When equipment cannot be repaired on site within 2 hours, it is moved to the rear (but only as far as necessary for repair) to a UMCP.

Unit Maintenance—Operator

Operator maintenance includes proper care, use, and maintenance of assigned vehicles and crew equipment such as weapons, NBC equipment, and night vision devices. The driver and other crewmembers perform daily services on the vehicle and equipment, to include inspecting, servicing, tightening, performing minor lubrication, cleaning, preserving, and adjusting. The driver and gunner are required to record the checks and services, as well as all equipment faults that they cannot immediately correct, on the equipment inspection and maintenance worksheet. The worksheet is the primary means of reporting equipment faults through the tank commander to the platoon sergeant and platoon leader and ultimately to organizational maintenance personnel.

Checks and services prescribed for the automotive system, weapon systems, and turret are divided into three groups: before-operation, during-operation, and after-operation. These checks and services are explained in every operator's manual and should be conducted as stated in the manual.

Unit Maintenance—Organizational

Organizational maintenance is the responsibility of the operators and unit mechanics whose unit is assigned the equipment. Organizational maintenance has become quicker for tank units because the M1A1's design allows rapid modular replacement of parts. Many equipment failures can be corrected without evacuating the tank for repairs and the vehicle is returned to combat with minimum delay.

When the operator identifies a problem that is beyond his level of maintenance capability, he notifies his chain of command so the problem can be corrected. The company maintenance team has trained mechanics who are authorized to perform unit maintenance tasks as prescribed in the tank's technical manuals. If the company or battalion maintenance team is not authorized to make a repair, arrangements are made for CSSG maintenance assets to perform the repair.

CSSG Maintenance

Personnel from the CSSG maintenance company, which normally supports a battalion or regiment, perform this level of maintenance. CSSG maintenance consists of repair and/or replacement of parts, assemblies, and components. Maintenance support teams from CSSG units are usually located forward with the battalion field trains. These support teams may go forward to fix disabled equipment on site, but they are limited in what they can fix and where they can go.

Evacuation

Evacuation is necessary when a damaged tank/vehicle cannot be repaired on site within 2 hours or when evacuation is the only means (besides friendly destruction) available to prevent capture or destruction by the enemy. When a tank/vehicle needs to be evacuated, the platoon leader or platoon sergeant reports its exact location, the vehicle type, and the extent of damage, if known, on the company net to the company maintenance chief. The crew remains with the vehicle to assist in evacuation and repair, to provide security, and to return the repaired vehicle to the platoon as soon as possible.

A recovery vehicle from the company or battalion maintenance team evacuates the damaged vehicle. The tank/vehicle is evacuated to an LRP, the main supply route, or the UMCP as necessary. The recovery team normally employs a M88A2 Hercules recovery vehicle. This vehicle travels with the company maintenance team under the direction of the maintenance chief. The location of the company maintenance team during operations is designated in the company OPORD.

If a recovery vehicle is not available or if time is critical, other platoon vehicles can evacuate the damaged vehicle for short distances—this decision is made by the platoon leader. Towing procedures are listed in the operator's manual. Self-evacuation by the platoon is a last resort that should be considered only to prevent losing the damaged tank/vehicle to the enemy.

Destruction

When damaged or inoperable equipment cannot be evacuated and it becomes apparent that enemy capture is imminent, the equipment must be destroyed. Platoon leaders must ensure that crews are trained to destroy their vehicles rather than allow them to fall into enemy hands. Instructions for destroying equipment are included in the operator's manual for each item.

The platoon leader should obtain the commander's permission before destroying any equipment. However, if the ability to communicate with the commander fails, the platoon leader must use his judgment to decide whether or not evacuation is possible. Every reasonable effort must be made to evacuate secure equipment, classified materials, and all weapons.

M1A1 Logistic Requirements

Fuel

Tanks require a large amount of fuel. To refuel a tank company, heavy expanded mobile tactical trucks are required to conduct refueling operations quickly and efficiently. The M1A1 tank engine can run on a variety of fuels: DF-1, DF-2, DF-A, JP-4, JP-5, or JP-8. JP-8 is the preferred fuel. Fuel requirements are as follows:

- One M1A1 tank: 504.4 gallons.
- Tank platoon (4 tanks): 2,107.6 gallons.
- Tank company (4 tanks): 7,061.6 gallons.

Additional POL

In addition to fuel, the M1A1 requires other lubricants to keep the tanks functioning properly. Table 6-1 shows the type of lubricants and amounts needed in each M1A1 tank. This table should be used as a guide for logistic planning.

Ammunition Resupply

Tanks carry a large amount of ammunition and can carry several different types of main gun rounds depending on the mission. For a discussion of the types of rounds and their specifications see appendix D. Table 6-2 is a matrix to help logisticians properly re-arm tank units. Not only must the main gun rounds be resupplied, but also the on board machine guns, the small arms of the tank crews, and the tank smoke discharger rounds must also be replenished. The frequency of resupply depends on the type of mission being conducted and the types of targets engaged by the tank units.

Table 6-1. POL Capacity for a Single M1A1 Tank.

POL Placement	Type of POL	Amount per Tank
Engine	Turbo shaft	25 qt
Transmission	30 weight (OEA/HDO)	45 gal
Final drives	30 weight (OEA/HDO)	5.5 qt
Suspension/shocks	30 weight (OEA/HDO)	30.6 qt
Suspension/hubs	30 weight (OEA/HDO)	20 qt
Hydraulic system	FRH	20 gal
Recoil mechanism	FRH	10.3 gal
Fire extinguisher	Halon	225 psi
Accumulator/LRU	Nitrogen	1000 lb bottle

Table 6-2. Arming Capacity for M1A1 Tank Units.

Type Ammunition	One M1A1	Tank Platoon (4 tanks)	Tank Company (14 tanks)
Main gun, 120mm	40	160	560
M2, .50 cal	1,000	4,000	14,000
Coax, 7.62mm	10,000	40,000	140,000
Loaders, 7.62mm	1,400	5,600	19,600
M16A2, 5.56mm	210	840	2,940
Pistol, 9mm	400	1,600	5,600
Phosphorous smoke	24	96	336

CHAPTER 7
AMPHIBIOUS OPERATIONS

An amphibious operation is launched from the sea by naval and landing forces with the primary purpose of introducing the landing force ashore to accomplish the assigned mission. Marine tank units normally participate in amphibious operations as part of an amphibious task force, maritime prepositioning force, or marine expeditionary unit (special operations capable). There are four types of amphibious operations, each designed to have a specific impact on the adversary: amphibious assault, raid, demonstration, and withdrawal.

Planning for the employment of tanks during the four types of amphibious operations differs little from planning for tank operations ashore. The operation plan provides basic information for a buildup of tanks ashore, their initial employment, and logistical support in combat operations ashore. Amphibious planning for tanks is conducted concurrently and in coordination with the planning of other units of the landing force.

Staff Planning Considerations

After receipt of planning guidance, the landing force's senior tank officer and his staff prepare estimates of supportability that are based on—

- Mission and concept of operations of the landing force.
- Enemy situation with particular attention to the enemy antitank defenses.
- Terrain, weather, and beach conditions.
- Shipping and landing craft availability.
- Tank strength available to the landing force.

Embarkation Plan

Upon receipt of the shipping allocation, the tank battalion begins planning. A listing of personnel and equipment to be assigned to each ship is created. During embarkation planning, it is determined whether tanks will be preboated prior to completing the embarkation plan. Final embarkation plans are developed after studying the assigned ships' characteristics pamphlets and direct liaison with the ships' officers.

Landing Plan

The landing plan is the basis upon which an orderly ship-to-shore movement is conducted by the landing force. The ship-to-shore movement plan includes the detailed plans, tables, diagrams, and schedules prepared by both Navy and landing force commanders, and the plans establish priorities for landing units of the landing force. Based on the method of landing, the tank battalion prepares all necessary forms. When subordinate units of the tank battalion are attached to infantry units, their plan for landing is reflected in the landing document of the units they are supporting. Plans for the landing of tactical units are found in the landing plan appendix to the amphibious operations annex of the operation plan.

Intelligence Requirements

The timely and continuous receipt of intelligence is critical to the employment of tanks. During amphibious planning, every effort is made to gain extensive information and intelligence relative to terrain, weather, and enemy situation. Intelligence for the employment of tanks during an amphibious operation should focus on what and where enemy antitank systems could be employed and the enemy's most likely COA to stop tanks from coming ashore and moving inland.

Terrain

Tank intelligence requires terrain information on beaches and terrain inland from the beaches. Required information about the beaches includes:

- Location, length, width, gradient, and composition of the beach and land adjacent to the beach.
- Trafficability of the land.
- Existing and reinforcing tank obstacles on and adjacent to the beach.
- Suitable exits.
- Sea approaches including underwater gradient and offshore obstacles.
- Surf, tide, and current conditions.

Weather

Weather affects the surf conditions and conditions of the sea, which are critical to the use of landing craft and landing ships attempting to place tanks on the shore. Winds and visibility influence control and coordination of tank units during landing. Rough seas have an adverse effect on the offloading of tanks. Precipitation affects not only visibility, but also trafficability. Extremes in temperature give added importance to the logistic requirement.

Enemy Situation

Amphibious planning requires current intelligence on the enemy at all stages of the planning process. However, the difficulty to alter plans once the assault has begun and the need of the tank battalion and its subordinate units to be well informed demands accurate and detailed intelligence. The following information is important to tank battalion planning:

- Beach antitank defenses.
- Enemy's overall countermechanized capability (including location of enemy armored units and reaction time against the landing force).
- Enemy air capability.
- Enemy electronic warfare capability.
- Enemy NBC capabilities.

Embarkation/Debarkation

Amphibious operations involving Marine Corps tank personnel and assets are normally characterized by movement from ship to shore via landing craft, utility (LCU) or landing craft air cushion (LCAC). Every tank has a fording kit that needs to be applied before conducting amphibious operations (see fig. 7-1).

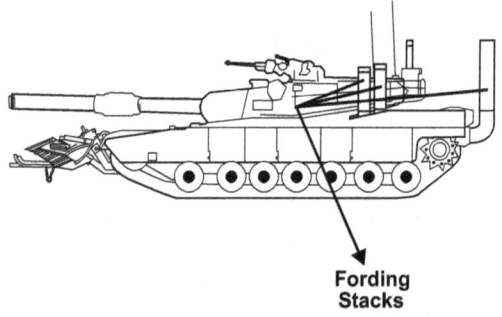

Fording Stacks

Figure 7-1. M1A1 Tank with Fording Kit.

Environmental Characteristics

Environmental characteristics that affect embarkation/debarkation are as follows:

- Fording depth: 78 inches (2 m).
- Additional wave action: 12 inches (30.48 cm).

- Fording depth capability: maintained on slopes up to 40 percent.
- Crosscurrent: 20 miles per hour (32 kph).
- Sea state: condition 2.
- Water: fresh or salt.

Equipment Characteristics

Equipment characteristics that affect embarkation/debarkation are as follows:

- Fording duration: 10 minutes.
- Automotive power performance degradation of M1A1: not more than 30 percent (acceleration and speed).
- Dimensions: not more than 24 inches (60.96 cm) (length increases with fording kit installed).
- Weight: 350 pounds (159 kg) (weight increases with fording kit installed).
- Installation or removal: 2 hours with three-man crew.
- M1A1 operating speed: 4 to 6 miles per hour (6 to 10 kph) at 78 inches (2 m) of water depth.

Planning Considerations

Planning considerations are as follow:

Beach
- Review the beach survey prior to embarkation or debarkation from landing craft. It is the beachmaster's responsibility to provide a copy of the survey to the craftmaster.
- Ensure the beach gradient is 40 percent or less.
- Ensure the path to and from the craft is void of obstacles.
LCU Loads
- When loading two M1A1 tanks, utilize rear and amidship spots and reposition LCU after first tank is off loaded.

- AVLBs and tanks with track-width mine plows must be loaded in the forward spot due to the width of the vehicles.
- Griping vehicles down is performed by the embarked crewman. It is the LCU craftmaster's decision when to gripe down.
- When practical, keep LCU loads tank-pure.
LCAC Loads
- One M1A1 can be loaded on an LCAC.
- Vehicles are always griped down.
- The tank crew rides in the crafts crew compartment, but the tank driver rides in the tank.
Tank With Mine Plows on LCUs
- The M1A1 with an attached plow must be positioned in the forward spot on an LCU.
- The tank must be on loaded and off loaded with a negative ramp (ramp angle below horizontal) on the LCU to prevent damage to the LCU.
- Dunnage must be placed parallel along the path of the track, under the craft ramp and perpendicular to the path of the tank with the plow (creating a speed bump), in order to raise the height of the mine plow to prevent damage to the ship when off loading vehicles from landing craft into the well deck.

Responsibilities

It is the responsibility of the tank commander to determine if the tank's embarkation/debarkation procedures are safe. The tank commander must ensure that there is a coordinated effort between the tank crews and Navy personnel. These responsibilities include:

Embarked Tank Crews
- Griping down.
- Remaining on the tank (LCU)/crew compartment (LCAC).

- Ensuring that the gun tube does not interfere with movement of the landing craft into or out of the ship.

Craftmaster

- Provides gripes.
- Provides depth soundings along the end of the ramp (3 feet is considered a good ramp) and at the hinge and aft of the wingwall.
- Grounds the craft prior to off loading.

Beachmaster

- Provides modified surf index and hydrographic survey to craftmaster.
- Salvages grounded equipment.

Ship

- Provides life jackets.
- Provides dunnage.

Operational Checks and Procedures

Pre-amphibious Operations Checks

The following must be coordinated prior to the amphibious operation:

- Complete installation of fording gear.
- Ensure that all communications cords are taped up.
- Ensure positive communication between the tank commander and driver.
- Use battery vice vehicle power when using the driver's night sight to prevent arching from leakage through the driver's hatch.
- Ensure that no gear is attached to the left turret sponson box that will interfere with fording stacks and not allow the turret to traverse to front. The gun should be at maximum elevation during on load and then leveled once it is griped down.

——————— **Caution** ———————

Once fording stacks are in place the tank can be run for approximately 10 minutes before overheating.

Before Embarking on an LCU

Ensure that the following are completed before embarking on an LCU:

- Turret seal is inflated.
- Loader's hatch is closed.
- Turret power is in the manual position at the loader station.
- Driver's hatch is correctly locked.
- Positive communications between the tank commander and driver.
- Hand-and-arm signals have been reviewed with naval personnel to ensure that there is a common understanding.
- Proper positioning of naval personnel to preclude them from being caught between the tank and a bulkhead.
- Loading instructions are taken from the boat commander.

Predisembarkation of the LCU

Ensure that the following is completed before predisembarkation of the LCU:

- Turret seal is inflated.
- Loader hatch is closed.
- Turret power is in the manual position at the loader station.
- Driver hatch is correctly locked.
- Positive communications between the tank commander and driver.
- The boat commander checks the depth in front of the entire ramp.
- The depth of the water from the bow ramp to the end of the wingwall is no more than 5 feet.
- Tank commander checks the depth of the water. If he feels that the water is too deep, tanks will not exit the landing craft.

Disembarkation of LCU

The following occurs during disembarkation of the LCU:

- Driver takes all commands from the tank commander.
- When disembarking from the LCU, the tank commander should time the movement of the tank to coincide with a lull in the wave swells.
- The tank moves forward slowly. Once two-thirds of the vehicle is off the ramp, the tank commander has the driver gradually increase speed to full throttle until the vehicle is out of the water.
- Drivers need to remember to listen to the tank commander and to expect some leakage through the driver's hatch as water comes over the front slope of the tank.

Procedures to Abandon the Tank

If the tank has aborted and will not restart, the tank is taking water in through the tank commander's hatch, and the tank commander feels that the crew is in danger of being trapped inside the tank, the tank commander gives the signal to abandon the tank. If the signal to abandon the tank is given, the following procedures are executed:

- Commander orders the crew to start emergency drill and exit the tank when flooding cannot be controlled by the bilge pump.
- Driver verifies that the parking brake is released and the engine is shut down.
- Driver unscrews the turret seal valve to deflate turret seal.
- Loader unlocks the turret lock.
- Commander positions AUX HYDR POWER switch to ON.

—————— **WARNING** ——————

Before traversing turret, alert crew and make sure all personnel are clear of turret. Crewman can be injured or killed if turret is traversed while body parts are extended between turret and hull.

- Gunner traverses the turret counterclockwise until turret opening is aligned with driver's station. If turret cannot be traversed with hydraulic power, traverse and align turret manually. If turret cannot be traversed, inform driver to exit through driver's hatch.
- Loader locks the turret lock.
- Commander turns off the VEHICLE MASTER POWER switch.
- Loader opens the driver's station access screen.
- Driver lowers the seat and headrest and disconnects helmet leads.

—————— **WARNING** ——————

Do not extend any part of the body from the turret into the driver's station unless the turret lock is set to LOCKED. A crewman may be killed if the turret is traversed while he is between the turret and the driver's station.

- Driver exits the driver's station to the turret through the turret opening.
- Crew exits the tank if flooding becomes excessive. If flooding is not excessive, wait in the tank until the tank is towed ashore or emergency personnel arrive.

The following steps are performed only after determining that the turret cannot be traversed:

- Driver disconnects the leads to the helmet at the quick-disconnect. Driver's hatch may be difficult to open until water has completely filled compartment. Once hatch is open, exit as quickly as possible.
- Gunner elevates the main gun tube to its maximum height.

In shallow water where only the hull is submerged, the following procedures apply:

- Driver lifts drain valve handle to open drain valves.
- Driver unscrews two wing nuts and removes middle periscope.
- Driver presses button on hatch, lifts handle, and pushes up on handle all the way, then releases.
- Driver turns crank clockwise to open driver's hatch.
- Driver assumes a safe position on hull or turret until tank is towed ashore or emergency personnel arrive.
- Remaining crew exits through the turret hatch.

Embarkation/Debarkation Communications

While backing onto the LCU, the driver stops and the crew attempts to re-establish communications. If communications cannot be re-established, and if the entire tank is on the boat, the crew with assistance from members of the boat crew will ground guide the tank onto the boat. If the tank is still partially in the water, the tank commander informs (the best way he can, SOPs should be established before the operation) the driver to move the tank straight off the ramp up onto shore and attempts to fix the communication problem.

While driving off the LCU, the driver stops and the tank crew attempts to re-establish communications. If communications cannot be re-established and if the entire tank is on the boat, the crew will stand fast until communication can be re-established. If the tank is partially on the ramp and the boat, the crew with assistance from members of the boat crew will ground guide the tank back onto the boat and stand fast until communications can be re-established. If the tank has already started to leave the ramp, the driver continues to drive straight until he is out of the water.

CHAPTER 8
MILITARY OPERATIONS OTHER THAN WAR

Military operations other than war (MOOTW) focus on deterring war, resolving conflict, promoting peace, and giving support to civil authorities in response to domestic crises. MOOTW may involve elements of both combat and noncombat. Tanks are employed in both offensive and defensive missions during MOOTW. Task-organized as part of a MAGTF, Marine tank units may be called upon to support a wide range of operations in various political and geographical environments. Because of the large amount of resources necessary to deploy, operate, and sustain mechanized forces, tank units are usually used to execute MOOTW activities that take maximum advantage of their inherent capabilities: armor protected firepower, cross-terrain mobility, and shock effect. Recently, Marine tank units have participated in MOOTW operations in Somalia and Haiti. During these operations, tanks were effective deterrents in lessening attacks towards Marines conducting peacekeeping operations. In addition, tanks served as powerful security escorts for food relief convoys carrying food to the local population, keeping them safe from convoy hijackers.

In MOOTW, tank units may be assigned missions traditionally handled by infantry or military police forces. For example, a tank unit could be tasked as a reaction force to support crowd and riot control; however, potential casualties to noncombatants and collateral damage of local infrastructure can occur if tank units are used in this type of role. To perform effectively and efficiently, tank crewmen should receive special equipment and training (e.g., the operational environment, rules of engagement [ROE], force protection, and civil affairs) before executing such operations. Disciplined, well-trained, combat-ready commanders and crewmen can adapt to the specialized demands of MOOTW. Flexibility and situational awareness are paramount requirements, especially for unit commanders.

The M1A1 tank's armor protection is well-suited to take the impact of small-arms fire and the rocks and bottles that might be encountered during a MOOTW operation. Tank units provide the MAGTF with a highly effective graduated response. Tanks can provide a graduated escalation in the use of force while providing a high level of protection to the tank crews. Graduated response options include using the tank's physical presence for crowd control or the use of the tank's main gun and machine guns to destroy barricades or engage snipers.

Environment

Note: In the following discussion of MOOTW, the term environment refers to both the cultural, political, and military context in which these operations take place and to the terrain and weather of the area of operation.

Tank units involved in MOOTW emphasize their psychological effects more than the offensive capabilities of the tank. Tanks can be viewed as a positive symbol of power and political resolve but they can also be viewed negatively and can insight violence if not carefully employed. Since MOOTW is often conducted in a politically sensitive environment, tank crewmen should realize that every individual action could have a significant political or operational impact. Tank commanders need to ensure consistent discipline, decentralized execution of lawful orders, cultural training, and, if necessary, the use of a language interpreter. One act of civil disturbance or intolerant treatment of civilians can turn a supportive populace against the force and can be exploited by potential adversaries. Marines should understand the military situation, especially the doctrine, tactics, and equipment that are employed by belligerent, guerrilla, terrorist, militant, or paramilitary forces. Orientation training should also clarify the following environmental conditions: the tempo of operations, local news media, and the United States' role in the operation.

The tank/mechanized commander must consider his activities in relation to similar activities carried out by agencies of the United States, its allies, and the host nation, as well as nongovernmental organizations. The presence of tanks or heavy mechanized forces in certain areas or situations could be counter to what other organizations are trying to achieve with the local population. MOOTW considerations for using tanks include the following:

- Media scrutiny may be extensive and tanks can be represented negatively.
- ROE may be more restrictive thereby limiting the tanks full offensive capabilities.
- Identification of hostile parties may be more difficult making security of tanks more difficult (e.g., concealed antitank weapons in large crowds).
- Tanks and other military assets may be routinely used to support noncombat functions (e.g., protection of civilian food, fuel convoys).
- Interaction with civilian noncombatants will be routine at every level of command.

Tempo

Although extreme tension may underlie MOOTW, the tempo of operations is generally slow. Therefore, the key to creating a secure tank environment is not only maintaining operational security but also varying security techniques and procedures to avoid predictability.

Rules of Engagement

ROE are directives issued by the military authority that delineate the circumstances and limitations under which United States' forces initiate and/or continue combat engagement with other encountered forces. ROE dictate when, where, against whom, and how force—especially lethal force—may be used. Key considerations in the design of ROE for tank employment include the following:

- United States policy.
- International law.
- Host nation law.
- The threat.
- Commander's intent.
- Operational considerations.
- Tactical capabilities.

Specific aspects of ROE may be intended to address force protection issues like combat identification, fratricide, or the use of a particular type of weapon in certain situations. Culture may be an important factor as well. ROE may forbid engagements in the vicinity of cultural or artistic sites, because such sites are often irreplaceable. For these reasons, tank crews must understand the lethality of the tank's weapon systems and destructive capabilities with regard to potential collateral damage to noncombatants, property, and local infrastructure (e.g., buildings, roads, rails, and bridges).

ROE issues are also greatly complicated by the urban environment. ROE designed for use in one area of a city may be irrelevant or counterproductive in another because of differences in the urban geometry, structural materials, and in the nature of the mission. For instance, the use of tank main gun rounds and coaxial machine rounds in a shantytown may pose more danger to adjacent friendly forces and to noncombatants than to the enemy. In other sections of the city, the use of tank high explosive rounds may threaten to disperse hazardous materials or contaminants into the air or water. The presence of adversary fighters dressed in civilian clothes, common in urban conflicts, will further complicate operations.

In all circumstances, ROE for tanks should be tactically sound, flexible, understandable, and enforceable. They must be disseminated and understood at all levels. Inappropriate or poorly enforced tank ROE may result in friendly casualties (including fratricide), collateral damage, and the deaths of noncombatants, all of which seriously hamper an operation. ROE CAN NEVER NEGATE THE RIGHT AND RESPONSIBILITY OF FRIENDLY FORCES TO SELF-PROTECTION.

Force Protection

Force protection is a primary responsibility for every commander involved in MOOTW. The armor protected firepower and automotive capabilities of the tank allow it to be employed in a number of MOOTW missions that provide the commander with options for minimal risk of personnel, equipment, and supplies because of the tank's inherent self-protection and security that it can provide to supported forces.

Antiterrorism protective measures training should include operational security, physical security, and personal security measures to protect tanks and their crews. Examples include avoiding employing tanks in patterns and routines; strict noise and light discipline; and use of cover and concealment, obstacles, observation posts, and early warning devices. Tanks can be viewed by terrorists or insurgents as powerful symbolic targets if they are able to destroy them and/or injure the crew. Commanders must protect armored vehicles and secure locations for eating, resting, and conducting maintenance while providing adequate force protection measures. For more information, see Marine Corps Reference Publication (MCRP) 3-02D, *Combating Terrorism*, and MCRP 3-02E, *The Individual's Guide for Understanding and Surviving Terrorism*.

Public Affairs and the Media

In many MOOTW environments, the local populace may view the presence of tank units as a highly visible and potentially intimidating military presence. Therefore, the employment of tanks infers a firm commitment and demonstration of American resolve in the respective crisis and often draws media attention. Consequently, the tank crew's actions may be highly visible, scrutinized and questioned by the media. See MCWP 3-33.3, *Marine Corps Public Affairs*, for more information.

Noncombatant Evacuation Operations

The tank unit in MOOTW can be used in a noncombatant evacuation operation scenario as an element of a security force or reaction force (see page 8-6 for details on the reaction force).

Security

The tank unit can establish a battle position or conduct a relief in place of a battle position as part of a MAGTF perimeter or strongpoint defense. (See chap. 3 for detailed information on defensive operations.) Dismounted infantry may or may not be integrated with the tank unit. Coordination with dismounted patrols and observation posts outside the perimeter is critical for situational awareness. See chapter 4 for detailed information on employment of tanks with infantry. In restricted terrain, commanders must understand that with each application of a tank in a static position, the danger and vulnerabilities of that tank are maximized. A team of four Marines is optimum to provide security for a tank in a defensive or overwatch position. The tank commander should be responsible for the team and their emplacement. In open terrain, such a team may not be required.

Clearing of Evacuation Routes

A tank unit can proof routes to detect and neutralize mines or improvised explosive devises (IEDs). Based on METT-T factors, the unit may use tactical movement techniques to provide overwatch for the proofing vehicle, which can be a tank (equipped with a mine roller, if available) or an engineer vehicle. If mines and/or IEDs are detected, the unit conducts breach force operations or bypasses within its capability. Whenever possible, the unit should be equipped with a mine plow and a breaching kit containing wire and bolt cutters, grappling hooks, and demolitions. If the mines and/or obstacles are not within the unit's breaching capability, engineers are called forward. While the breaching is occurring, the proofing and overwatch vehicles should take notice of anything that is out of the ordinary, such as new construction, repairs to damaged buildings, plants or trees that seem new or out of place, and freshly dug earth. These conditions may indicate the presence of newly emplaced or command-detonated mines or IEDs. The tank unit conducts tactical movement breaching operations as discussed in appendix E.

Foreign Humanitarian Operations

The tank's intimidation factor is always present; therefore, the tank unit is normally positioned as far away as possible from those who are benefiting from foreign humanitarian efforts. Tanks can be used to man a battle position as part of a MAGTF foreign humanitarian supply site providing security from insurgents who wish to confiscate the supplies or destroy them. (See chap. 3 for detailed information on defensive operations.) When tanks are used for this purpose, coordination with dismounted patrols and observation posts outside the perimeter is critical for security. Signs, in the local language, should be posted as necessary around the supply site to identify movement restrictions for the local populace.

Convoy Security Operations

Because of the tank's mobility, firepower, and armor protection, tank units can provide convoy security and close-in protection from direct fire to convoys while they are on the move. Depending on a variety of factors (e.g., size of the convoy, escort assets available, METT-T), convoy escort missions are normally conducted by Marine tank units at the platoon level, either independently or as part of a larger unit's convoy security mission. See MCRP 4-11.3F, *Convoy Operations Handbook,* for detailed tactics, techniques, and procedures.

Command and Control

The relationship between the tank platoon and the convoy commander must provide for unity of command. In most cases, the tank unit commander may serve as the security element or support the security force commander.

Tactical Disposition

During escort missions, the tank unit leader supports the convoy commander by positioning his tanks to provide security in all directions and throughout the length of the convoy. The convoy commander adjusts the disposition of the tank unit, either as a unit or dispersed, to fit the security requirements of each particular situation.

Escort Missions

When the tank unit is deployed during an escort operation, it can provide forward, flank, rear, or close-in security. In such situations, it executes tactical movement based on the factors of METT-T. Figures 8-1 and 8-2 show the platoon using various formations while performing escort duties as a unit. These formations can also be used by the platoon while part of a large-scale escort mission.

Large-scale Escort Missions

If sufficient escort assets are available, the convoy commander usually organizes the convoy into three distinct elements: advance guard, close-in protective group, and rear guard.

The tank unit is normally best employed as an element of the close-in protective group. This group provides immediate, close-in protection for the main body of the vehicle column with escort vehicles positioned either within the column or

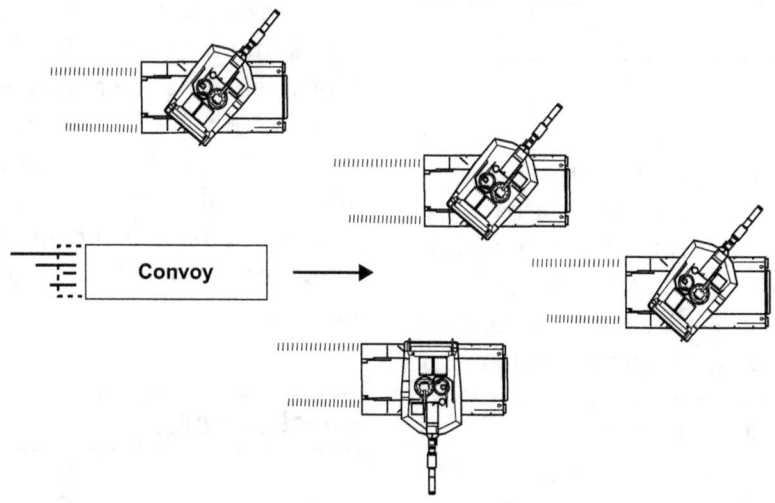

Convoy Escort Using Platoon Wedge Formation

Figure 8-1. Tanks Performing Forward Security for a Convoy.

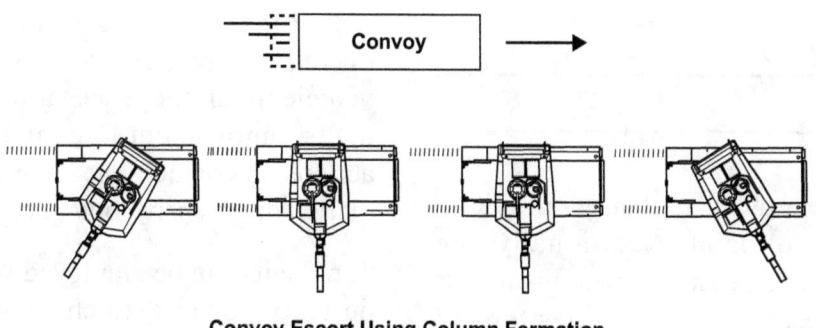

Convoy Escort Using Column Formation

Figure 8-2. Tanks Performing Flank Security for a Convoy.

on the flanks. The convoy commander's vehicle is located within this group.

The advance guard reconnoiters and proofs the convoy route and searches for signs of enemy activity, such as ambushes and obstacles. Within its capabilities, it attempts to clear the route and provide the convoy commander with early warning before the arrival of the vehicle column. A tank section or the entire platoon may be designated as part of the advance guard. The platoon commander may also be required to attach a mine plow or mine roller to the tank unit.

The rear guard follows the convoy and provides security in the area behind the main body of the vehicle column, often moving with medical and recovery assets. A tank section or the entire tank platoon may be part of this element.

Note: The convoy commander may also designate the tank as part of a reserve (quick reaction) force for additional firepower in the event of enemy contact. The reserve will either move with the convoy or be located at a staging area close enough to provide immediate interdiction against the enemy.

Mounted Patrols

Mounted patrols should be carefully planned to ensure that chosen routes do not canalize tanks (i.e., tanks unable to maneuver without backing up or waiting for vehicles behind them to move). Choosing such routes makes a tank an easy target for insurgents armed with antitank weapons. When selecting a route, tanks should avoid areas that are culturally sensitive or that their presence would escalate the level of violence.

The tank unit, when patrolling urban areas or close terrain, normally overwatches and/or follows in support of dismounted infantry. Procedures for operating with infantry are discussed in chapter 4 and are very similar for operating in a MOOTW environment.

Checkpoints

A tank unit can overwatch an infantry or military police traffic control point. Additionally, the overwatch element must ensure it coordinates for its own local security; it usually does this by coordinating with dismounted infantry for observation posts and dismounted patrols. See chapter 3 for more information on overwatch and occupation of a defensive position.

The tank unit (supported by infantry) can be employed to occupy a perimeter defense to protect traffic and facilitate movement through a chokepoint along the main supply route. Infantry is normally integrated into the perimeter defense to augment the tank unit's firepower and to provide security by means of dismounted patrols and observation posts.

The tank unit can be employed to overwatch a blockade or roadblock. The blockade or roadblock can either be a manned position or a reinforcing obstacle covered by fires only. It coordinates with dismounted infantry for local security (observation posts and dismounted patrols). Positions are improved using procedures for deliberate occupation of a battle position (see chap. 3).

Reaction Force

Tank units can be employed as an element of the MAGTF reserve (sometimes referred to as the quick reaction force) during tactical recovery of aircraft and personnel (TRAP) missions. Typical missions include reinforcement and relief of encircled friendly forces that are conducting the TRAP mission or securing an objective in an operation to rescue a downed aircraft or stranded vehicle. In all these scenarios, the tank unit conducts a movement to contact and, if required, actions on contact. See chapter 2 for more information on offensive operations.

Tank units can be employed with infantry to conduct a cordon and search mission. During the cordon and search, the tank unit normally occupies overwatch and/or hasty defensive positions to isolate a search area. Close coordination and communication with the dismounted elements conducting the search is critical. Dismounted forces are also employed in observation posts and patrols to maintain surveillance of dead space and gaps in the cordoned area. The tank unit must be prepared to take immediate action if the search team or observation posts identify enemy elements. Enemy contact may require the unit to execute tactical maneuver and deliver fires directed by the dismounted elements (see chap. 4).

CHAPTER 9
MILITARY OPERATIONS ON URBANIZED TERRAIN

The powerful, high-velocity cannon mounted on the M1A1 tank provides Marines with a key requirement—a highly survivable direct-fire asset—for victory in urban areas. Although the infantry assumes the lead role during combat in urban areas, tanks and infantry work as a close team. Tanks move down streets after the infantry has cleared the street of any suspected ATGM positions. Tanks, in turn, support the infantry with fires. The tank is one of the most effective weapons for heavy fire against structures. The primary role of the tank cannon during combat in urban areas is to provide heavy direct fire against buildings and strongpoints that are identified as targets by the infantry. The quick, accurate, and devastating effects of the 120mm tank cannon, coaxial 7.62mm machine gun, and .50 caliber machine gun are major assets to Marines fighting in urban areas.

The tank provides an all-weather, direct-fire platform. Crewmen have the ability to utilize the tank's thermal viewer to engage targets in low illumination and limited visibility conditions, which often accompanies urban fighting environments. Precision engagement systems enable our forces to locate the objective or target with enhanced optics, engage with desired effect, and retain the flexibility to re-engage when required. Even from extended ranges, a tank unit's precision engagement capability provides a degree of force protection for the GCE and can limit collateral damage to noncombatants (such as civilians in adjoining buildings from being engaged) and local infrastructure. The wide arrays of responsive and accurate weapons on the tank provide the commander with flexible options.

Tank Units and the Infantry

Tanks have been the primary fire and maneuver force on the armor heavy battlefield, but they have also begun to play a major role in the lower end of the range of military operations. In the military operations in urban terrain (MOUT) environment, the tank clearly is in a support role for infantry. If properly integrated in the scheme of maneuver, the tank is also a great combat multiplier and can provide a tremendous advantage to combined-arms forces engaged in urban combat.

Some key considerations for tanks and infantry working together in urban areas are as follows:

- Situational awareness must exist between the tanker and the infantry. Crosstalk between tankers and the infantry fosters a good working team. Communications between elements can take many forms (e.g., radio communication, use of field phones externally mounted on the right rear fender of the tank, visual signals such as hand-and-arm signals and pyrotechnics).
- Both the infantry and tankers must exercise tactical patience. Tanks, indoctrinated in moving quickly from one position to another, must remember that they are in a support role to the infantry and that they also depend on infantrymen for support and protection against close ambush.
- Terrain can create mobility restrictions for a tank and the terrain that is easily trafficable by the infantry may be impassable by a tank.
- The use of tanks does not negate the need to use smoke, obscurants, and indirect fire when moving up to an obstacle and support-by fire positions.

- It is essential that tankers attached to the infantry unit be involved in every step of the OPORD development, especially rehearsals.
- To be effective, the tank and infantry units are organized as a combined-arms team.

When the mechanized Marine force is employed in an urban area that is very restricted, tank units may have to be task-organized into sections. Marine tank units support Marine infantry in urban areas by—

- Providing overwhelming firepower and shock effect using both its main gun and/or machine guns.
- Isolating objectives with direct fire to prevent enemy withdrawal, reinforcement, or counterattack.
- Neutralizing or suppressing enemy positions with smoke, high explosive, and automatic weapon fire as infantry closes with and destroys the enemy.
- Assisting opposed entry of infantry into buildings when debris, obstacles, or enemy fire blocks doorways by firing breaching holes into buildings.
- Breaking through street barricades or reducing barricades by fires.
- Using fires to reduce enemy strongpoints in buildings.
- Holding cleared portions of the objective by covering avenues of approach.
- Attacking by fire any other targets designated by the infantry.
- Establishing roadblocks.
- Suppressing identified sniper positions.

Marine infantry facilitates tank employment in urban terrain by—

- Locating targets for engagement by the tank.
- Suppressing and destroying antiarmor weapons with mortars, automatic weapons, and grenades.

- Assaulting positions and clearing buildings.
- Providing local security for tanks.

Planning

Compared to combat in open terrain, urban operations are compressed in space and time. This compression limits observation distances; engagement ranges; weapons effectiveness; mobility; and time to maneuver, generate more fires, anticipate enemy actions, plan and conduct operations, and, if necessary, respond to enemy actions. These limitations tend to force extremely close combat with troops fighting from building to building and from room to room. Command and control is difficult because small-unit leaders cannot see their troops and radio communications is subject to interference caused by the presence of structures. Historically, urban combat has required a high degree of initiative by small-unit leaders who were directing the employment of task-organized special assault teams, of which tanks were a part.

When tanks are to be task-organized for MOUT, it is vital that tank unit representatives be integrated into the planning process as early as possible. Familiarity with unit SOPs must be achieved down to infantry squad and tank section levels for effective tank-infantry employment in MOUT operations. Additionally, the tank unit leader must keep the infantry commander informed regarding his units; supply, crew, and weapons status; and any special equipment available (e.g., mine plows and rollers).

When planning a mission, commanders must consider the capabilities, limitations, and likely COAs available to the enemy. The commander and staff must consider the strength, composition, disposition, and activities of the enemy forces. Enemy tactics may range from ambushes, snipers, and urban terrorism to large-scale conventional operations.

Therefore, the tactics and techniques utilized by tanks and infantry may require different tactics, techniques, and procedures. The addition of armor creates the following planning considerations for the infantry commander:

- Conducting full dress rehearsals utilizing tanks whenever possible.
- Standardizing reporting formats for both tanks and the infantry.
- Establishing SOPs for tanks working with infantry emphasizing safety of friendly infantry maneuvering with tanks, signals between tanks and infantry, marking of cleared buildings/areas, ROEs, and mutual security between tanks and the infantry.
- Determining tank maintenance and logistical support requirements to the supported unit.
- Considering battle damage assessment and recovery, resupply, and casualty evacuation of tank crew personnel.

Employment Considerations

Marine infantry and/or tank commanders should consider the following when employing the M1A1 in urban terrain:

- Tank main gun fire is an effective method for eliminating a sniper in a building or creating a psychological effect that destroys the enemy's will to continue, but this method creates a higher degree of collateral damage.
- Streets and alleys constitute ready-made fire lanes and firing zones that can greatly restrict and canalize vehicular traffic.
- Tanks should be employed by section. All fundamental fire and movement techniques are conducted at the section level, so tanks should never be employed individually. In extreme cases, tanks can work separately, but it is not recommended.
- Typically, a tank and an infantry squad work in intimate support of each other. The infantry

furnishes local security and designates targets for the tank.
- SINCGARS radios are utilized for intervehicular communications and should be the primary means of communications between the infantry and the vehicle commander. If SINCGARS radios are unavailable, a rigged external TA-1 phone or hand-and-arm signals can be used.
- The tank should use multipurpose antitank (MPAT) ammunition to create holes in the walls of buildings so the infantry can enter. High explosive antitank (HEAT) ammunition may also be used but is less effective in creating holes.
- The tank should use MPAT ammunition against barricades. MPAT rounds can be used to demolish towers, steeples, chimneys, and other tall structures likely to contain enemy artillery observers. This technique depends on established ROEs.
- Tank sabot ammunition has limited utility against most nonvehicular targets and the discarding sabot petals can endanger friendly infantry or civilians nearby. The hazard area extends 70 meters to each side of the tank gun out to 1 kilometer.
- The tank main gun has an overpressure that, when fired, can kill friendly troops. The danger to dismounted troops is a 90-degree arc out to 200 meters from the end of the tank main gun.
- Tanks should avoid stopping or moving slowly near nonsecure buildings due to the threat of possible enemy close range ATGM fires.
- Tanks should mount the fording kit elbow exhaust plenum pipe attachment or the heat deflector to allow Marine infantry to safely approach the rear of the M1A1 tank without being burned by the tank's hot exhaust.
- Units should check all bridges and overpasses for mines and determine the bridge's weight-carrying capacity.
- Tanks should stay near buildings held by friendly troops. Crewmembers should watch for signals from the infantry inside the buildings on their flanks.

- Tank crewmembers should keep their personal weapons ready for close-in combat.
- Tanks should be used to destroy enemy strong-points with main gun fire:
  - Firing armor-piercing ammunition to penetrate the reinforced wall of a building followed by MPAT or HEAT rounds to kill or neutralize the enemy.
  - Firing into the ground floor to drive the enemy into the basement, where infantry can attack them, or to higher floors, where the wing tank can destroy them.
- Tanks are sometimes at a disadvantage because their main guns cannot depress or elevate sufficiently to fire into basements and upper floors at close range (see fig. 9-1). The M1A1 can depress to –10 degrees or elevate to a height of +20 degrees.
- The M1A1 has a coaxial M240 machine gun and can use it to engage enemy troops and enemy positions behind light cover while the tank crew remains protected. The coaxial machine gun has the same elevation and depression restrictions as the main gun.

- Tanks can use the tank commander's .50 caliber machine gun but it can only elevate to +36 degrees.
- When buttoned up, tank crews have limited visibility. Security infantry for the tank must help the tank crew "see" by communicating to the tank crew possible targets relative to the tanks position and orientation.

Control Measures

Combat in urban areas requires control measures with which all troops must be familiar. One of the keys to ensuring ease of coordination of fires, linkup points, and patrol routes is the use of an effective map system. Intelligence sections should provide an accurate map, down to exact buildings if possible. Buildings and roads can be sectioned off and labeled alpha-numerically. Without an effective and universally used map, MOUT operations verge on impossible. MOUT control measures include boundaries; objectives; frontages, formations, and zones of actions; and phase lines.

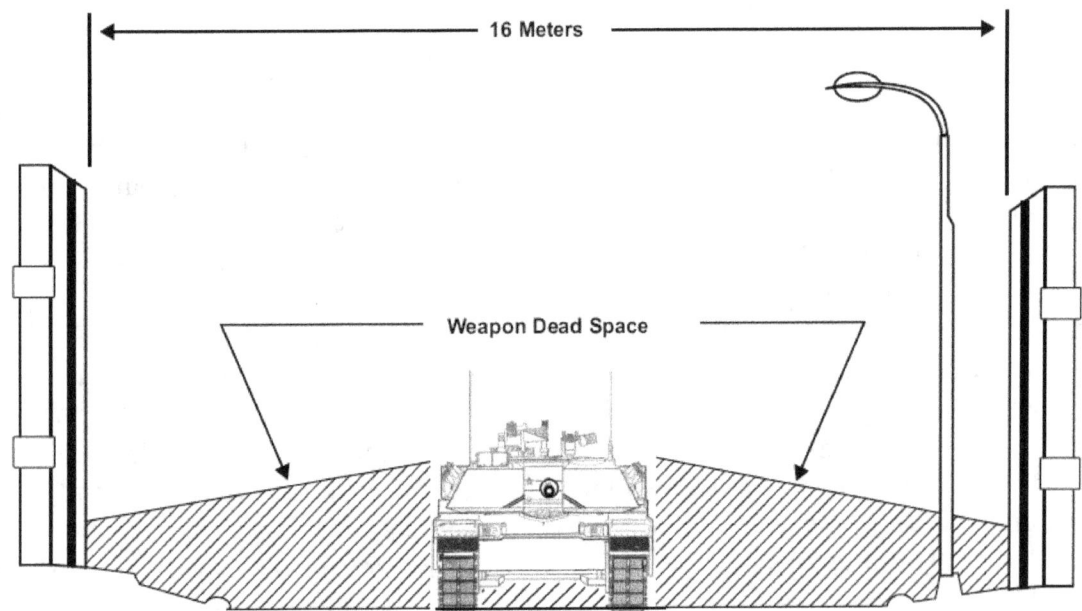

Figure 9-1. Tank Cannon Dead Space at Street Level.

Boundaries

In dense urban areas, units should place boundaries along one side of the street to provide easy and definite identification. In areas where observation and movement are less restricted, they may place boundaries in alleys or within blocks so that one unit's zone includes both sides of the street.

Objectives

Objectives are specific and limited. Choosing major intersections, choosing and numbering principal buildings, and choosing other readily identifiable physical features along the route of attack improve control. As the unit moves forward through an area, unit commanders should designate the near side of the street as the objective. If they choose the far side of the street, the unit will have to secure buildings on both sides of the street to take the objective. Units must promptly report seizure of objectives.

Frontages, Formations, and Zones of Action

Attacking battalions normally operate within relatively narrow zones of action. The frontages depend on the enemy's strength, the size of the buildings, and the anticipated resistance. Normally, a battalion-sized unit has a frontage of three to six blocks and companies one to two blocks.

Frontages and zones of action influence tank employment. The tanks should be well forward to add momentum to the attack, exploit success, repel counterattacks, and protect the flanks and rear against enemy action.

Phase Lines

Phase lines increase control by regulating the advance of attacking forces. Phase lines are less restrictive than objectives, and they encourage the rapid exploitation of success without halting. Principal streets, rivers, and trolley or railroad lines make good phase lines.

Checkpoints and Contact Points

Street corners, buildings, railway crossings, bridges, and easily identifiable features can be checkpoints or contact points, and they facilitate the reporting of locations. The commander can use them as specific points where he desires units to make physical contact.

Offensive MOUT Operations

Because of the nature of the terrain, offensive urban area operations are typically conducted by dismounted infantry. Tanks should be employed as much as possible in close support of dismounted infantry in order to secure locations and provide direct fire support. Formations depend on the composition of the combined-arms force. The best formation for command and control for security purposes is a column. The column must be flexible and provide 360 degrees of spherical security. The combined-arms column travels within the security bubble, with dismounted infantry clearing buildings and providing security along the route. Once enemy contact is made, expedient coordination is done to use the proper weapons system to engage the enemy. Buildings and terrain will most likely not permit an on-line formation.

Attacking in Urban Areas

A detailed study of the city and the enemy's dispositions in and around it forms the basis for planning the attack and seizure of an urban area. Planning may include tanks for both maneuver and fire support. The attacking force is normally separated into two forces: the enveloping force (tank-heavy) and the direct assault force (infantry-heavy). Follow the procedures and considerations listed below when attacking in an urban area:

- Dissipate the enemy's strength by causing him to react to demonstrations, feints, or ruses.
- Concentrate overwhelming combat power to force a quick and violent disruption of the defenses, envelop the urban area, and move rapidly to the enemy's rear.

- Reduce strongpoints with fires only (if possible), secure them with follow-on forces, and maintain the momentum of the attack.
- Cut lines of communications and defeat the enemy through isolation.
- Attack at night to gain surprise or to take objectives whose assault during daylight would be too costly.
- Attack continuously once the momentum has been gained and continue to attack until defenses have been splintered.

Obliquity

The tank cannon produces its best urban target effects when fired perpendicular to the hard surface (zero obliquity). However, during combat in built-up areas, finding a covered firing position that permits low-oblique firing is unlikely. Most shots strike the target at an angle that normally reduces penetration. With tank cannon armor-piercing, fin-stabilized, discarding sabot (APFSDS) rounds, oblique angles of up to 25 degrees have little effect in reducing penetration, but angles greater than 45 degrees greatly reduce penetration.

Ammunition

APFSDS rounds are the most commonly carried tank ammunition. These rounds work best against armored vehicles. However, the 120mm cannon also fires an effective HEAT round. Tank units conducting MOUT should carry a HEAT/MPAT heavy mix. A detailed discussion of each round's composition and capabilities can be found in appendix D.

M1A1 Tank Fires Dead Space Characteristics

The M1A1 tank has limited elevation in an urban environment; it can elevate its cannon 20 degrees and depress it 10 degrees. This lower depression limit creates a 35-foot dead space around a tank (see fig. 9-1). There is also a zone overhead in which the tank cannot fire (see fig. 9-2). This dead space offers ideal locations for short-range antiarmor weapons and allows hidden enemy

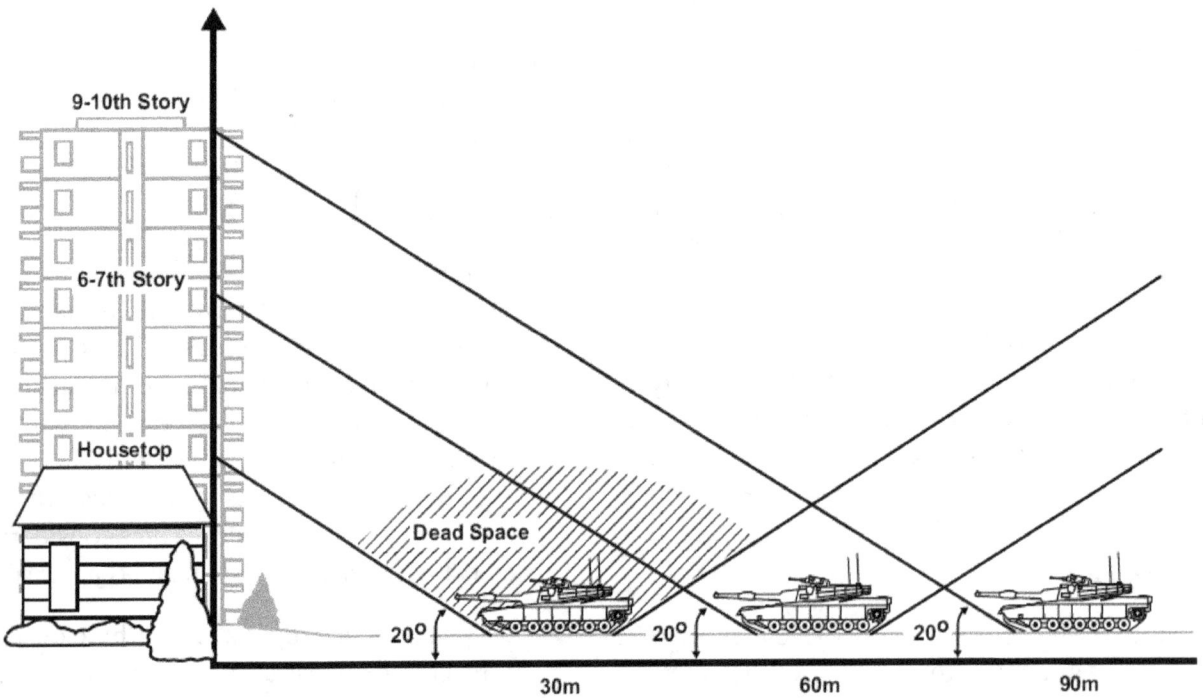

Figure 9-2. Tank Cannon Dead Space Above Street Level.

gunners to fire at the tank when the tank cannot fire back. It also exposes the tank's most vulnerable areas: the flanks, rear, and top. Infantry must move ahead, alongside, and to the rear of tanks to provide close protection. The M1A1 tank also has a blind spot caused by the zero-degree depression available over part of the back deck. To engage any target in this area, the tank must pivot to convert the rear target to a flank target.

The 120mm MPAT has a short arming range; it arms a round at about 60 feet. This arming distance allows the tank to engage targets from short ranges. The armor of the tank protects the crew from both the blowback effects of the round and enemy return fire. The APFSDS round does not need to arm and can; therefore, it can be fired at very close targets at almost any range. The discarding portions of the round can be lethal to exposed infantry forward of the tank.

When the tank main gun fires, it creates a large fireball and smoke cloud. In the confines of a built-up area, dirt and masonry dust are also picked up and added to the cloud and the target is further obscured by the smoke and dust of the explosion. Depending on the conditions, this obscuration could last as long as 2 or 3 minutes. Marines can use this period to reposition or advance unseen by the enemy.

A tank cannon creates an overpressure and noise hazard to exposed Marines. All dismounted Marines working near tanks should wear Kevlar helmets and protective vests, as well as ballistic eye protection. If possible, they should also wear earplugs and avoid the tank's frontal 60-degree arc during firing. The overpressure can also cause glass in surrounding buildings to shatter. Falling glass can cause injury to Marines if they are not warned to stay clear of windows.

————————— WARNING —————————

The overpressure from the tank's 120mm cannon can kill a Marine within a 90-degree arc that extends from the muzzle of the gun tube out to 200 meters. From 200 to 1,000 meters along the line of fire and on a frontage of about 400 meters, dismounted Marines must be aware of the danger from discarding sabot petals, which can kill or seriously injure personnel. Personnel outside the tank should remain at least 50 meters from the tank in all directions as they may receive damaging effects from firing noise and overpressure. Personnel must also wear hearing protection when operating within 704 meters of a tank that is firing its main gun.

Tanks are equipped with powerful thermal sights that can be used to detect enemy personnel and weapons that are hidden in shadows and behind openings. Dust, fires, and thick smoke can degrade this sight capability.

Tanks have turret-mounted grenade launchers that project screening smoke grenades. The grenades use a bursting charge and burning red phosphorous particles to create the screen. Burning particles can easily start uncontrolled fires and are hazardous to dismounted Marines near the tank. The tank commander and the infantry small-unit leader must coordinate when and under what conditions these launchers can be used. Grenade launchers are a useful feature for protecting the tank, but can cause problems if unwisely used.

The tank's size and armor can provide dismounted Marines with cover from direct-fire weapons and fragments. With coordination, tanks can provide moving cover for Marines as they advance across small open areas. However, enemy fire that strikes but does not penetrate a tank is a major threat to nearby Marines. Fragmentation generated by antitank rounds and ricochets off of a tank's armor have been a prime cause of casualties while infantry were working with tanks in built-up areas.

Target Effects

MPAT rounds are most effective against masonry walls. The APFSDS round can penetrate deeply into a structure but does not create as large a hole or displace as much spall behind the target. In contrast, tank MPAT or HEAT rounds are large enough to displace enough spall to inflict casualties inside a building. One MPAT round normally creates a breach hole in all but the thickest masonry construction—a single round demolishes brick veneer and wood-framed constructions. Even the 120mm MPAT round cannot cut all of the building's reinforcing rods, which are usually left in place, often hindering entry through the breach hole. MPAT, HEAT, and APFSDS rounds are effective against field fortifications. Only large earth berms and heavy mass-construction buildings can provide protection against tank fire.

Security

Tanks need infantry to provide security in built-up areas and to designate targets. If targets are protected by structures, tanks should be escorted forward to the most covered location that provides a clear shot. On-the-spot instructions by infantry commanders ensure that the tank's fire is accurate and its exposure is limited. The tank commander may have to halt in a covered position, dismount, and reconnoiter his forward route into a firing position.

Attack Phases

Reconnoiter the Objective

Intelligence gathering and reconnaissance and surveillance are critical to the planning process. Whenever possible, leaders should make a personal reconnaissance of the objective area to collect first-hand information regarding the area to be attacked. Avenues of approach for both infantry and the tanks, observation posts, supply routes, and the emplacement positions of direct and indirect fire weapons systems for both tanks and/or infantry are all examples of information that can be obtained during reconnaissance. Likely enemy ATGM positions can also be determined as danger areas for tanks. Composition and structure of buildings and roadbeds, cover and concealment opportunities, and other information not apparent in a map study may have a significant impact on the plan. For example, determining that the buildings that are to be attacked are made of brick means tanks will have an easier time making building breach holes for infantry then if the building walls contained reinforced rebar.

Isolate the Objective

Seizing natural and manmade features that dominate the area can isolate the objective. Isolation may also be accomplished by coordinated use of supporting arms to seal off enemy lines of communication. This phase may be conducted simultaneously with the third phase, which is securing a foothold.

To isolate an urban objective, tanks can be used two ways. Tanks can be used to isolate an enemy objective by becoming a support element or they can be employed as part of the attack. By using tanks as a support element they can be held in reserve or given a mission to keep enemy reinforcements from moving into the isolated attack objective (such as a main avenue of approach into a town). When tanks are used in the attack force they may be employed to directly support the attacking infantry to help clear buildings and/or areas. They can also engage enemy forces trying to hinder the attack. Tanks should always be aware of enemy mounted avenues of approach.

Once the attacker has isolated the city, he can either continue the attack or fix the defender and force him to capitulate. If necessary, the unit then secures positions outside the urban area from which to support entrance into the city itself. If tanks are of limited use within a town due to the inability to maneuver, they can be employ just outside the urban area to restrict further enemy forces from entering. The tactics and techniques for this phase of the operation are similar to those used in an attack against an enemy strongpoint.

Secure a Foothold

Once the objective is isolated, a foothold should be secured as soon as possible in order to maintain tempo. Dismounted forces can be employed to attack from any direction. If infantry is working with tanks, areas above, at, and below the street level (e.g., cellars, building, sewers, subways) must be cleared before tanks move through the area in order to ensure that enemy antitank teams are not able to move around the attacker and engage the tanks. Both tanks and infantry should ensure that areas are cleared for possible mines and/or IEDs. The attacking force uses the foothold area to reorganize, regain control, and emplace units to supporting positions. After seizing a foothold, the attacking force continues the attack through the objective area. Normally, the attacking force penetrates the enemy defenses on a narrow front. The assault is supported by all available supporting arms and usually maximizes use of smoke to screen the attacking forces movement.

The tank or mechanized unit commander may employ variations of the column formation to better maneuver into urban areas. For example, a tank battalion may use a column, with each of its companies in a line, wedge, or echelon. These formations tend to shorten the length of the column, reducing the time necessary to move into the urban area. The leading tank elements normally use a formation that speeds the delivery of maximum fire on the point of penetration. Air-bursting artillery and mortar fires are usually

placed over the entry point to prevent the enemy from manning crew-served or individual antitank weapons. The infantry moves as close to the objective as possible. When the infantry attacks a strongly defended area, it provides close-in protection for the tanks. Unit leaders may assign fire teams or squads to work with each tank. If radios are not available, visual signals and TA-1 phones external to the tank may help maintain direct communication between the infantry leaders and the tank commanders. The infantry maneuvers to suppress or destroy the enemy, and tanks move forward as soon as possible to support them. Suppressive tank fires can be used to cover the attacking forces exposed flanks.

Seizing the Objective

Once a foothold is seized and consolidated, supporting forces move to the built-up area to support the seizing of the objective area. To maintain tempo, the transition between the phases should be seamless. Once the foothold has been established, forward units continue the attack through the objective area. The attack can vary from a systematic block-by-block, house-to-house reduction of the urban area to a rapid advance with clearance of critical areas and buildings. Clearance and seizure techniques depend on the mission; the size of the town, construction and building arrangement; and the enemy's disposition, strength, and objective. The momentum of the assault is continued until the objective area is cleared or controlled.

When the urban area is small or lightly defended, the attacking force should drive through or into it as rapidly as possible. Marine armor should lead the column in this instance, closely followed and supported by infantry. It will rarely be possible to employ more than two tanks at the head of the column except when advancing on a wide street. Tanks continuously concentrate main gun and automatic weapons fire on windows and the rooftops of buildings (see fig. 9-3). The infantry protects the tank from close-in enemy fire. When required to protect tanks from fire from nearby buildings, an infantry squad moves along each side of the street, keeping abreast of the lead vehicles. Depending on the resistance, the infantry may challenge every doorway or ground floor window by throwing in hand grenades and spraying the interior with small-arms fire. Unit leaders will usually assign Marines in each squad to locate and engage targets on the upper floors and rooftops of the buildings. The infantry may also assist in the removal of obstacles or barriers halting the advance. Lead tank crews must continually be aware of where the infantry is in order to avoid possible fratricide or moving forward of their infantry security and being engaged by enemy antitank teams.

The assault force should establish limited objectives to ensure that the attacking forces do not become strung out along the axis of advance. Gaps give the enemy the opportunity to infiltrate along the line of advance or make isolated friendly forces vulnerable to attack.

Defensive MOUT Operations

In urban combat, the defender possesses key advantages over the attacker. The defender can shape the battlespace to his advantage by maximizing the natural restrictions and obstacles found in the urban environment. Knowledge of the terrain and time available for preparing defensive positions are advantages that may enable the defender to successfully resist a numerically superior force. Defensive operations in a built-up

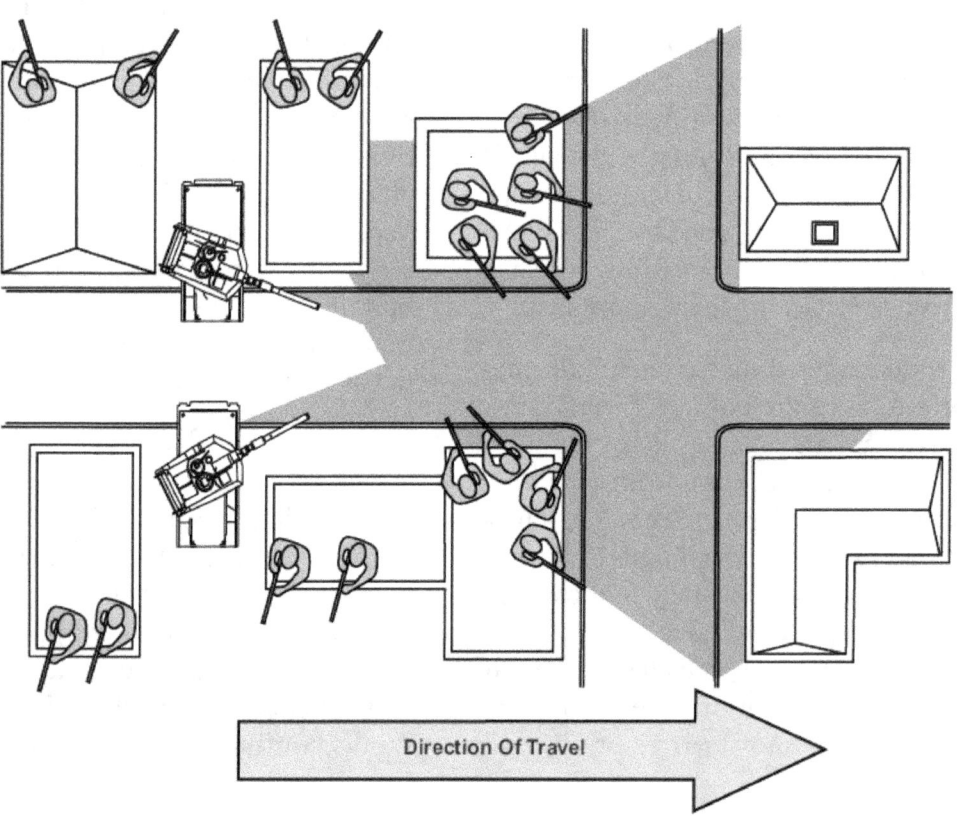

Figure 9-3. M1A1s Advancing with Infantry.

area require thorough planning and precise execution based on METT-T. This discussion examines MOUT considerations that affect the tank unit in the defense.

Defensive Techniques

In the defense, Marine tanks provide the MOUT commander with a mobile force that can respond quickly to enemy threats. They should be located on likely enemy avenues of approach in positions that allow them to take advantage of their long-range fires. Effective positioning allows the commander to employ the armored vehicles in a number of ways:

- On the edge of the city in mutually supporting positions.
- On key terrain on the flanks of towns and villages.
- In positions from which they can cover barricades and obstacles by fire.
- As part of the reserve.

The commander may also employ sections or individual armored vehicles with infantry platoons and squads; this allows the tank crew to take advantage of the close security provided by the infantry.

Fighting Positions

Fighting positions for tanks are an essential component of a complete and effective defensive plan in built-up areas. Vehicle positions must be selected and developed to afford the best possible cover, concealment, observation, and fields of fire; at the same time, they must not restrict the vehicle's ability to move when necessary.

If fields of fire are restricted to the street area, hull-down positions should be used to provide cover and to enable tanks to fire directly down the streets (see fig. 9-4). From these positions, the armored vehicles are protected while retaining their ability to rapidly move to alternate positions. Buildings

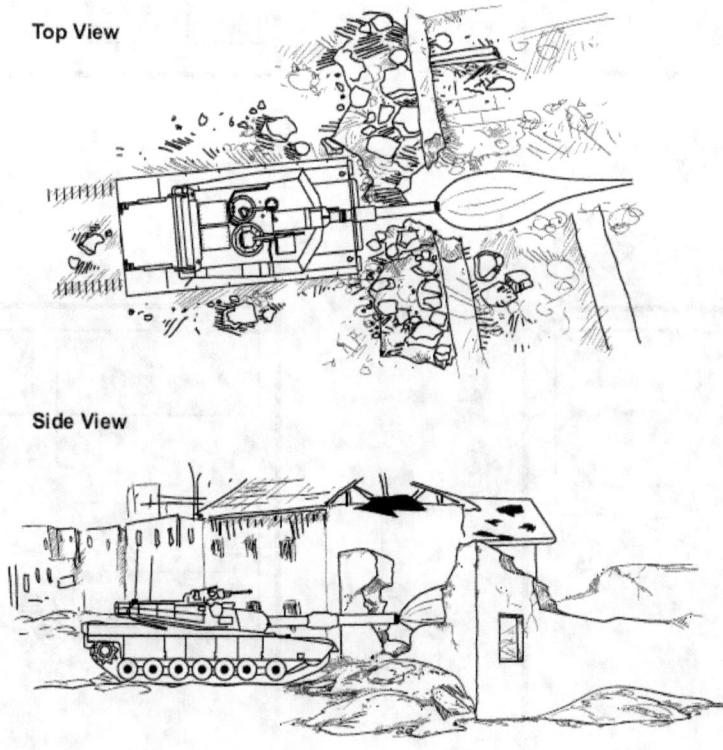

Figure 9-4. Hull-Down Position.

collapsing from enemy fires are a minimal hazard to the armored vehicles and their crews.

Before moving into position to engage the enemy, a tank can occupy a hide position for cover and concealment. Hide positions for armored vehicles may be located inside buildings or underground garages, adjacent to buildings (using the buildings to mask enemy observation), or in large ditches.

Since the crew will not be able to see the advancing enemy from the hide position, an observer from the vehicle or a nearby infantry unit must be concealed in an adjacent building to alert the crew (see fig. 9-5). When the observer acquires a target, he signals the armored vehicle to move to the firing position and firing at the proper time. After firing, the tank moves to an alternate position to avoid compromising its location.

Infantry are usually employed abreast of the tanks so that they can fire toward the expected direction of attack. Too much separation between the tanks and infantry does not allow them to easily support one another. However, in a company team battle position, the limited number of available infantrymen may require infantry fighting

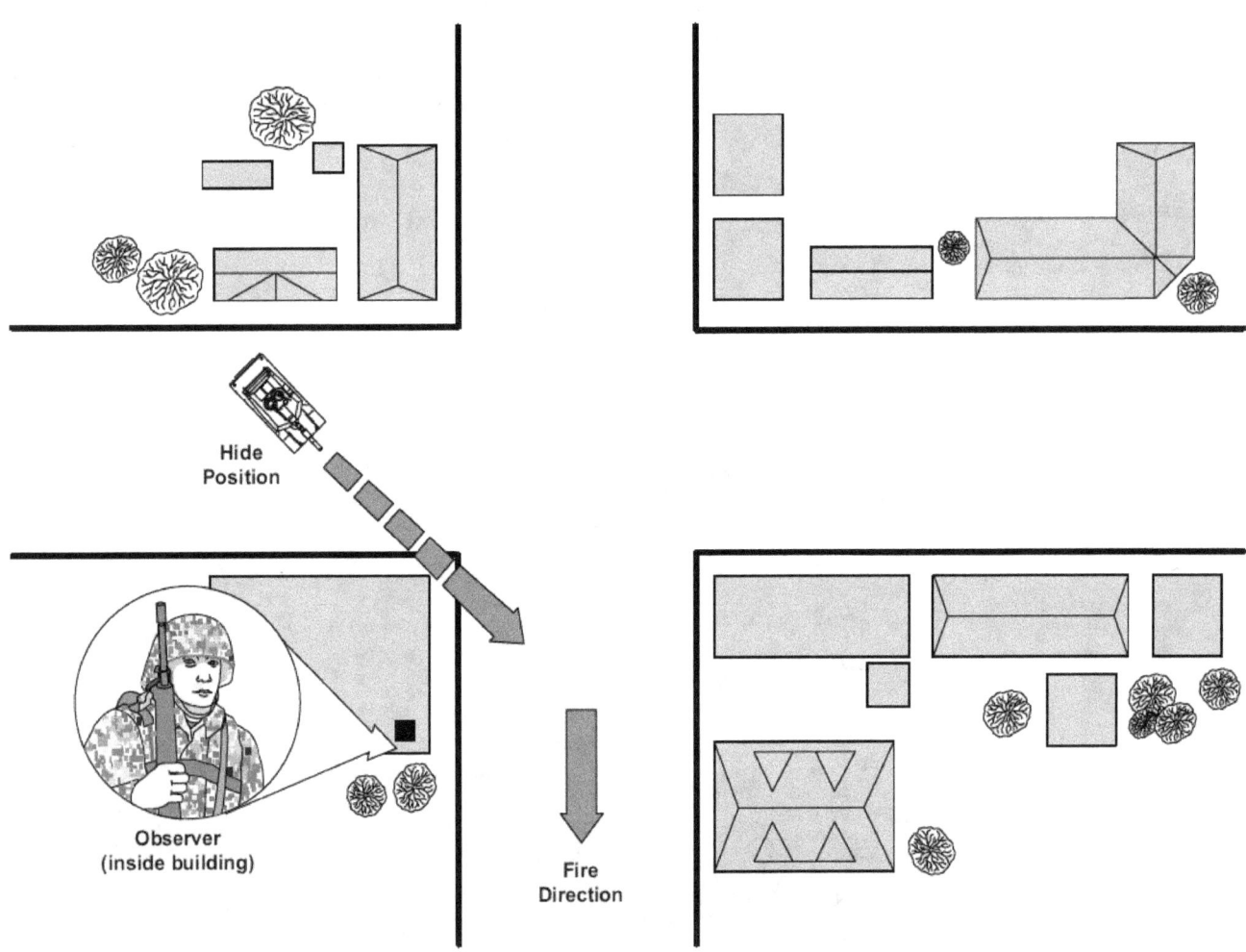

Figure 9-5. Hide Position.

positions to be interspersed with vehicle positions. In urban areas, rooms within a building may separate small units such as platoons, squads, and fire teams, or they may be positioned in different buildings. Infantry positions must be mutually supporting and allow for overlapping sectors of fire, even when they are in separate buildings or are divided by walls.

The commander's defensive scheme of maneuver in MOUT must always include the employment of a reserve force. This force should be prepared to counterattack to regain key positions, block enemy penetrations, protect the flanks of the friendly force, or provide a base of fire for disengaging elements. For combat in urban areas, the reserve force has these characteristics:

- Normally consists of infantry elements.
- Must be as mobile as possible.
- May be supported by tanks, light armored vehicles (LAVs) and/or AAVs.

CHAPTER 10
SCOUT AND TOW PLATOONS

The scout and TOW platoons found in Marine tank battalions are unique and provide the tank units with organic reconnaissance, security, and countermechanized capabilities while operating. These capabilities are an integral part of Marine Corps tank battalion operations and they perform a number of important roles in helping to shape the battlefield.

Scout Platoon

Mission

The tank battalion's scout platoon performs reconnaissance, provides limited security, and assists in controlling the battalion's movements. The platoon is not organized or equipped to conduct independent offensive, defensive, or retrograde operations. It operates as part of the tank battalion and should be assigned missions that capitalize on its reconnaissance capabilities. The scout platoon is one of the battalion commander's primary sources of organic combat intelligence both before and during the battle. Although the platoon has an antitank capability, it cannot perform its scouting roles when employed as an antitank force.

Organization

The scout platoon is organized into a headquarters section and two other sections. The headquarters section consists of the platoon commander and platoon sergeant and their vehicles. Each section contains a section leader and two other vehicles. See figure 10-1.

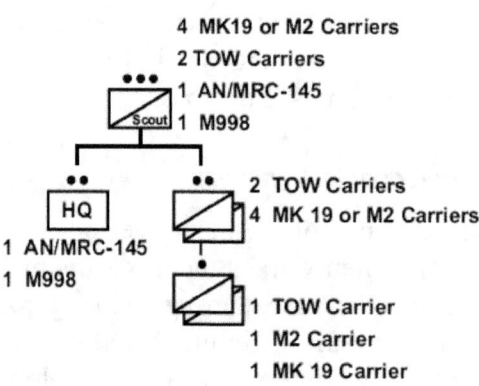

Figure 10-1. Scout Platoon Organization.

Employment

There are six fundamentals required for the successful employment of the tank battalion scout platoon:

- Use maximum reconnaissance force forward.
- Orient on the reconnaissance objective.
- Report all information rapidly and accurately.
- Retain freedom of maneuver.
- Gain and maintain enemy contact.
- Develop the situation rapidly.

Use Maximum Reconnaissance Force Forward

Do not keep scouts in reserve. This does not mean scouts must be on line and oriented forward; rather, all available scouts must be employed executing reconnaissance tasks.

Orient on the Reconnaissance Objective

The platoon's scheme of maneuver is focused toward a specific objective or set of objectives based on the OPORD and the battalion commander's intent.

Report all Information Rapidly and Accurately

Commanders base their decisions and plans on the battlefield information that scouts provide during reconnaissance. Since information loses value over time, scouts must report all information exactly as it is seen and as fast as possible. They must never assume, distort, or exaggerate information—inaccurate information is dangerous.

Retain Freedom to Maneuver

Scouts must be able to maneuver on the battlefield. If the enemy fixes them, scouts must free themselves; otherwise, they can no longer accomplish their mission. Scouts must continually maintain an awareness of tactical developments. They must employ the proper tactical movement and react appropriately to unexpected situations. If contact is made, the platoon commander develops the situation at the lowest possible level while retaining the initiative, the ability to continue the mission, and the ability to maneuver his other elements.

Gain and Maintain Enemy Contact

Scouts seek visual contact with the enemy on favorable terms. They employ sound tactical movement, target acquisition methods, and appropriate actions in order to see the enemy first, thereby retaining the initiative and control of the situation. Once scouts find the enemy, they use all available means to maintain contact until directed to do otherwise.

Develop the Situation

Whether scouts encounter an obstacle or the enemy, they must quickly assess the situation. If scouts encounter the enemy, they—

- Determine the enemy's size, composition, and activity.
- Find the enemy's flanks.
- Find any barriers or obstacles surrounding the enemy position and determine if any other enemy forces can support the position.

If the scouts encounter an obstacle, they find and mark a bypass or, if appropriate, execute or assist in a breach. This must be accomplished with minimum guidance from higher headquarters.

Capabilities and Limitations

In addition to its primary missions, the scout platoon can conduct other missions such as:

- Conduct liaison between units.
- Perform quartering party duties.
- Provide traffic control.
- Conduct chemical detection and radiological survey and monitoring operations as part of a NBC defense.
- Conduct limited pioneer and demolition work.
- Participate in area security.

The following identifies some of the scout platoon's limitations:

- The scout platoon depends on its parent unit for combat support and CSS augmentation.
- The high mobility multipurpose wheeled vehicle (HMMWV) scout platoon can reconnoiter only two routes simultaneously (reconnoitering for trafficability only).
- The scout platoon reconnoiters a zone 3 to 5 kilometers wide. METT-T conditions may increase or decrease the size of the zone.
- During screening operations, all scout platoons are limited in their ability to destroy or repel enemy reconnaissance units.
- The HMMWV scout platoon can man up to six observation posts for short durations or up to three observation posts for long durations.
- When properly organized, scouts can conduct effective reconnaissance and security patrols. The HMMWV scout platoon has a very limited dismounted capability. It must be properly task-organized to conduct dismounted operations.
- The distance the scouts can operate away from the main body is restricted to the range of communications and the range of supporting indirect fire.

- The scout platoon has limited obstacle creation ability and carries a basic load of demolitions.
- The scout platoon has a very limited obstacle breaching capability (limited to hasty point obstacles).

TOW Platoon

Mission

The primary mission of the antitank TOW platoon is to provide countermechanized support that utilizes the TOW to engage and destroy enemy armored vehicles, particularly tanks. When not performing its primary mission, the antitank TOW platoon may assume a secondary mission of engaging other point targets or providing limited security to the commander in the form of a screen or observation posts.

Organization

The TOW platoon has three squads and a headquarters section. See figure 10-2.

Employment

The TOW platoon may be employed as an organic unit for a specific mission such as setting

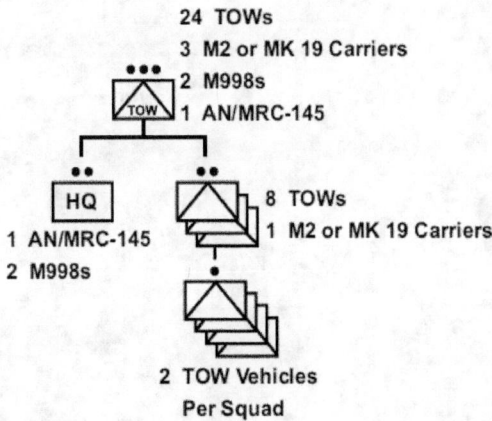

Figure 10-2. TOW Platoon Organization.

a screen or a blocking position; but it will typically be broken down into sections that are then attached in direct or general support to individual tank or infantry companies. The TOW's long standoff range allows it to cover likely avenues of approach for armored vehicles, which allows tanks to conduct offensive missions.

Capabilities and Limitations

Some advantages of the TOW weapon systems are as follows:

- Can be manpacked to obtain an advantageous firing position not accessible while mounted, but only for short distances due to the heavy weight of the system.
- Engagement of the maximum effective range does not significantly decrease its accuracy.
- Has a fire down munition that can penetrate a vehicle's armor at its thinnest point (on the top).
- Contains a thermal sight that provides enhanced capability at night and during limited visibility.
- Does not lose power in direct proportion to the engagement range.

The TOW's limitations are as follows:

- Employed in squads with two launchers at a minimum so that the crews can provide mutual support.
- Vulnerable to both direct and indirect fire; therefore, cover and concealment are extremely important.
- Large amount of backblast are produced, which must be taken into consideration when planning firing positions. Clearing the backblast area of loose debris or watering the area down can help reduce the signature.
- Reduced range when firing over water obstacles.
- Cannot fire on the move and the gunner must keep his sights on the target throughout the time of flight (14 to16 seconds to reach maximum range).

APPENDIX A
ARMOR VEHICLE CHARACTERISTICS

1. M1A1 Tank

The M1A1 combat (main battle) tank uses high speed, maneuverability, and a variety of weapons to attack and destroy enemy tanks, equipment, and forces. See figure A-1 on pages A-2 and A-3. The M1A1 combat tank consists of the hull and turret assemblies. The turret can rotate a full 360 degrees.

The tank is equipped with a laser rangefinder. The laser rangefinder can range on targets 200 to 7,990 meters from the tank with an accuracy of plus/minus 10 meters. It is also equipped with a thermal imaging system. The thermal imaging system provides the M1A1's fire control system with a night vision capability by presenting a thermal scene in the gunner's primary sight eyepiece. The thermal imaging system picture can be viewed at 3- or 10-times magnification.

Crew: 4 (commander, gunner, loader, and driver)

Armament:
    Main gun, M256, 120mm
    Ammunition, 120mm combustible cartridge

Machine Guns:
    Coaxial machine gun, M240, 7.62mm
    Loader's machine gun, M240, 7.62mm
        Maximum effective range: 900 meters (tracer burnout)
        Maximum range: 3,725 meters
    Commander's machine gun: M2 heavy-barrel, caliber .50
        Maximum effective range: 1,200 to 1,600 meters (tracer burnout)
        Maximum range: 6,700 m
    M16 A2, 5.56mm rifle
    Grenade launcher, M250
Ammunition Quantity:
    120mm (main gun), 40 rounds
    M240, 7.62mm (coaxial machine gun), 10,000 rounds
    M240, 7.62mm (loader's machine gun), 1,400 rounds
    .50 cal (commander's machine gun), 900 rounds
    UKL8 series (smoke grenades for grenade launcher), 24 grenades
    5.56mm rifle, M-16, 210 rounds

Engine: Turbine engine

Transmission:
    Model X1100-3B
    Range: four speeds forward, two reverse, with pivot and neutral selections

Performance and Specifications:
    Forward speed, maximum (paved level surface): 42 mph
    Reverse speed, maximum (paved level surface): 25 mph
    Range (dry level secondary roads without refueling): 273 to 298 mi
    Forward climb of a vertical obstacle: 49 in

Maximum width of forward crossable ditch: 108 in
Fording depth:
    Without kit: 48 in
    With kit: turret roof

Weight:
    Combat loaded: 67.6 tons
    Military load classification (MLC): 68 tons

Dimensions:
    Length (overall, main gun rearward): 356 in
    Length (gun forward): 387 in
    Width: 144 in
    Height (ground to turret roof): 96 in
    Height (maximum overall): 114 in
    Ground clearance (center portion of the hull): 19 in
    Ground clearance (other portion of hull structure): 16.5 in
    Ground pressure: 15.00 psi

Fuels and Oils:
    Fuel tanks (total in tank): 504.4 gal
    Transmission, initial fill: 40 to 45 gal
    Transmission, refill approximate: 30 to 35 gal
    Engine lubrication oil tank (refill, approximate): 17 qt
    Recommended fuel types: DF-1
        DF-2
        JP-8
        DF-A
        JP-4 may be used in an emergency

For more information concerning the M1A1 tank refer to technical manual (TM) 08953A-10, *Tank M1A1 (120mm Gun)*.

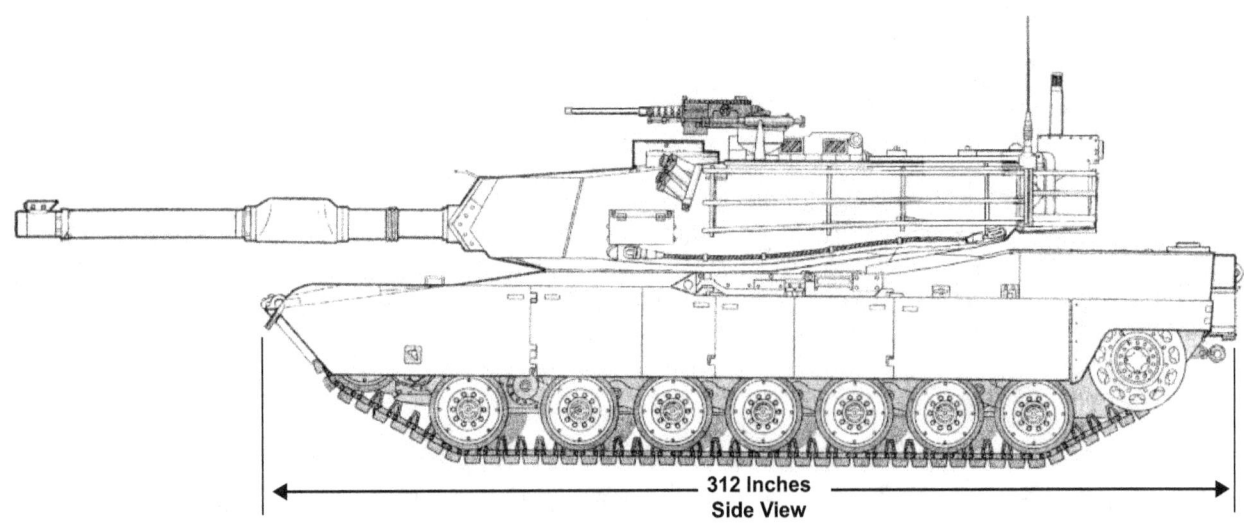

Figure A-1. M1A1 Tank.

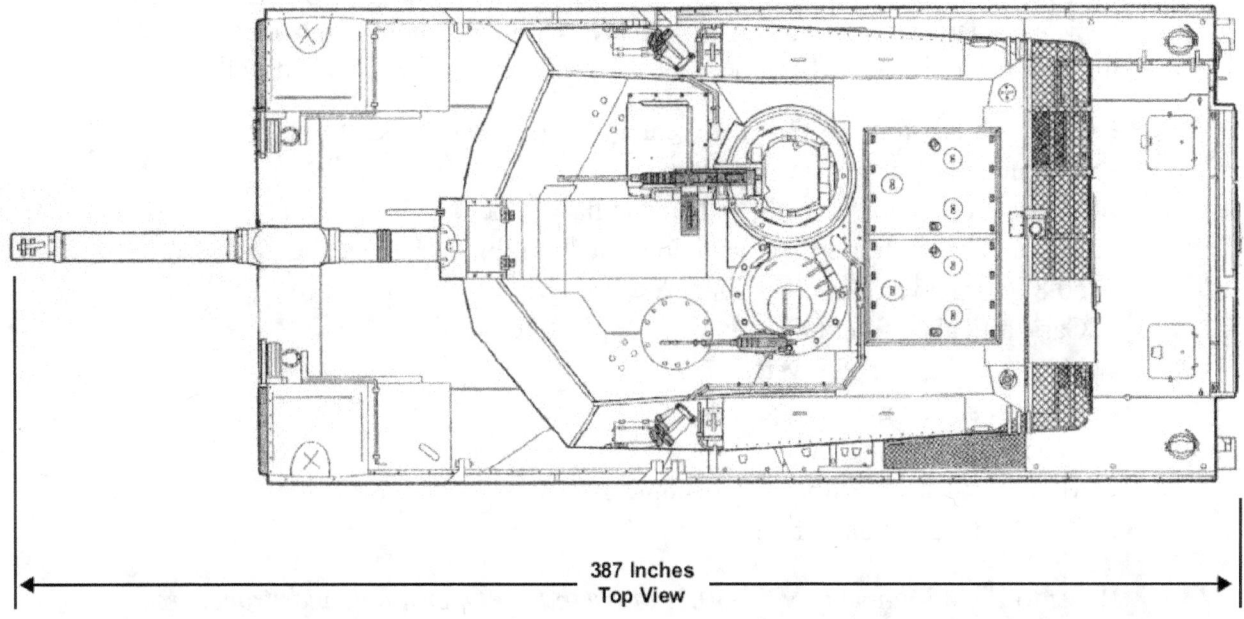

387 Inches
Top View

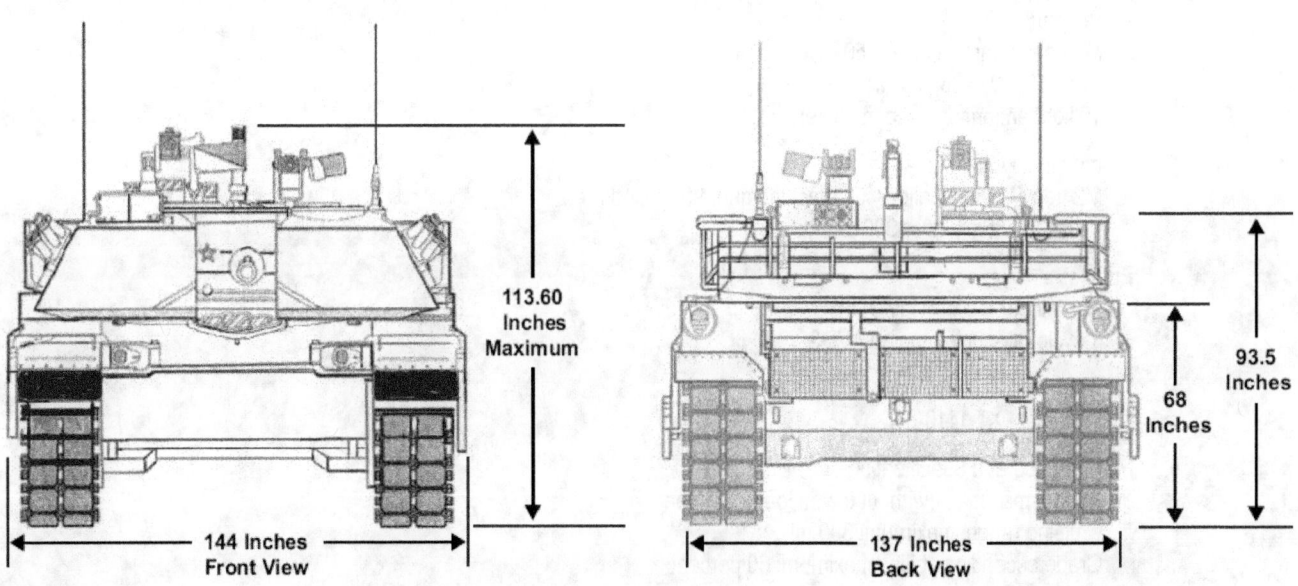

113.60
Inches
Maximum

144 Inches
Front View

93.5
Inches

68
Inches

137 Inches
Back View

Figure A-1. M1A1 Tank (Continued).

2. M88A2 Recovery Vehicle, Fully Tracked: Heavy

The M88A2 heavy recovery vehicle is an armored, full-tracked, low silhouette vehicle (see fig. A-2). It is used for hoisting, winching, and towing operations for all vehicles up to 70 tons (63.49 metric tons). It is equipped to assist in repairing disabled vehicles under field conditions. The vehicle has a crew of three: commander, operator, and mechanic/rigger. Specific vehicle capabilities and features are as follows:

- Combination transmission, differential, steering, and braking unit.
- Hydraulic power-assisted braking.
- Main winch, a hoist winch, and an auxiliary winch.
- Hull and cab armor protect vehicle from 30 millimeter direct fire.
- 10.8 horsepower, diesel auxiliary power unit.
- Gas-particulate filter unit.
- M239 smoke grenade system.
- Exhaust smoke generating system.
- Deep water fording kit.
- M2 heavy-barrel, caliber. 50 machine gun.
- Two M16A2, 5.56mm rifle.

Refer to Field Manual (FM) 4-30.3, *Maintenance Operations and Procedures*, for recovery methods using the vehicle's equipment.

Crew: 3 (commander, operator, and mechanic)

Armament:
    M2 heavy-barrel, caliber .50 machine gun
    Two M16A2, 5.56mm rifle
    10 light antiarmor weapon rockets

Ammunitions Quantity:
    M2 heavy-barrel, caliber .50 machine gun, 900 rounds
    M16A2, 5.56mm rifle, 300 rounds

Engine:
    12-cylinder diesel engine
    4-cycle, air-cooled model AVDS-1790-8CR

Transmission:
    Twin disc, XT-1410-5A

Performance and Specifications:
    Speed, maximum (without towed load): 25 mph
    Cruising range, maximum: 300 mi
    Grade ascending ability, maximum: 60 percent
    Grade descending ability, maximum: 60 percent
    Side slope grade, maximum: 30 percent
    Maximum vertical wall: 42 in
    Maximum trench crossing width: 8.5 ft
    Minimum turning radius: pivots in one vehicle length

Draw bar pull: 107,000 lb
Boom lift height:
    At 8-ft reach: 22.5 ft
    At 4-ft reach: 25.0 ft
Hoist winch capacity, (four-part line): 70,000 lb
Boom capacity:
    Spade up, 4 part line, with lockout blocks installed: 50,000 lb
    Spade down: 70,000 lb
Main winch capacity, single line, continuous pull: 140,000 lb
Auxiliary winch capacity, single line: 6,000 lb
Fording depth:
    Without fording kit: 56 in
    With fording kit: 90 in

Weight, Combat Loaded: 139,000 lb

Dimensions:
    Length: 28.33 ft
    Width: 12 ft
    Height: 9.75 ft
    Ground pressure: 13.7 psi

Fuels and Oils:
    Fuel tanks: 413 gal
    Main engine crankcase (refill): 18.5 gal
    Transmission (refill): 17 gal
    Main winch: 9.5 gal
    Hoist winch: 9 pt
    Auxiliary winch: 6 pt
    Hydraulic system: 80 gal
    Electromagnetic clutch: 5.2 qts

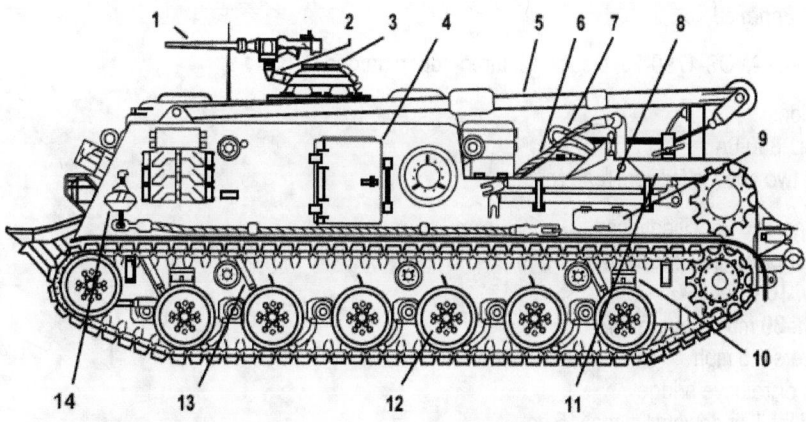

1. M2 heavy-barrel, caliber .50, machine gun
2. Machine gun mount
3. Commander's cupola
4. Personnel door, left side
5. Boom
6. Tarpaulin and 100 ft rope
7. Snatch block, 90-ton
8. Tow bar
9. Left side stowage compartment door
10. Bumper sprint (4)
11. Crow bar (2)
12. Roadwheel (12)
13. Shock absorber (6)
14. Snatch block, 10-ton

Figure A-2. M88A2 Recovery Vehicle.

3. Armored Vehicle-Launched Bridge

The M60A1 AVLB is primarily employed to cross short gaps (e.g., narrow streams), antitank ditches, craters, canals, or partially-blown bridges. It provides heavy armor protection for personnel and can provide a limited smoke screen from either the smoke grenade launcher or engine smoke generator (if equipped). The AVLB can operate in an NBC environment and on rough ground. See figure A-3 on page A-8.

The M60A1 AVLB is divided into two sections: hull and launching mechanism. The hull contains the following:

- Crew compartment with all controls for operating the launching mechanism.
- Engine compartment with engine and transmission that supplies power for operating hull and launching mechanism.
- Operator and commander cupolas to enter crew compartment.
- Cupola vision blocks and periscopes for visual operation when hatches are closed.
- Bridge seat on which bridge rests during transporting.

The launcher mechanism contains the following:

- Hydraulic system (pump, fluid, cylinders, hoses, and other parts for moving the bridge, outrigger, and tongue during launch and retrieval).
- Outrigger (steadies vehicle during bridge launch and retrieval).
- Tongue (connects vehicle to bridge).

Crew: 2 (commander, operator)

Armament: unarmed

Engine: Model AVOS-1790-20, type V-12, turbo-supercharged

Transmission:
    Type CD-850-6A
    Range: two speeds forward, one reverse

Performance and Specifications:
    Land performance speeds (maximum):
        Low: 10 mph
        High: 30 mph (governed)
        Reverse: 5 mph
    Launch or retrieve bridge
            Uphill or downhill slope: 15 pct
            Side slope: 8 pct
    Fording depth: up to 4 ft without special equipment

Weight:
    Vehicle (without bridge): 92,200 lb (46.1 tons)
    Vehicle (with bridge): 121,700 lb (61 tons)

Dimensions (travel position):
    Length:
        Without bridge: 28.3 ft

With bridge: 37.0 ft
Height:
    Without bridge: 10.0 ft
    With bridge 12.8 ft
Width:
    Without bridge: 12.0 ft
    With bridge: 13.2 ft
Ground clearance: 14 in
Ground pressure, vehicle:
    Without bridge: 9.0 psi
    With bridge: 12.2 psi
Brakes: hydraulic, mechanical foot pedal
Steering:
        Type: hydraulic mechanical
        Turning capability: 360-degree pivot

Fuels and Oils:
    Fuel: diesel oil
    Fuel consumption: 1.13 gpm (gal per mile)
    Fuel tanks (total): 375 gal
    Hydraulic system:
        Without bridge: 115 gal
        With bridge: 135 gal

Bridge:
    Length:
        Extended: 63 ft
        Folded: 32 ft
    Bridge span:
        60 ft with prepared abutments
        17 ft with unprepared abutments
    Height: unfolded, 3.1 ft
    Weight: 14.65 tons
    Weight capacity: one MLC 60 vehicle (waived for M1 series tank during combat operations)
    Launching time: 2 to 5 minutes using only the two-man AVLB crew

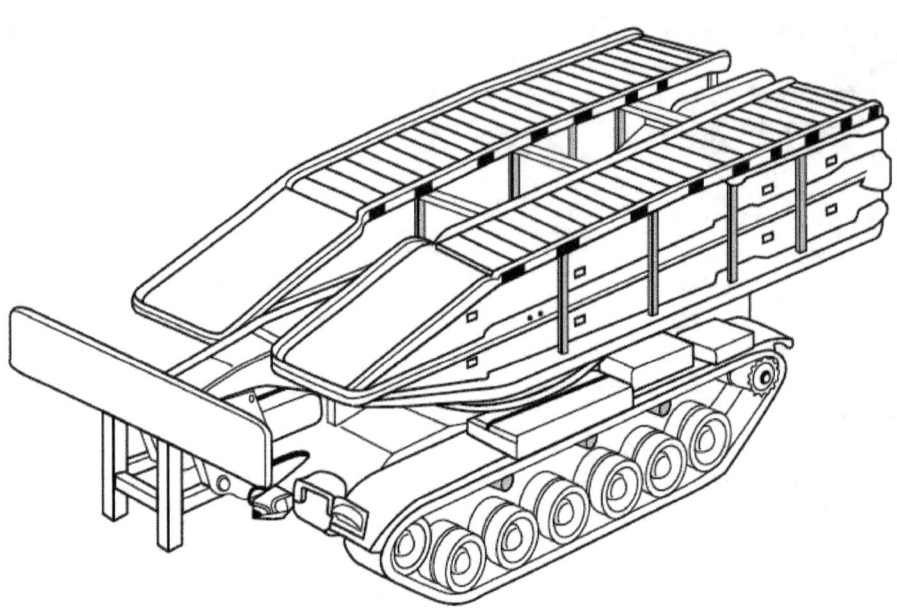

Figure A-3. AVLB.

Appendix B
Operations in Extreme Environments

Tank employment in changing operational conditions and environments presents special problems, challenges, and situations. Planners must consider the tank's capabilities and limitations, the principles of tank employment, and the environmental conditions. Each operation may require modification in tactics and augmentation in equipment in order to support the environmental conditions. For detailed discussions on operating tanks in varying environmental conditions refer to the M1A1's technical manuals.

Jungle Operations

MCWP 3-35.5, *Jungle Operations*, addresses jungle operations in depth. Jungle combat involves operations with such impediments as swamps, undulating terrain, extreme heat, heavy rains, and areas largely overgrown with thick tropical foliage. Marine tank crews need to be acclimated to live and fight in the jungle because tank maintenance and operations are exhausting in jungle operations. The basics of successful jungle operations are decentralized control, flexibility, security, and intelligence.

Cover and concealment are excellent in this type of terrain and increase the possibility of achieving surprise. As a result, both the attacker and the defender usually commit large portions of available forces to security missions. However, the restrictive nature of a jungle environment impedes typical tank operations.

In the offense, security elements prevent surprise and protect the MAGTF. In jungles, successful security force operations depend on proper implementation of security elements. Units find their direction of movement hard to maintain without navigation aids such as global positioning system receivers. The thick foliage and rugged terrain of most jungles limit fields of fire ground movement speed and the range of combat net radios and automated command information systems. Restrictions on observation and fields of fire may reduce the capabilities of tanks to acquire targets and deliver accurate direct fires. Additionally, the difficulties associated with jungle operations increase in proportion to the size of the force involved. These limitations drive the conduct of operations to the company, platoon, and individual tank crew level.

Despite their limitations, tank employment can still be effective in jungle operations. Although tanks must move slower in the jungle due to difficult trafficability, they are one of the few vehicles capable of traversing through thick foliage and undergrowth where wheeled vehicles could never operate. In addition, tanks can provide effective reconnaissance by fire and suppressive fires for supported infantry. The tank's ability to produce a large volume of fire from its machine guns and main gun antipersonnel rounds can be devastating to the enemy as long as the tank is protected by a good infantry security element.

The critical aspect of a defensive operation in a jungle environment is the security of the line of communications sustaining the MAGTF. To guard against surprise, the defending commander organizes his forces in depth. He secures or provides alternative routes around chokepoints and provides for the security of resupply convoys. He also ensures the all-around defense of units and installations operating in jungles and installations. The commander establishes a mobile reserve to counter unanticipated enemy actions, to block enemy penetrations of his defensive perimeter, to counterattack, or to pursue a detected enemy. Tanks are best suited as a mobile reserve in most situations.

Tank considerations during a jungle operation include the following:

- The dense foliage and weather alter the effective range of a weapon system. Engagements for tanks are usually at close ranges requiring quick target recognition by the tank crews.
- Units must allow for slower movement and restricted fire support. The jungle's limited visibility may make the observation and adjustment of indirect fires difficult.
- Heat, thick vegetation, and rugged terrain will tire Marines rapidly. Supported infantry may want to ride on the back of the tanks if enemy contact is not expected.
- Lack of roads hinder resupply and evacuation in the absence of helicopter support.

Desert Operations

Desert terrain varies considerably from place to place. Certain environmental characteristics (e.g., extreme temperature ranges, lack of water, absence of vegetation, dust /sandstorms) are common to all deserts, and their adverse effect must be considered during planning. Highly mobile forces play a dominant role in operations in desert regions. Tanks provide the freedom of maneuver in the vastness of these regions that favor a fluid type of warfare characterized by dispersed formations on extended frontages with considerable depth. Properly employed and maintained, the tank can be the most decisive supporting arm available to the MAGTF commander during desert operations.

Desert topography may consist of loose sand and sand dunes that greatly impede the movement of vehicles or it may have a hard surface that facilitates large mechanized formations. Successful desert operations require adaptation to the environment and to the limitations of its terrain and climate. Units must modify and adapt their equipment and tactics to a dusty and

rugged landscape. See MCWP 3-35.6, *Desert Operations,* for detailed information.

Desert offensive operations tend to favor wide envelopments and fast and wide flanking movements by armored formations because of the freedom of maneuver. Because of the limited concealment offered by the bare terrain, units must attain surprise by use of deception, appropriate security measures, and rapid movement and commanders must exploit periods of limited visibility.

Defensive operations in desert regions emphasize mobility and flexibility. Commanders should make provisions for long-range direct fire weapons, construction of extensive obstacle systems to canalize or slow the enemy, a high degree of mobility, and secure communications. The organization of the defense should emphasize measures against both air and armored attack.

The following additional considerations are necessary when planning tactical operations:

- Long-range direct fire capability makes the tank an ideal weapon in desert terrain. The long-range fields of fire common to desert areas tend to allow all weapons systems to engage at their maximum range. However, these same extended engagement ranges hinder positive target identification.
- Dust is an observational, control, and maintenance hazard to a maneuvering force.
- Land navigation may be difficult in the absence of navigation aids and current maps due to changing terrain features and minimal key landmarks.

Mountain Operations

Rugged, compartmented terrain with steep slopes and few natural or manmade lines of communications generally characterize military-significant mountains. The compartmented terrain causes a corresponding compartmentalization of military operations. Successful mountain operations require special equipment, training, acclimating personnel to altitude conditions, self-discipline, and modifications of standard tactics and procedures. MCWP 3-35.2, *Mountain Operations*, provides additional information.

The focal point of mountain operations is to control the heights. Key terrain features normally include those heights that dominate lines of communications, mountain passes, roads, bridges, and railroads. Fighting from higher ground gives the possessor distinct tactical advantages. Tanks are best used in this environment to control key terrain. Restricted mechanized routes in the mountains do not lend themselves to maneuver warfare of mechanized units. Tightly channelized routes should be anticipated by mechanized units and recognized as danger areas that require good infantry security until the units are clear of the area. Inherent in mountain operations are the difficulties that the terrain offers to movement. Operations in mountainous regions take longer than normal to plan and execute. Key mountain operational characteristics include the following:

- Communications and sustainment are increasing difficult to execute in rugged terrain. In general, operations in mountainous terrain retard and restrict maneuver and make communications and resupply of tanks difficult.
- Defenses may have to locate on the military crest to fire into an engagement area. Mountainous terrain can be either a dangerous obstacle to operations or a valuable aid, according to how well it is understood and to what extent the tank commander takes advantage of its peculiar characteristics.
- Night and periods of limited visibility are the best movement times due to the extended range of observation from enemy positions. Movement times are slower due to terrain and altitude effects. Any differences in elevation over the march route also have an impact on unit movement times.
- The terrain reduces the effectiveness of firepower. The M1A1 tank has only a limited ability to depress its main gun. The ability to elevate its main gun should also be considered when employing the tanks.
- Centralized planning and decentralized small unit execution characterize operations because the terrain limits the commander's capability to directly control operations. Command and control of tanks is therefore decentralized with small units often operating independently.

Operations in Deep Snow and Extreme Cold

Deep snow and extreme cold weather present employment problems in operations involving tanks, which increases engineer support requirements and may require the extensive use of lines of communications. Combat operations in deep snow or extreme cold weather present two opponents: the enemy (who must be defeated) and nature (who must be made an ally). Planning and training can reduce the effect of the climatic conditions, but commanders and their staffs must understand the impact that these severe conditions impose on tank operations. Many of the missions assigned to tanks are the same as those assigned in normal operations and the tactics and techniques employed in offensive and defensive operations are also similar. See MCWP 3-35.1, *Cold Weather Operations,* for detailed information on cold weather operations.

Tactical employment is modified to offset the characteristics of the area and its weather. When planning tactical operations for execution during rigorous winter weather, commanders must carefully consider the probable effects of weather upon operations, the health of Marines, supply, evacuation, and also the maintenance of lines of communication. Ice, deep snow, and extreme cold weather modify the normal use of terrain features. Planning considerations during operations in snow or extreme cold weather are as follows:

- Operations take longer than normal to plan and execute.

- Tanks are mostly metal which can become difficult to work around in extreme cold. Gloves have to be worn at all times by the crews and this in turn slows the ability to operate/maintain the tank.
- Cold weather impacts a weapons' reliability; therefore the M1A1's machine guns require the same cold weather considerations as ground mounted machine guns.
- Tanks can generally negotiate deep snow better than wheeled vehicles. However, packed snow and ice will often cause tracked vehicles to slide and possibly lose control. This is particularly true on hills or roads with steep inclines. Tank drivers must be trained how to properly steer, brake, and accelerate under these conditions. Infantry on roads should stay clear of heavy tracked vehicles in these conditions while they are moving.
- Concealment and camouflage is more difficult due to the white snow. Depending of the mission and environment, tanks may need to be painted white for better camouflaging.
- Increased requirements for CSS.

APPENDIX C
NBC OPERATIONS

Planning

Planning is critical to the success of any operation; therefore, all staff sections must make NBC an integral part of their operational planning process. One major factor that must be considered is the NBC effect on individuals and operations once the unit enters a mission-oriented protective posture (MOPP): the operational tempo will slow, Marines will require more rest and hydration to recover from physical exertion, and the possibility of heat casualties will increase. Proper planning must address threat analysis, vulnerability analysis, MOPP analysis, and the decontamination site.

Threat Analysis

A threat analysis focuses on the enemy's capabilities and willingness to use NBC weapons and includes the following:

- History of NBC weapons use.
- Availability of NBC weapons and support equipment.
- Production and stockpile of NBC weapons.
- Delivery systems.
- Doctrine and training.

Vulnerability Analysis

A vulnerability analysis focuses on United States forces and our weaknesses and includes the following:

- Effects of weapons on personnel and equipment.
- Type and size of weapons within range.
- Detection/warning systems available.
- Unit protection available.
- Personnel training levels.
- Unit location in relationship to the battlefield.

- Weather, climate, terrain.
- Medical supplies and services available.

For more information on NBC vulnerability assessments, see MCRP 3-37.1A, *Nuclear, Biological, and Chemical (NBC) Vulnerability Analysis.*

MOPP Analysis

A MOPP analysis focuses on the effects of placing the unit into MOPP and includes the following:

- The mission.
- Likelihood of a follow-on mission.
- Commander's acceptable degree of risk/percent of casualties.
- Likelihood and types of agents to be employed.
- Additional protection afforded/required.
- Expected warning time.
- Mental demands of work.
- Physical demands of work.
- Duration of mission.

See MCWP 3-37.2, *Multiservice Tactics, Techniques, and Procedures for Nuclear, Biological, and Chemical (NBC) Protection,* for detailed information on performing a MOPP analysis.

Decontamination Site

The battalion scout platoon can be tasked to locate a decontamination site. The following are characteristics of a good decontamination site:

- Easy to find.
- Located on or along a hard stance road network.

- Access to a potable water source.
- Removed from the main battle area.
- Good cover and concealment.
- Access to a clean route out for decontaminated units.

For further information on decontamination see MCWP 3-37.1, *Multiservice Tactics, Techniques, and Procedures for Nuclear, Biological, and Chemical Defense Operations*, and MCWP 3-37.3, *NBC Decontamination*.

React to a Nuclear Attack

When a tank crew observes a brilliant flash of light and a mushroom-shaped cloud, crewmen must act quickly to minimize the effects of a nuclear detonation. The nuclear attack drill involves four steps:

Step 1. Take immediate protective actions, including the following:

- If mounted, button up and close the breech and ballistic doors. If time permits, position the vehicle behind a protective terrain feature and turn off the master power until the effects of the blast have passed.
- Dismounted crewmen drop to the ground and cover exposed skin until blast effects have passed.

Step 2. Implement SOPs and accomplish related actions in the following areas:

- Re-establish communications.
- Prepare and forward an NBC-1 report.
- Implement continuous monitoring.
- Submit a situation report to the commander.

Step 3. Re-organize the platoon:

- Evacuate casualties and fatalities.
- Redistribute personnel as needed.
- Conduct essential maintenance.

Step 4. Continue the mission that is given at the end of the monitoring phase.

React to a Chemical/Biological Attack

During an operation, the tank crew initiates the following steps whenever an automatic masking event occurs, the chemical agent alarm sounds, M8 and M9 detection paper indicates the presence of chemical agents, or a Marine suspects the presence of chemical or biological agents:

Step 1. Crewmen recognize and then react to the hazard:

- Put on protective mask (and hood) within 15 seconds.
- Alert remainder of the platoon and company.
- Within 8 minutes, assume MOPP 4, then button up/activate the tank over pressurization system.
- Perform immediate decontamination of any possibly contaminated, exposed skin using the M291 individual decontamination kit.

Step 2. Implement SOPs in these areas:

- Administer self-aid and buddy-aid to platoon members with symptoms of chemical/biological agent poisoning.
- Conduct operator's spray-down and decontamination of equipment as necessary.
- Submit NBC-1 and follow-up reports as needed.

Step 3. Continue the mission.

Step 4. Monitor for chemical/biological agents and, as the situation warrants, initiate actions to reduce MOPP levels and discontinue agent monitoring.

Note: If the M256 detection kit records a negative reading inside an over pressurized M1A1 tank, the crew can initiate unmasking procedures.

Decontamination

Successful avoidance and protection may prevent the need for decontamination; however, due to the large area of coverage of NBC weapons, the unit must be prepared to conduct decontamination operations. The primary purpose of decontamination is to restore the unit's combat power and reduce the number of casualties caused by NBC weapons. When planning and conducting decontamination operations, the following decontamination principles will be the controlling factor:

- Decontaminate as soon as possible. This limits the effects of NBC agents by reducing exposure time and concentration on personnel and equipment.
- Decontaminate as far forward as possible. This limits the spread of contamination, thus reducing the possibility of contaminating units and personnel that have not been affected previously.
- Decontaminate only what is necessary. Decontaminate only those items, or areas of equipment, that are considered essential for mission accomplishment. Do not attempt to decontaminate personal items or equipment that is not normally used.

- Decontaminate by priority. Set priorities for decontamination according to the unit's mission and the threat.

Decontamination operations are conducted on four levels based upon decontamination principals and METT-T. The four levels of decontamination are immediate/operational and thorough/clearance (see table C-1). Immediate and operational decontamination are time-critical and designed to remove life-threatening contamination on personnel and equipment as quickly as possible in order to save lives and regenerate combat power. Thorough and clearance decontamination are time and resource intensive, designed to remove virtually all of the contamination and are usually conducted as part of a reconstitution effort. Decontamination is not a sequential process that requires the conduct (in order) of immediate, operational, and thorough decontamination. For example, conducting operational decontamination to remove gross contamination in order to continue the mission, combined with the natural weathering process may alleviate the requirement to conduct thorough decontamination. The detailed procedures and techniques for the following decontamination operations are contained in MCWP 3-37.3.

Table C-1. Decontamination Levels/Techniques.

Levels	Techniques[1]	Purpose	Best Start Time	Performed By
Immediate	Skin decontamination	Saves lives and stops agent from penetrating	Before 1 min	Individual
	Personal wipedown		Within 15 min	Individual or crew
	Operator spraydown		Within 15 min	Individual or crew
Operational	MOPP gear exchange[2]	Provides temporary MOPP4 and limits agent spread	Within 6 hr	Unit
	Vehicle washdown[3]			Battalion crew or decontamination platoon
Thorough	Detailed equipment decontamination and detailed aircraft decontamination	Provides probability long-term MOPP reduction with less risk	When mission allows reconstitution	Decontamination platoon
	Detailed troop decontamination			Unit
Clearance	Unrestricted use of resources	METT-T depending on type of equipment contaminated	When mission permits	Supporting strategic resources
1. The techniques become less effective the longer they are delayed.				
2. Performance degradation and risk assessment must be considered when exceeding 6 hours.				
3. Vehicle washdown is most effective if started within 1 hour.				

Immediate

Immediately upon becoming contaminated, individuals must carry out immediate decontamination. This may include decontamination of some personnel, clothing, and equipment. Immediate decontamination consists of skin decontamination and personal and operator wipe down. It is designed to prevent casualties and permit the use of individual equipment and key systems.

Operational

Operational decontamination is carried out by an individual and/or a unit and is restricted to specific parts of operationally essential equipment, materiel, and/or work areas in order to minimize contact and transfer hazards and to sustain operations. Operational decontamination reduces the spread and the level of contamination. In some cases, when combined with weathering, MOPP levels may be reduced without further decontamination, depending on the surface or material being decontaminated. Operational decontamination consists of MOPP gear exchange and vehicle washdown.

A MOPP gear exchange should be performed within 6 hours of being contaminated due to the inherent performance degradation that occurs the longer a unit is in MOPP 4. MOPP gear exchange allows a unit to remove the gross contamination from personnel and equipment and provides temporary relief from MOPP 4 and a return to an increased operational tempo in pursuit of mission accomplishment.

Vehicle washdown should be performed within 6 hours of being contaminated if the mission does not permit a thorough decontamination. This process removes gross contamination and limits its spread.

Thorough

Thorough decontamination operations reduce and sometimes eliminate contamination. They restore combat power by reducing or removing nearly all of the contamination on personnel, equipment, and materiel; permitting the partial or total removal of individual protection equipment; and allowing units to maintain operations with minimum degradation. Detailed troop and detailed equipment decontamination are conducted as part of a reconstitution effort during breaks in combat operations. These operations require immense logistical support and are manpower intensive. Thorough decontamination removes the unit from performing its primary mission but allows it to return with restored effectiveness.

Clearance

Clearance decontamination of equipment and/or personnel accomplishes the decontamination process to a standard that allows *unrestricted* transportation, maintenance, employment, and disposal. Clearance decontamination consists of a combination of all of the techniques and procedures known to reduce contamination to levels below that which can be detected using current detection suites

Unmasking Procedures

Once the unit goes into MOPP 4, unmasking will not be conducted unless approved by the battalion commander. Once approval to unmask is received, the following procedures will be executed:

Selective Unmasking with a Chemical Detector:
- At least two separate detection samples are taken from different locations within unit position. All results must be negative.
- The senior man present selects two/three Marines of different size/weight/ethnic backgrounds and checks their physical condition.
- The Marines disarm and are placed in a shaded area. Ensure a corpsman is present if available.
- The Marines remove their mask for 5 minutes. Keep a close and constant watch for chemical agent symptoms while Marines are unmasked.

- After 5 minutes, have the Marines don and clear their masks. Monitor them for 10 minutes.
- After 10 minutes, if no symptoms appear, begin selective unmasking within the unit.
- If at any time symptoms appear, stop the unmasking process and treat as appropriate.

Selective Unmasking Without a Chemical Detector:

- The senior man present selects two/three Marines of different size/weight/ethnic backgrounds.
- The Marines disarm and are placed in a shaded area. Ensure a corpsman is present if available.
- The Marines break the seal of their masks for 15 seconds, keeping their eyes open and holding their breath.
- After 15 seconds, have the Marines don and clear their masks. Monitor these Marines for 10 minutes. If no symptoms appear, continue. If symptoms appear, stop selective unmasking.
- Have the Marines break the seal of their masks once again and take two to three normal breaths.
- After taking two to three breaths, they will don and clear their masks. Monitor these Marines for 10 minutes. If no symptoms appear, continue. If symptoms appear, stop selective unmasking.
- Have the Marines remove their masks for 5 minutes.
- After 5 minutes they will don and clear their masks. Monitor these Marines for 10 minutes.
- After 10 minutes, if no symptoms appear, continue. If symptoms appear, stop selective unmasking.
- Selective unmasking within the unit can begin.

APPENDIX D
AMMUNITION

Main Gun Ammunition

Classification

Conventional main gun ammunition is classified according to type and use:

- Armor-defeating ammunition:
  - Kinetic energy ammunition (sabot) is the primary round used against tank and tank-like targets.
  - Chemical energy ammunition (HEAT and MPAT) is the primary round used against lightly armored targets, field fortifications, and personnel. It is also used against tank and tank-like targets. MPAT is also used against helicopters.

- Beehive and high explosive plastic ammunition are used against troops or field fortifications.
- White phosphorus ammunition is used for marking, screening, and incendiary purposes.
- Target practice ammunition is used for gunnery training. These rounds have ballistic characteristics similar to service ammunition.
- Dummy ammunition is used for practicing gunnery-related tasks and has no propellant or explosive charge.

Identification

Main gun ammunition can be identified by shape and the projectile's color code and markings. A standard NATO color code is used for main gun ammunition (see fig. D-1 for example of 120mm

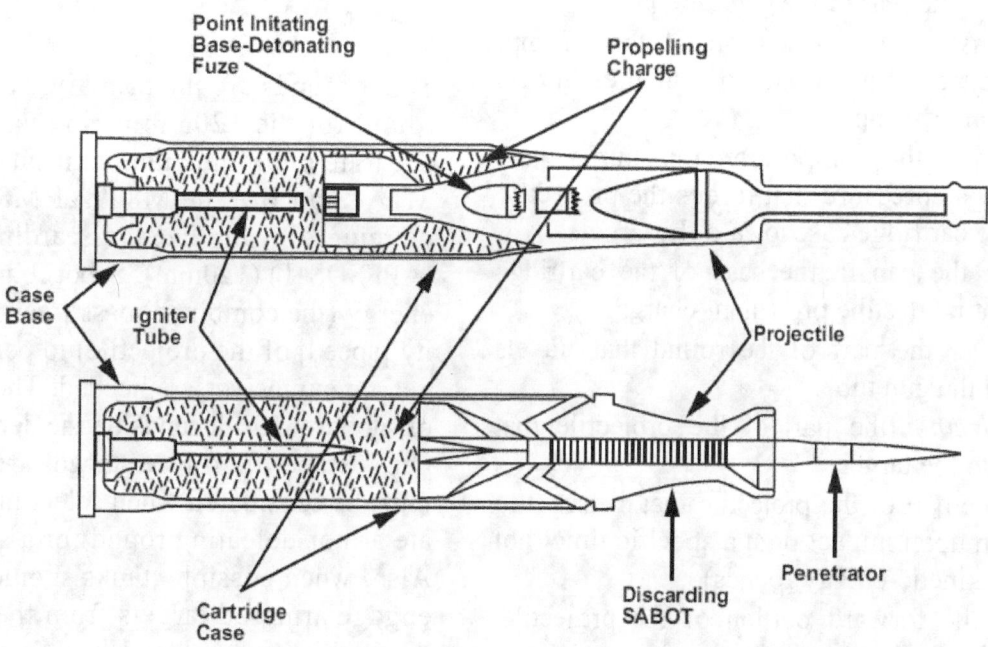

Figure D-1. Example of 120mm Main Gun Ammunition Markings.

main gun ammunition markings). The projectile and the cartridge case have markings that provide additional information about the ammunition and the firing weapon. Marking information is as follows:

- Tracer.
- Caliber and type of weapon.
- Type of filler.
- Type of projectile (round).
- Model of projectile (round).
- Ammunition lot number.

Components of a Main Gun Round

A complete round of main gun ammunition is usually composed of the following basic parts:

Note: Not every type of round will have all the parts listed, and every possible part is listed.

- *Cartridge case:* the brass, steel, or combustible casing that contains the propellant and primer. When the round is fired, the cartridge case expands to seal the rear of the gun tube. (On the 120mm round, the obturator on the base stub seals the rear of the gun tube.)
- *Case base:* the rear portion of the 120mm ammunition that houses the primer and is ejected after firing.
- *Propellant:* the composition that burns, producing gas pressure that forces the projectile from the cartridge case toward the target.
- *Primer:* the cap in the base of the cartridge case that ignites the propellant charge.
- *Projectile:* the part of the round that travels through the gun tube.
- *Subprojectile:* the part of the projectile that travels to the target.
- *Fuze:* the part of the projectile that causes it to function upon impact or at a specific time (not used in kinetic-energy rounds).
- *Ogive:* the forward portion of the projectile. The ogive is designed to reduce air resistance and provide aerodynamic stability.

- *Bourrelet:* a raised metal or plastic ring around the outer forward surface of the projectile. Its purpose is to center the forward part of the projectile as it travels through the bore.
- *Body:* the part of the projectile between the bourrelet and the rotating bands. It contains either a subprojectile or an explosive chemical filler and fuze; it can also contain all three.
- *Rotating band:* the hard plastic or metallic ring(s) around the base of the projectile. It seals the propellant gas behind the base of the projectile and imparts spin (for rifled guns) to a spin-stabilized round or absorbs spin on fin-stabilized rounds.
- *Obturator:* the rubber seal that helps the rotating band seal the propellant gas behind the projectile.
- *Tracer:* an element inserted in the base of projectiles that, when ignited, burns and allows both the projectile's trajectory and the impact to be observed during flight.

Armor-Defeating Ammunition

Sabot Rounds

Sabot rounds are the primary, armor-defeating round for the 120mm main gun and the most accurate of all tank ammunition. Currently the M1A1 can fire the M829A1/M829A2 armor-piercing, fin-stabilized, discarding sabot-tracer (APFSDS-T) (120mm). Sabot rounds use kinetic energy (the combined mass [weight] and velocity [speed] of the projectile) to penetrate the target, no explosives are needed. The effectiveness of sabot rounds depends on the density of the target surface; therefore, target armor thickness must be considered when selecting the appropriate armor-defeating round for a specific target. Also, when possible, tanks should maneuver to engage armored targets from the flank or rear where the armor is less dense. See figure D-2 and D-3 on page D-4.

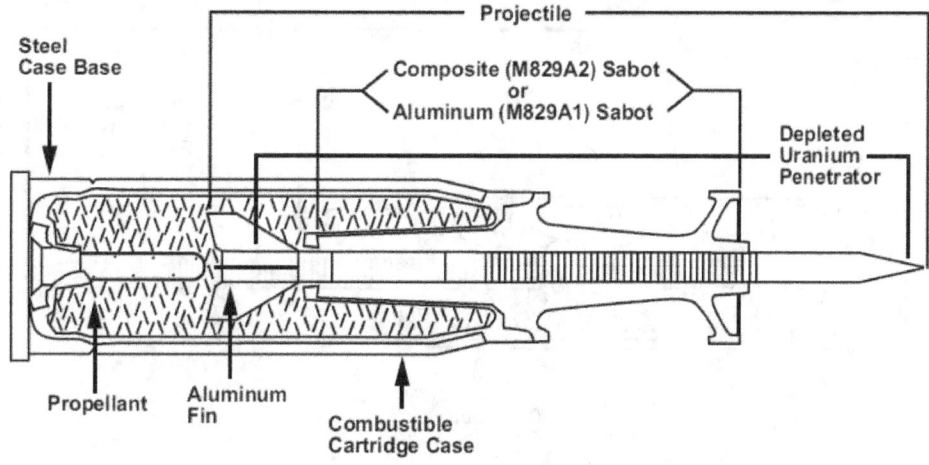

Muzzle Velocity:	1,575 m/s (M829A1)
	1,680 m/s (M829A2)
Penetrator Composition:	Depleted uranium
Announced in Fire Command as:	Sabot (pronounced SAY-BO)
Fuze:	None
Employment:	Primary armor-defeating round against tanks or tank-like targets
Projectile Color Code:	Black with white letters
Weight:	46.2 lb (M829A1)
	44.9 lb (M829A2)
Length:	38.7 in
Storage Temperature Limits:	-50°F to 145°F
Safe-to-Fire Temperature Limits:	-25°F to 125°F
Performance Temperature Limits:	-25°F to 125°F

Figure D-2. M829A1/M829A2 APFSDS-T (120mm).

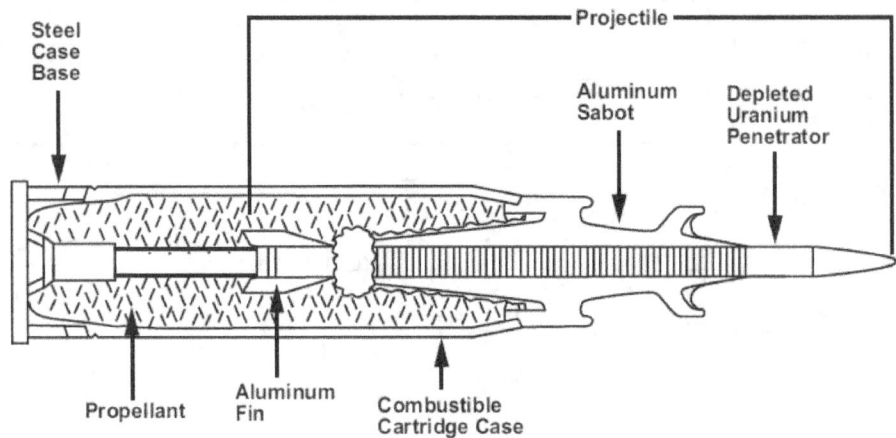

Muzzle Velocity:	1.670 m/s
Penetrator Composition:	Depleted uranium
Announced in Fire Command as:	Sabot (pronounced SAY-BO)
Fuze:	None
Employment:	Primary armor-defeating round against tanks or tank-like targets
Projectile Color Code:	Black with white letters
Weight:	41.2 lb
Length:	38.8 in
Storage Temperature Limits:	-50°F to 145°F
Safe-to-Fire Temperature Limits:	-50°F to 145°F
Performance Temperature Limits:	-25°F to 125°F

Figure D-3. M829 APFSDS-T (120mm).

HEAT Rounds

HEAT rounds are the secondary armor-defeating ammunition. The HEAT round is used primarily against lightly armored targets, field fortifications, and personnel. Each round consists of a steel body that contains a high explosive shaped charge, formed by a copper shaped charge liner; the M830 (high explosive antitank, multipurpose-tracer [HEAT-MP-T] includes a wave shaper (see fig. D-4). The projectile embodies a steel spike with a shoulder and nose switching mechanism for full frontal area functioning. Upon impact, one of the fuze sensors is activated. The fuze then detonates the high-explosive shaped charge, which collapses the cone assembly creating a high-velocity focused shock wave and a jet of metal particles that penetrate the target. Fragmentation of the projectile body sidewall provides an antipersonnel capability.

Due to its slower muzzle velocity, HEAT rounds are not as accurate as sabot rounds at ranges beyond 2,000 meters. However, this round depends on chemical energy and not striking velocity; therefore, its ability to penetrate armor is as effective at 4,000 meters as it is at 200 meters.

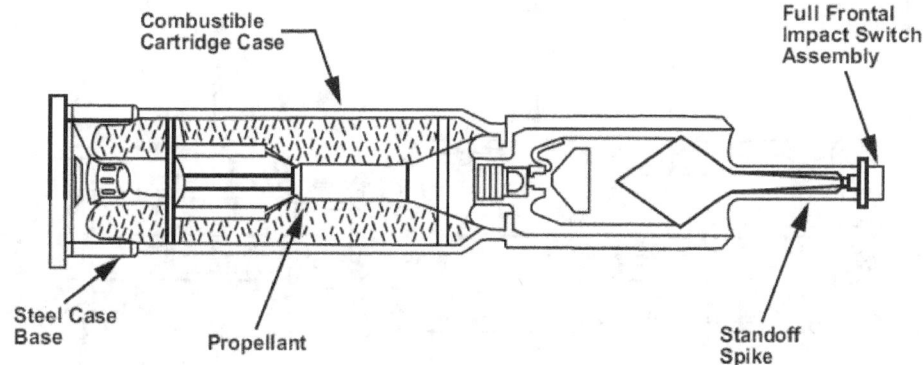

Muzzle Velocity:	1,410 m/s
Announced in Fire Command as:	HEAT
Fuze:	Point-initiating, base-detonating and full frontal area impact switch.
Employment:	Light-armored targets and field fortifications. Secondary round for tanks or tank-like targets.
Projectile Color Code:	Black with yellow letters
Weight:	53.4 lb
Length:	38.6 in
Storage Temperature Limits:	-50°F to 145°F
Safe-to-Fire Temperature Limits:	-50°F to 145°F
Performance Temperature Limits:	-25°F to 125°F

Figure D-4. M830 HEAT-MP-T (120mm).

MPAT Ammunition

The 120mm M830A1 MPAT round contains a high explosive warhead equipped with a proximity fuze that allows it to be fired in either an air or ground mode (see fig. D-5 on page D-6). Its primary targets are light armored ground targets, which are engaged with the fuze set to ground mode. MPAT ammunition may also be used against bunkers, buildings, the side and rear of enemy tanks, and enemy personnel. When the fuze is set in the air mode, the round can be used in a self-defense role against enemy helicopters. When fired in the air mode, a black puff of smoke is produced when the proximity sensor and fuze function. This permits the crew to observe when and where the round functions in relation to the target. M830A1 cartridges are shipped to units with the fuze set in the ground mode. The MPAT round is a fin-stabilized round with a three-piece discarding sabot and is used in the 120mm M256A1 smooth-bore cannon.

——————————— **WARNING** ———————————

The nose of the M830A1 contains the air/ ground sensor. This sensor can be damaged if it is struck on hard surfaces inside the turret (turret strut, breech, etc.) with moderate force. Loaders must take precaution to avoid striking the nose during the loading process.

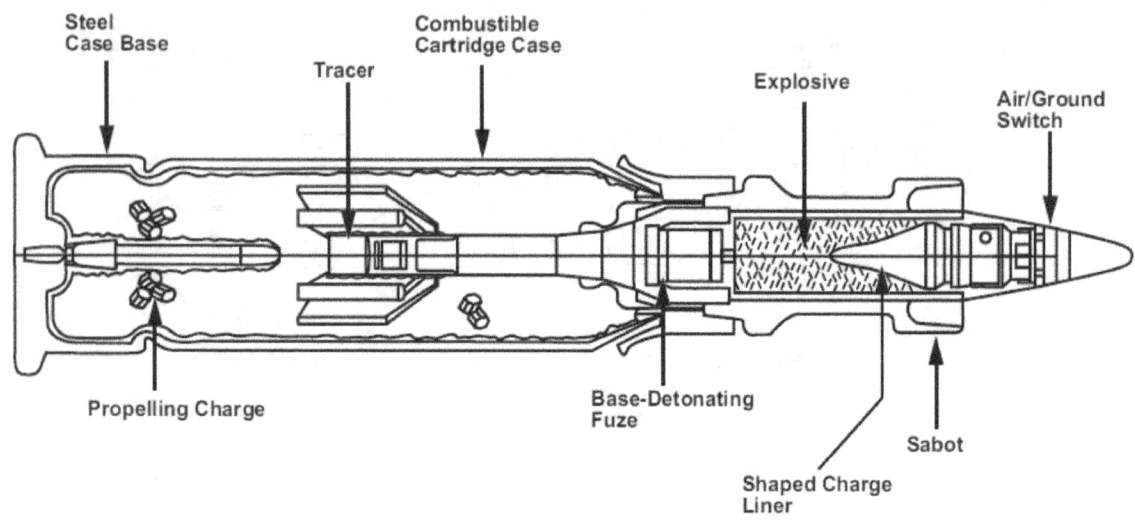

Muzzle Velocity:	1,410 m/s
Announced in Fire Command as:	MPAT (ground mode)
	MPAT AIR (air mode)
Fuze:	Point-initiating, base-detonating (ground mode)
	Proximity or point-initiating, base-detonating (air mode)
Employment MPAT GROUND:	LAVs, buildings, bunkers, ATGM platforms, and personnel.
	Secondary round for tanks or tank-like targets.
Employment MPAT AIR:	Helicopters
Projectile Color Code:	Black with yellow letters
Weight:	50.1 lb
Length:	38.7 in
Storage Temperature Limits:	-50°F to 145°F
Safe-to-Fire Temperature Limits:	-25°F to 120°F
Performance Temperature Limits:	-25°F to 120°F

Figure D-5. M830A1 HEAT-MP-T (120mm).

Ammunition Stowage Plan

The ammunition stowage plan for all tanks within a battalion-size unit is part of the unit SOP. The stowage plan should include the location of all ammunition, by type and number of rounds, authorized for the basic load. During darkness, when lights inside the turret reduce the crew's night vision or give away the tank's position, a standardized stowage plan helps the loader rapidly locate the ammunition announced in the initial fire command. The stowage plan also helps the crew keep track of the number of rounds (by type) that have been fired.

When loading the M1A1, the loader should place sabot rounds along the sides and across the top in the turret and hull compartments. HEAT rounds should be loaded in the center racks of the compartments.

Machine Gun Ammunition

Link Belts

Machine gun ammunition is belted in disintegrating metallic link belts. The .50 caliber machine gun ammunition is linked with the M9 closed link. Both the 7.62mm coax machine gun and the loader's machine gun use the M13 clip-type open link. See figure D-6.

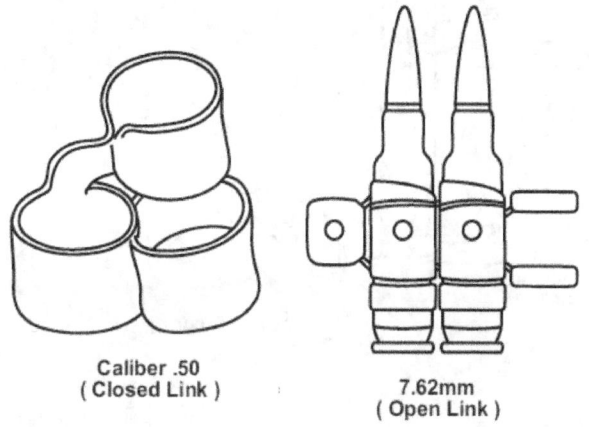

Caliber .50
(Closed Link)

7.62mm
(Open Link)

Figure D-6. Link Belts.

Color Code Identification

Machine gun ammunition is identified by type, caliber, model, and lot number. A color code on the bullet tip or band identifies the type. Markings are also located on packing containers. See figure D-7.

Smoke Grenade Ammunition

The L8A1, L8A3, and M76 infrared smoke grenades are fired from the M250 grenade launcher mounted on the M1A1 to provide screening protection for the tank and crew. The M82 smoke grenade is designed to simulate the L8A3 and M76 smoke grenade. The M250 grenade launcher

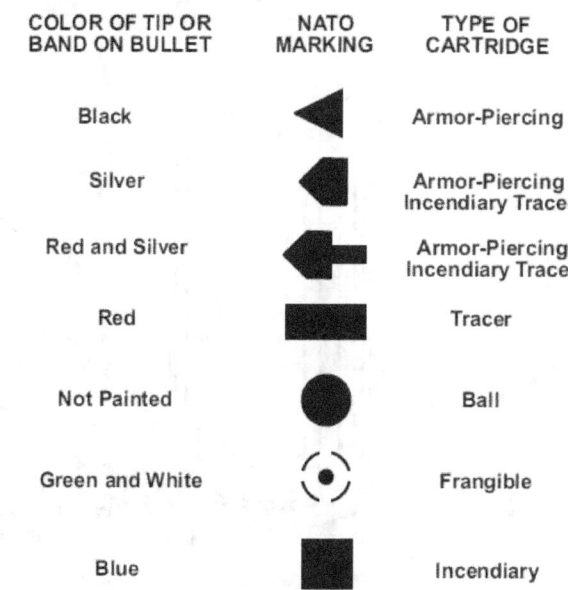

COLOR OF TIP OR BAND ON BULLET	NATO MARKING	TYPE OF CARTRIDGE
Black		Armor-Piercing
Silver		Armor-Piercing Incendiary Tracer
Red and Silver		Armor-Piercing Incendiary Tracer
Red		Tracer
Not Painted		Ball
Green and White		Frangible
Blue		Incendiary

Notes: Dummy ammunition is identified by a corrugated or perforated cartridge case. It is used to train clearing, loading, and immediate action on the machine gun.

Blank ammunition is identified by a colored plug or crimped forward end in place of the projectile for caliber .50 ammunition and an elongated case and plug for 7.62mm ammunition.

Figure D-7. Ammunition Color Code/NATO Marking Chart.

consists of two dischargers (one on either side of the turret), mounting hardware, arming and firing switches on the tank commander panel, and wiring. Six smoke grenades are loaded in each discharger.

——————— **Caution** ———————

Smoke grenades contain fire-producing chemicals and are dangerous to exposed personnel outside the vehicle.

L8A1 and L8A3 Grenades

The L8A1 and L8A3 red phosphorus screening smoke grenades are identified by the markings at the base of the casing (see fig. D-8 on page D-8).

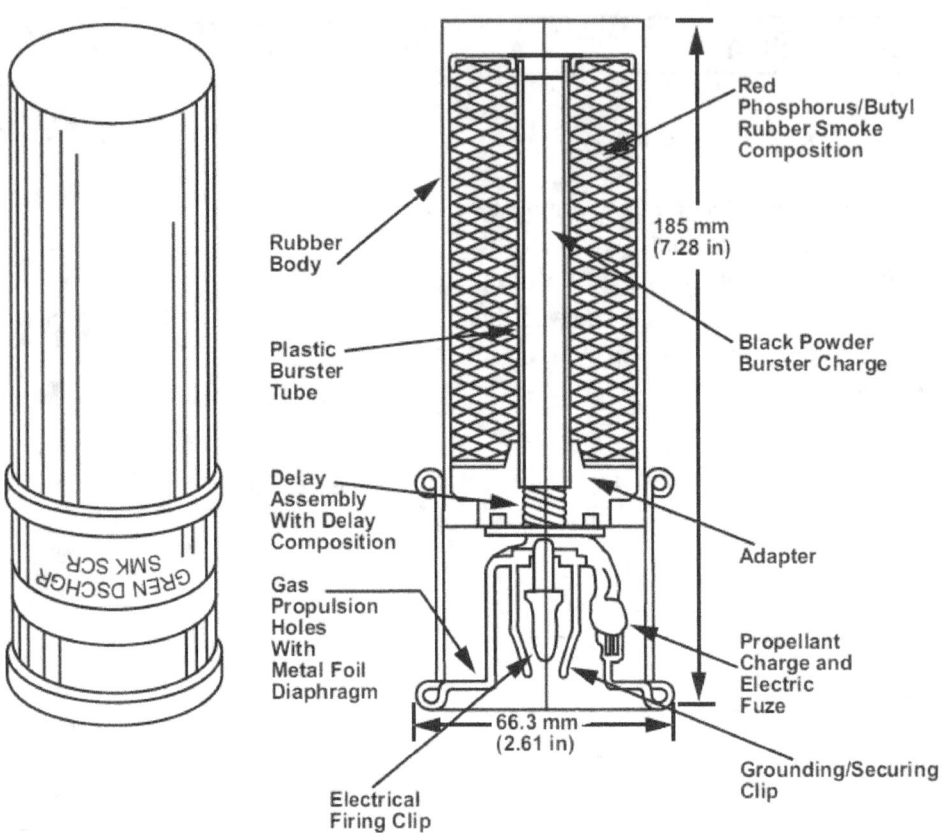

Figure D-8. L8A1 and L8A3 Smoke Grenade.

The grenade is propelled from the discharger by pressure build-up in the metal base when electrical current at the electrical firing clip ignites the squib-type electric fuze and propellant charge. The propellant charge simultaneously ignites the delay composition within the delay holder. During flight, the delay composition burns through and ignites the black powder bursting charge. The bursting charge ignites the red phosphorus and butyl rubber composition and bursts the rubber body, dispensing the burning red phosphorus and butyl rubber pellets to produce a smoke cloud.

M76 Grenade

The M76 infrared screening smoke grenade is identified by the markings at the base of the casing. The grenade is propelled from the discharger when an electrical current at the firing contact activates the electrical match. The electrical match ignites the propellant, which both launches the grenade and ignites the pyrotechnic time delay detonator. Launch acceleration causes the setback lock to displace aft, out of engagement with the safe and arm slider/bore rider. When the slider/bore rider clears the launch tube, it moves into the armed position, which aligns the transfer lead with the time delay detonator and the booster lead. When the time delay detonator ignites the transfer lead, booster lead, and central burster, the grenade bursts, creating an infrared obscuring cloud. See figure D-9.

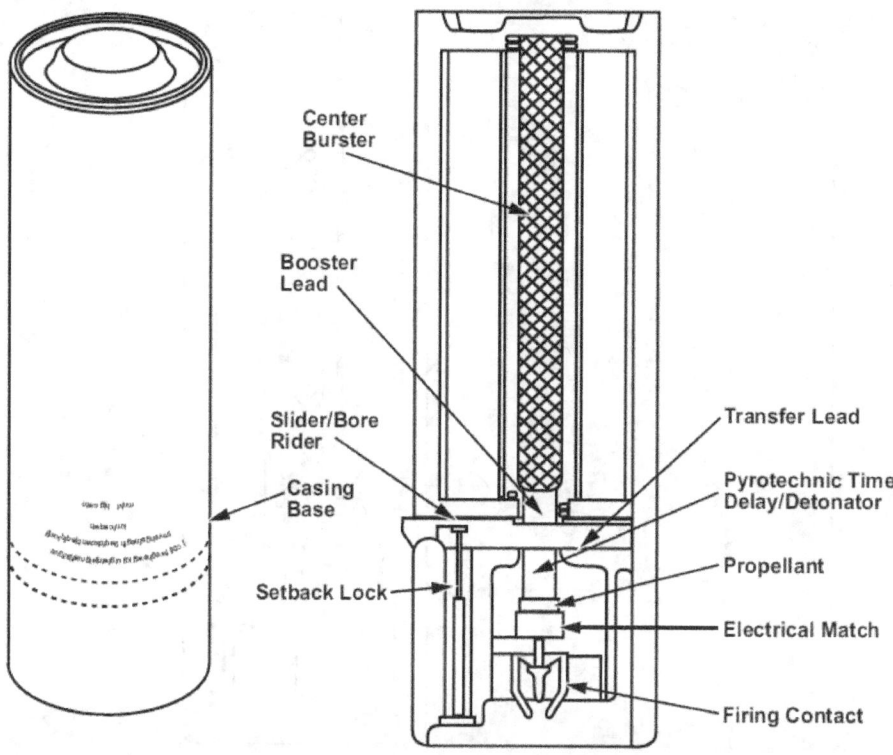

Figure D-9. M76 Smoke Grenade.

M82 Grenade

The M82 smoke grenade is identified by the markings at the base of the casing. The M82 is an electronically-initiated, propellant-launched grenade that functions to disseminate a screening cloud 30 meters forward of the firing vehicle. The environmentally acceptable smoke composition consists of 1.8 pounds of titanium dioxide. The grenade's plastic body houses the launch system, the safe and arming mechanism, the explosive booster and burster, and the smoke composition. The M82 is designed to simulate the L8A3 and M76 smoke grenade and can be used during gunnery or force-on-force training. See figure D-10 on page D-10.

Limited-Issue 120mm Ammunition

The XM908 is a highly explosive, obstacle reducing round with tracer (see fig. D-11 on page D-11). It is a full-service, tactical, 120mm round fired from the M256 cannon system. The round is similar in appearance to the M830A1 MPAT round. Major differences include:

- A steel nose cap painted yellow in place of the proximity sensor.
- Markings on the projectile.
- Markings on the case base that identify the round as the HE-OR-T XM908.

The weight of the round and center of gravity are nearly identical to the M830A1 MPAT round.

Loading and firing procedures for the XM908 are basically the same as those used for all 120mm tank rounds. The XM908 contains a high-explosive filler with a three-part fusing system. This fusing system consists of the M774 base element, flexible communications circuit, and frontal impact switch assembly. Upon impact, the steel nose penetrates the target, and a firing signal is sent to the M774 fuze. This initiates the firing sequence and full detonation occurs. The steel

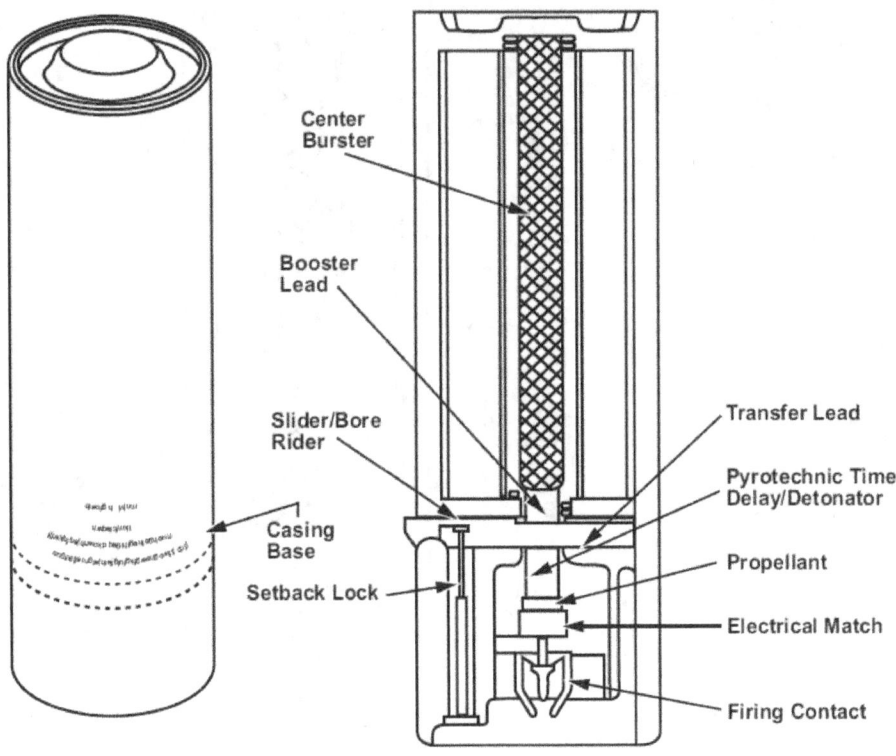

Figure D-10. M82 Smoke Grenade.

nose penetration allows the munition to explode inside the target. When firing at concrete obstacles, this penetration will reduce the obstacle more efficiently.

The XM908 round is primarily used to reduce concrete obstacles into rubble that is small enough to be cleared by either unit organic equipment or external support. Live-fire test results have shown that this round is also effective against concrete bridge pylons. Units now have the capability to destroy bridges or damage them enough to greatly hinder their carrying capacities. This action could be used to create an obstacle that would greatly restrict or impede enemy movement.

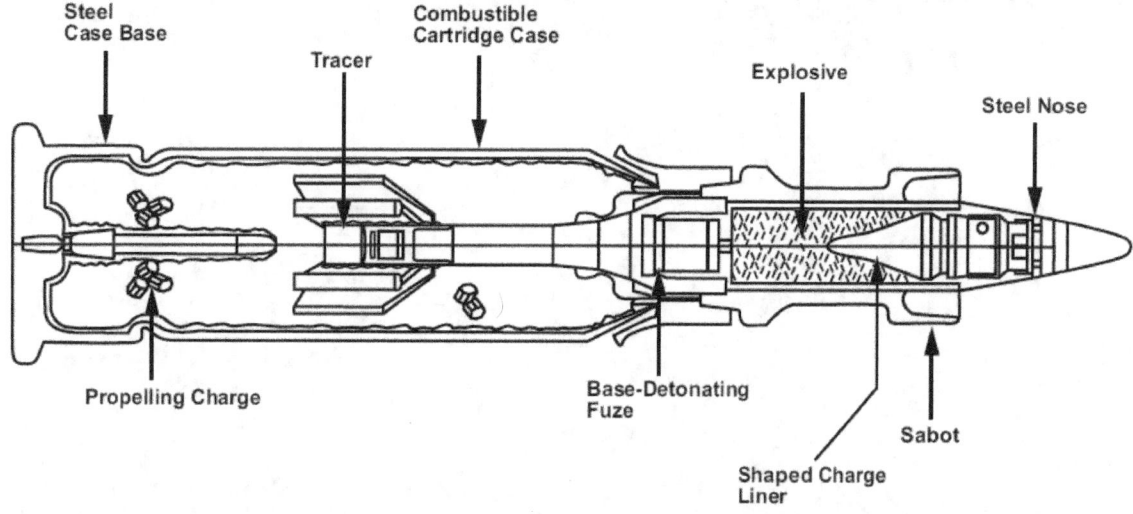

Muzzle Velocity:	1,410 m/s
Announced in Fire Command as:	OR (pronounced Oh Are)
Fuze:	Point-initiating, base-detonating
Employment:	To reduce concrete structures
Projectile Color Code:	Black with yellow letters and a yellow steel nose
Weight:	50.1 lb
Length:	38.7 in
Storage Temperature Limits:	-50°F to 145°F
Safe-to-Fire Temperature Limits:	-25°F to 120°F
Performance Temperature Limits:	-25°F to 120°F

Figure D-11. XM908 HE-OR-T (120mm).

APPENDIX E
BREACHING OPERATIONS

Obstacle breaching is conducted during offensive operations with the goal of projecting combat power to the far side of an obstacle. Key considerations for the commander include an understanding of the various types of obstacles and the capabilities and limitations of available mobility assets.

Fundamentals

Breaching fundamentals are suppress, obscure, secure, reduce, and reconstitute:

- Sufficient support elements are employed to suppress enemy elements that are overwatching the obstacle.
- The support force requests smoke to obscure breach force operations.
- The breach force creates and proofs a lane through the obstacle, allowing the assault force to secure the far side of the obstacle.
- The required actions are taken to further reduce and mark obstacles in order to allow the assault force, main attack force, and any follow-on forces to continue the attack.
- The reconstitution of personnel and assets are executed as necessary in order to conduct subsequent breaches.

These fundamentals are the same for all breaches, but they may vary in degree based on the situation. Tanks have the capability to be the support force, part of the breach force or the assault force.

Suppress

Suppression is focusing all available fire on enemy personnel, weapons, or equipment in order to prevent the enemy from prohibitively interfering with friendly forces during breaching operations. It includes the full range of lethal and nonlethal fires from direct and indirect fire weapons, aviation, and electronic warfare. Suppression helps to isolate the breaching site and fix the enemy in position thus providing protection to forces reducing and maneuvering through the obstacles. Suppression is primarily the responsibility of the support force; therefore, tanks and their ability to mass fires quickly and to engage targets at long ranges using sophisticated sights and thermal targeting are effective suppression tools. Tanks in the support force make it difficult for the enemy to engage the breach force because he must expose himself, making him vulnerable to accurate and effective tank fire. (See the breaching elements paragraph on page E-4 for a discussion of forces.)

Obscure

The most effective obstacles are those covered by fire and observation and obscured during breaching. While the primary obscuration means is smoke, electronic warfare is also a way to obscure breaching activities by providing protection from direction finding and jamming. Obstacle reduction efforts should be hidden from enemy observation as much as possible. Consideration is always given to selecting a breaching site where the terrain provides natural concealment from enemy observation. Obscuring smoke placed on the breaching area and screening smoke placed between the breaching area and the enemy conceals friendly activities, intentions, and obstacle reduction activities. Smoke should be employed across a wide front in order to deceive the enemy as to the actual breach site(s) Tanks can use their smoke dischargers to help obscure their movement but this capability is limited and designed as a defensive measure. Once the smoke rounds are discharged, they must be manually reloaded, which is time-consuming. Therefore, smoke rounds from artillery units provide a higher volume of smoke for obscuration, builds up quickly, is thicker, and lasts longer than using smoke from a vehicle.

Secure

The breaching site is secured to prevent the enemy from interfering with obstacle reduction and exploitation of the breach force. A friendly force must control the breaching site, to include enemy listening/observation posts, before it can reduce the obstacle. This is accomplished by suppressive fire and/or physical occupation. Generally, tactical obstacles are secured by fires and protective obstacles are secured by force. The support force is responsible for securing the nearside of the obstacle. The breach force creates and proofs a lane through the obstacle, allowing the assault force to secure the far side of the obstacle. The breach force must also contain sufficient assets to provide local security against forces that the support force cannot sufficiently engage due to terrain or other cover. Tanks contribute to the breach force by using plows attached to the front of the tank to either plow and/or proof a breach lane. They also provide effective armor-protected firepower to the breach force by engaging the enemy with their main guns and/or machine guns while being impervious to small-arms and indirect fires directed at the breach force. Tanks in the assault force are effective for the same reasons.

Reduce

Reduction is the creation and marking of lanes through a minefield or obstacle to allow passage of the attacking ground force. The number and width of lanes created varies with the situation and type of breaching operation. Lanes must be wide enough to allow a force to pass through the obstacle rapidly and continue the attack. The unit reducing the obstacle marks and reports obstacle and lane locations and conditions to higher headquarters. Lanes are normally handed over to follow-on forces that will further reduce or clear the obstacle when possible, but they will not reduce or clear the obstacle when under enemy fire.

Reconstitute

Upon completion of the breach, the breaching task force normally has seriously depleted, yet essential, class V and possibly personnel and breaching equipment. The commander is normally faced with two options: reconstitute forces for continued breaching operations or release the elements back to their respective commands. If the commander intends to continue breaching operations, resupply of critical materiel must be conducted and assets redistributed for future breaching operations. See appendix A for the M1A1 tank's class V requirements.

Types of Breaching Operations

The following paragraphs cover the major types of breaching operations: hasty, deliberate and covert. Amphibious breaches are covered in MCWP 3-17.3, *MAGTF Breaching Operations*. Also included is a discussion of the bypass operation, which the commander must consider as an alternative to conducting an actual breach.

Bypass

When a unit bypasses an obstacle, it physically changes direction, moving along a route that avoids the obstacle. Obstacles should be bypassed whenever possible to maintain the momentum of the operation. Commanders, however, must ensure that conducting the bypass provides a tactical advantage without exposing the unit to unnecessary danger. Previously unreported obstacles and bypassed enemy forces should be reported to higher headquarters. If possible, they should conduct a reconnaissance to evaluate tactical considerations such as—

- The limits of the obstacle.
- Physical aspects of the bypass route, including location, availability of cover and concealment, and key terrain influencing the route.
- Confirmation that the bypass route will take the unit where it needs to go while avoiding possible enemy ambush sites and engagement areas (also known as kill sacks).

Tank units should expect to be engaged by enemy antitank weapons while trying to find an obstacle bypass. The enemy obstacle may have been designed to stop, slow, or turn the tanks and direct them into his kill sacks.

Hasty Breach

A hasty breach or in-stride breach is the rapid creation of a route through a minefield, barrier, or fortification by any expedient method. A hasty breach is used against a weak defender when the enemy situation is vague or changes rapidly or against very simple obstacles. Little or no time may be available in which to plan or prepare for this type of breach, particularly during the conduct phase of an attack; therefore, well-rehearsed, pre-planned standard battle drills must be used. To maintain momentum and take advantage of the enemy situation, the hasty breach is normally conducted with the resources that are immediately available. Because tanks can carry mine plows or mine rollers, tank units have the ability to conduct hasty breaches without the assistance of engineers. When tanks are attached to other units, SOPs and rehearsals for breaching are essential to ensure quick and effective breaching when confronting obstacles.

Deliberate Breach

A deliberate or assault breach is used against a strong defense or complex obstacle system. It is similar to a deliberate attack, requiring detailed knowledge of both the defense and the obstacle systems. With this knowledge, forces conducting the deliberate breach can develop detailed plans, task-organize to accomplish the mission, and execute rehearsals. A deliberate breach is further characterized by a buildup of combat power on the near side of obstacles. The term deliberate breach does not apply to the speed or tempo with which the attack is executed. Deliberate breaching operations require significant planning, coordination, and preparation.

In a battalion deliberate breach, the tank company is most likely to be part of the support or assault force. The engineer company, task-organized with plow and roller tanks, serves as the breach force. The battalion commander may also form the breach force by task-organizing a tank or mounted infantry company with one or more engineer platoons.

Overt and Clandestine Breaching

Breaches can be conducted either overtly or clandestinely. Overt operations are conducted in the open without concealment. Clandestine operations are conducted in secret or under limited visibility. Thorough reconnaissance and detailed intelligence assists the commander in determining the best location to breach, concealed routes to the obstacle, and the type of breaching equipment and number of personnel required. The covert breach relies on stealth and dismounted maneuver, with the breach force employing quiet, manual lane reduction techniques. Coordination is of the utmost importance. All forces must know what event triggers the shift from clandestine to overt breaching, without this information they may be prematurely exposed to the enemy or to friendly fire. Because surprise is critical, the key to conducting a breach clandestinely may require delaying suppression of the enemy until the last possible moment (depending on the enemy situation). For example, suppression of the enemy may be delayed until:

- The breach force is detected by enemy forces.
- The breach force is close to the obstacle and must expose itself in order to reduce the obstacle.
- Lanes are open and the assault force attacks.
- The breach force completes lane reduction and detonates charges to clear obstacles, signaling direct and indirect suppressive fire to support the assault force.

Clandestine breaching also requires withholding the use of obscuring smoke. Weather and darkness are the best concealment for clandestine operations. Security is achieved through stealth, which outweighs the need for speed. Silently eliminating enemy outposts provides additional security, but may give away friendly activity. Obstacle reduction must be conducted as silently as possible by using manual techniques vice mechanical equipment.

Breaching Elements

Support Force

The support force's mission is to suppress the enemy's ability to interfere with the actions of the breach force. The support force usually leads movement of the breach elements. After identifying the obstacle, the support force moves to covered and concealed areas and establishes support by fire positions. The support force leader sends a spot report to the commander. This report describes the location and complexity of the obstacle, the composition of enemy forces that are overwatching the obstacle, and the location of possible bypasses. The commander decides whether to bypass or to breach the obstacle and

must keep in mind that a bypass may lead to an enemy kill zone.

Whether the decision is made to breach or bypass, the support force suppresses any enemy elements that are overwatching the obstacle to allow the breach force to breach or bypass the obstacle. All available assets, including artillery, air, electronic warfare, naval surface fire support, and direct fire weapon systems should be used to suppress and obscure the enemy. As the breach and assault forces execute their missions, the support force lifts or shifts supporting fires. Because the enemy is likely to engage the support force with artillery, the support force must be prepared to move to alternate positions while maintaining suppressive fires. The support force may have reserve breaching and assault assets (e.g., line charges, track width mine plows, AVLBs, armored combat earthmovers) that are intended for use only in the event the breach and assault forces become ineffective and to expedite reconstitution where multiple obstacles must be breached in quick succession.

The M1A1's range, armor protection, and magnified sights allow it to carry out the support force role very efficiently.

Breach Force

The mission of the breach force is to create and mark lanes that enable the main attack force to pass through an obstacle in order to continue the attack. It is normally a combined-arms force that may include engineers, infantry, tanks, AAVs, LAVs, and AVLBs. The breach force must be capable of overcoming an enemy counterattack. Assets are allocated based on the number of lanes required. Two breached lanes per each battalion-sized task force are highly recommended. The commander of the breaching force should also plan for at least 50 percent redundancy in breaching equipment due to expected losses during opposed breaching operations. The breach force is organized into an engineer reconnaissance team, security team, obstacle reduction team, and a lane marking team:

- The engineer reconnaissance team verifies intelligence about the obstacles, locates the forward edge of obstacle zones so the rest of the breach force does not inadvertently enter the obstacle, and marks the standoff distance for explosive reduction.
- If the support force cannot provide local security to the breach force, the security force will provide local security. Infantry, LAVs, tanks, and AAVs normally provide security while the engineers are reducing obstacles.
- The obstacle reduction team physically creates the lanes and proofs the lanes for mines, if required.
- The lane marking team initially marks the newly created lanes for passage of the assault force, the main attack force, and follow-on forces. The lane marking team is also ready to assume the mission of obstacle reduction if the obstacle reduction team is rendered ineffective.

Once the breach force has reduced the obstacle and the assault force has passed through the lanes, guides are employed to conduct the handover to follow-on units. At a minimum, lanes must be marked and their locations and conditions reported to higher headquarters and follow-on units.

Proofing is verifying that a breached lane is free of live mines. This can be accomplished by checking the breached lane with a secondary breaching means other than explosives, such as probing, mine detectors, mine plows, or mine rollers. Proofing is done only when the potential risk of live mines remaining in the lane exceeds the risk of loss to enemy fire while a lane is being proofed. It is important to remember, obstacle reduction is the physical creation of a lane through or over obstacles.

Tank units may be some of the first units to move through the lane to provide security for the assault force on the far side of the obstacle. In some instances, the breach force may move to a hull-down firing position that allows it to suppress enemy elements overwatching the obstacle. At other times, it may assault the enemy with suppressive fires provided by the support force.

A tank platoon can create a lane by itself if it is equipped with the assets required to breach the type of obstacle encountered. If the tank unit does not have this capability, it may be required to provide close-in protection for attached engineers with breaching assets. Three breaching methods are available to the platoon:

- Mechanical breaching, usually with mine plows.
- Explosive breaching, employing such means as the mine-clearing line charge (MICLIC), M173 line charge, or 1/4-pound blocks of TNT.
- Manual breaching, with Marines probing by hand or using such items as grappling hooks, shovels, picks, axes, and chain saws. Manual breaching is the least preferred method for the tank platoon.

In extreme cases, the commander may order the tank platoon to force through an obstacle. This technique requires the breach force to move in column formation through the obstacle location. If available, a disabled vehicle can be pushed ahead of the lead breach vehicle in an attempt to detonate mines.

The mine plow is the breaching device most commonly employed by the tank platoon. The battalion or company commander may allocate one to three plows per platoon. When properly equipped and supported, the platoon can create up to two lanes through an obstacle.

Plow tanks lead the breach force. Immediately following them are vehicles that proof the lanes;

these are usually tanks equipped with mine rollers. This process ensures that the lane is clear.

Note: If the location and/or dimensions of the obstacle are unknown, the platoon leader may choose to lead with tanks equipped with mine rollers to identify the beginning of the obstacle.

If the platoon is allocated one plow, the platoon sergeant's wingman normally serves as the breach tank. The platoon sergeant follows immediately behind to proof the lane and provide overwatch. The platoon leader's section follows the platoon sergeant.

If the platoon has two or more plows, it can create multiple lanes, usually 75 to 100 meters apart. The wingman tanks are normally equipped with the plows and the section leaders' tanks follow to proof the lanes and provide overwatch (see fig. E-1).

To create a wider lane, two plow tanks can stagger their movement along a single lane (see fig. E-2). This technique is also used in order to clear a lane that HMMWVs and other wheeled vehicles can go through without a center lane of mine-ridden spoil. Using figure E-2 as a literal example, a wide lane with no center lane would be created on the right side of the double proofed lane.

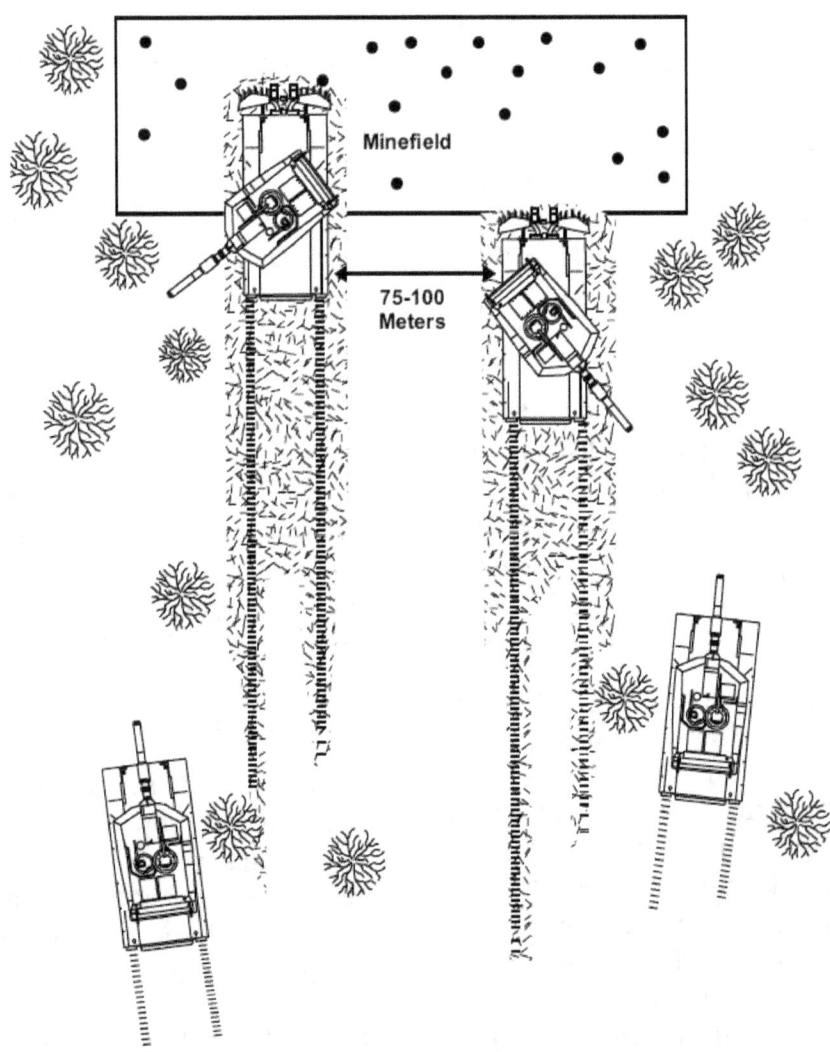

**Figure E-1. Plow Tanks Create Multiple Lanes
While the Section Leaders' Tanks Provide Overwatch.**

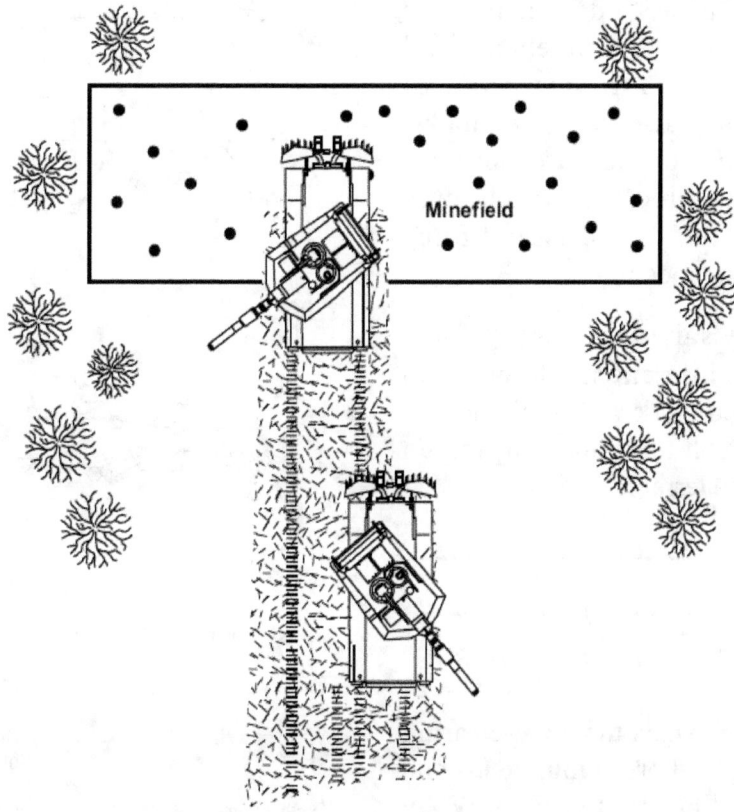

Minefield

**Figure E-2. Plow Tanks use Staggered
Movement to Create a Wider Lane.**

*Note: The lanes created on the left side
would not be doubled proofed, and spoil
from the second tank through would be put
into the first tank's right lane.*

After a lane is created and proofed, it is normally turned over to attached engineers for marking. The platoon leader reports the location of the lane and the method of marking to higher headquarters in order to expedite the movement of the assault force. If no engineers are available, an attempt should be made to at least mark the entrance and exit of the breach using NATO marking procedures. Unit SOPs will dictate marking methods and materials, which commonly include engineer stakes with tape, guides, and chemical lights.

Throughout the operation, the platoon leader provides continuous updates of the breach force's progress to higher headquarters and other ele-

ments involved in the breach. He also coordinates with the support force for suppressive fires.

The assault force will often move behind the breach force and closely follow the breach vehicles through the new lane.

Assault Force

The mission of the assault force is to destroy or dislodge the enemy on the far side of the obstacle, or in between obstacle belts, in order to allow other combat forces to continue the attack. While the breach is in progress, the assault force assists the support force or follows the breach force while maintaining cover and dispersion. Once a lane is cleared through the obstacle, the assault force moves through the breach. It secures the far side of the obstacle by physical occupation and/or continues the attack in accordance with the scheme of maneuver. The assault force must be of sufficient size to eliminate the enemy and should be a combined-arms force consisting of elements such as infantry, LAVs, AAVs, tanks, and engineers. Fire control measures must be coordinated so support force and breach force fires are lifted and shifted as the assault force maneuvers into the enemy position.

Tank units are ideally suited for assault force operations against mobile enemy defenses in open terrain. Tanks also work well with mechanized infantry as an assault force attacking dug-in enemy positions in close terrain.

Mobility Assets

Mine Plow

The mine plow, also known as the mine-clearing blade, is used to breach and proof minefields and affords good survivability (see fig. E-3). When fully operational, a tank equipped with a mine plow can quickly clear two, 58-inch wide lanes, one in front of each track.

> *Note: The plow's dogbone assembly will detonate the tilt rods of mines in the area between the two plowed lanes; however, only plows equipped with the improved dogbone assembly (IDA) will defeat magnetically activated mines.*

The plow must be dropped at least 100 meters before the tank reaches the minefield, and it is not lifted until the tank is at least 100 meters past the far edge of the minefield. The plow must have 18 inches of spoil to be effective, which limits the tank's speed to 10 miles per hour or less in the lane. The mine plow should be used only in a straight line; it does not work well on hard, rocky, or uneven ground where it cannot maintain adequate spoil. Mine detonation can cause violent upward movement of the blade; therefore, the crew traverses the tank's main gun to the side during plowing to prevent damage to the gun tube. The crew must also ensure the plow's lifting straps don't become entangled in wire obstacles.

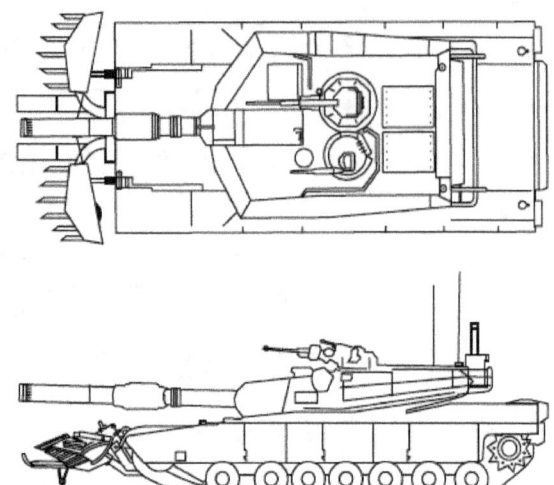

Weight:	3 tons
Speed when mounted and lowered:	<10 kph
Primary use:	Clearing path through minefield
Width of path:	Creates 58-in cleared path in front of each track
Depth of path:	Lifts and pushes surface-laid mines or buried mines up to 4 in deep in front of its path.

Figure E-3. Track Width Mine Plow for M1A1.

Mine Roller

The mine roller is used to identify the forward edges of a minefield and to proof lanes. The roller sweeps a 44-inch path in front of each track and is also equipped with a dogbone assembly. It is also effective at breaching wire obstacles. The roller, however, is not effective on broken or uneven ground. The mine roller, like the mine plow, will not defeat magnetically fuzed mines unless equipped with the IDA. The main gun must be traversed to the side or rear when contact with a mine is possible or imminent; detonation can throw the roller (or pieces of it) violently upward, possibly damaging the 120mm main gun. The mine roller can usually withstand two mine explosions before needing repairs or replacement.

AVLB

The AVLB is primarily employed to cross short gaps (such as narrow streams), antitank ditches, craters, canals, or partially blown bridges. Its span is 18 meters (60 feet) using prepared abutments and 17 meters with unprepared abutments. The capacity of the bridge is one MLC 60 vehicle (this is waived for M1-series tanks during combat operations). The AVLB launcher, which requires 10 meters of overhead clearance for transportation and operation, is most visible and vulnerable during launching of the bridge. An experienced crew can launch the bridge in 2 to 5 minutes. Technical characteristics of the AVLB are provided in appendix A.

MICLIC

Used to breach wire and mine obstacles, the MICLIC clears a lane 100 meters deep and 14 meters wide.

Note: The MICLIC must be fired 62 meters from the obstacle to get the full 100 meters of depth.

The charge may create two skip zones, where the mines are not detonated, on the right and left side of the centerline of the cleared lane. The skip zones, which are about 1.5 meters wide, require all MICLIC lanes to be proofed. The MICLIC is effective against pressure-activated antitank mines and against mechanically activated antipersonnel mines. Effectiveness is limited against magnetically activated mines, including scatterable mines and those with multi-impulse (double-impact) or time-delay fuzes. The MICLIC is not effective on severely broken ground where the line charge cannot lay flat. When detonated, the MICLIC has a danger area with a radius of 1,600 meters.

Armored Combat Earthmover

The armored combat earthmover uses its blade to defeat berms and antitank ditches. It can also skim a minefield with its blade; however, it is slow and vulnerable in this role and should be employed this way only as a last resort. Its one-man crew further limits the vehicle's capability.

Engineer Attachment

The engineer attachment is the most versatile of all breaching assets. It can be used to conduct explosive or manual breaches and proofs and to mark lanes through an obstacle. However, while it is conducting these breaching and proofing operations, the attachment is extremely vulnerable to enemy direct and indirect fires.

If other breaching assets are unavailable, an infantry or tank platoon can conduct explosive breaches (with hand-emplaced charges) and/or use manual breaching kits (normally consisting of grappling hooks, gloves, and wire cutters). At the same time, however, employment of either type of platoon organization in breaching operations has distinct disadvantages. The pace of the breach will be slow, and the operation will leave the platoon vulnerable to enemy attack.

APPENDIX F
GLOSSARY

Section I. Acronyms

AAV . . . . amphibious assault vehicle

AAVC7 . . . . assault amphibian
vehicle command model 7

AAVP7 . . . . assault amphibian
vehicle personnel model 7

APFSDS . . . . armor-piercing,
fin-stabilized, discarding sabot

APFSDS-T . . . . . . armor-piercing, fin-stabilized,
discarding sabot-tracer

ATGM . . . . antitank guided missile

AVLB . . . . .armored vehicle-launched bridge

BHL . . . . battle handover line

C2 . . . . .command and control

cal . . . . .caliber

CAS .close air support

cm . . . . .centimeter

CO . . . . .company

COA . . . . course of action

COC . . . . combat operations center

CSS . . . . combat service support

CSSE . . . . .combat service support element

CSSG . . . . combat service support group

DLIC . . . . detachment left in contact

EA . . . . .engagement area

EPW . . . . enemy prisoner of war

°F . . . . .degree Fahrenheit

FAC . . . . forward air controller

FEBA . . . . .forward edge of the battle area

FM . . . . field manual

FPF . . . . final protective fires

FRH . . . . fire resistant hydraulic

FSC . . . . fire support coordinator

FSCC . . . . fire support coordination center

ft . . . . feet

gal . . . . gallon(s)

GCE . . . . ground combat element

GPM . . . . gallons per minute

HEAT . . . . high explosive antitank

HEAT-MP-T . . . . .high explosive antitank,
multipurpose-tracer

HMMWV . . . . high mobility multipurpose
wheeled vehicle

hp . . . . .horsepower

HQ . . . . .headquarters

hr . . . . hour

H&S CO . . . . headquarters and service company

IDA . . . . improved dogbone assembly

IED . . . . improvised explosive device

in . . . . .inch

JP . . . . .joint publication

kg . . . . .kilogram

km . . . . kilometer

kph . . . . kilometers per hour

LAV . . . . light armored vehicle

lb . . . . pound

LCAC . . . . .landing craft air cushion

LCU . . . . landing craft, utility

LOGPAC . . . . logistics package

LRP . . . . logistic resupply point

LRU . . . . line replaceable unit

m . . . . meter

MAGTF . . . . Marine air-ground task force

MCRP . . . . . .Marine Corps reference publication

MCWP . . . . Marine Corps
warfighting publication

MEF . . . . Marine expeditionary force

METT-T . . . . mission, enemy, terrain and
weather, troops and support
available—time available

mi . . . . .miles

MICLIC . . . . .mine-clearing line charge

min . . . . minute

MLC . . . . .military load classification
mm . . . . .millimeter
MMO . . . . maintenance management officer
MOOTW. . . . . military operations other than war
MOPP . . . . . .mission-oriented protective posture
MOUT. . . . . . military operations in urban terrain
MPAT . . . . .multipurpose antitank
mph . . . . miles per hour
m/s. .meters per second
MTO . . . . motor transport officer

NATO . . . . .North Atlantic Treaty Organization
NBC . . . . .nuclear, biological, and chemical

OP . . . . .observation post
OPORD .operation order

pct . . . . percent
PlSgt . . . . .platoon sergeant
plt . . . . platoon
POL . . . . .petroleum, oils, and lubricants
psi . . . . .pounds per square inch
pt . . . . .pint

qt . . . . quart

RECON. . . . . reconnaissance
ROE . . . . .rules of engagement
RSTA . . . . .reconnaissance, surveillance,
and target acquisition

S1 . . . . personnel staff officer (adjutant)
S1A . . . . personnel staff officer
(adjutant) assistant
S2 . . . . .intelligence staff officer
S2A . . . . .intelligence staff officer assistant
S3 . . . . .operations staff officer
S3A . . . . .operations staff officer assistant
S4 . . . . logistics staff officer
S4 . . . . logistics staff officer assistant
S6 . . . . communications staff officer
SAW . . . . .surface-to-air weapon
sct . . . . .scout
Sgt. . . . . sergeant
SINCGARS. . . . . single-channel ground
and airborne radio system
SOP. . . . . .standing operating procedure

TM . . . . technical manual
TMO . . . . tank maintenance officer
TNT. .trinitrotoluene
T/O . . . . table of organization
TOW . . . . .tube-launched, optically tracked,
wire-command link
guided missile
TRAP . . . . .tactical recovery of
aircraft and personnel
TRP . . . . target reference point

UMCP. unit maintenance
collection point

Section II. Definitions

armor—Steel, iron, or other materials used as a protective covering on tanks.

avenue of approach—An air or ground route of an attacking force of a given size leading to its objective or to key terrain in its path. (JP 1-02)

axis of advance—A line of advance assigned for purposes of control; often a road or a group of roads, or a designated series of locations, extending in the direction of the enemy. (JP 1-02)

basic load (ammunition) —That quantity of ammunition authorized to be on hand in a unit to meet combat needs until resupply can be accomplished. Size of the basic load is normally determined by corps or the major overseas commander.

battle position—1. In ground operations, a defensive location oriented on an enemy avenue of approach from which a unit may defend. 2. In air operations, an airspace coordination area containing firing points for attack helicopters. Also called **BP**. (MCRP 5-12C)

Beehive—A term associated with antipersonnel projectiles, loaded with flechettes.

bounding overwatch—A tactical movement technique used when contact with enemy ground forces is expected. The unit moves by bounds. One element is in position to overwatch the other element's move. The overwatching element is always positioned to support the moving unit by fire or fire and maneuver. This is the slowest but most secure movement technique. (MCRP 5-12A)

caliber—1. The diameter of the bore of a gun. In rifled gun barrels, the caliber is obtained by measuring between opposite lands. 2. The diameter of a projectile. Also called **cal**.

cartridge case—A container that holds the primer, propellant, and projectile.

coax machine gun—A machine gun mounted in the turret of a tank in a way that its line of fire is parallel (coaxial) to that of the cannon set on the same mounting.

command post—A unit's or subunit's headquarters where the commander and the staff perform their activities. In combat, a unit's or subunit's headquarters is often divided into echelons; the echelon in which the unit or subunit commander is located or from which such commander operates is called a command post. Also called **CP**. (JP 1-02)

company team—A combined arms organization formed by attaching one or more nonorganic tank, mechanized infantry, or light infantry platoons to a tank, mechanized infantry, or light infantry company either in exchange for or in addition to organic platoons. (MCRP 5-12A)

concealment—The protection from observation or surveillance. (JP 1-02, part 4 of a 6 part definition)

cover—Shelter or protection, either natural or artificial. (JP 1-02, part 4 of a 6 part definition)

covering force—1. A force operating apart from the main force for the purpose of intercepting, engaging, delaying, disorganizing, and deceiving the enemy before the enemy can attack the force covered. 2. Any body or detachment of troops which provides security for a larger force by observation, reconnaissance, attack, or defense, or by any combination of these methods. (JP 1-02)

dead space—1. An area within the maximum range of a weapon, radar, or observer, which cannot be covered by fire or observation from a particular position because of intervening obstacles, the nature of the ground, or the characteristics of the trajectory, or the limitations of the pointing capabilities of the weapon. 2. An area or zone which is within range of a radio transmitter, but in which a signal is not received. 3. The volume of space above and around a gun or guided missile system into which it cannot fire because of mechanical or electronic limitations. (JP 1-02)

defilade—Protection from hostile observation and fire provided by an obstacle such as a hill, ridge, or bank. (JP 1-02, part 1 of a 3 part definition)

direct fire—Gunfire delivered on a target using the target itself as a point of aim for either the weapon or the director. (JP 1-02)

dummy ammunition—Ammunition that is used for practicing gunnery-related tasks; it has no propellant or explosive charge.

elevation—The degree above the horizon to which a gun is aimed. Also called **EL**.

fire control system—A group of interrelated fire control equipments and/or instruments designed for use with a weapon or group of weapons. (JP 1-02)

fire support—In Marine Corps usage, assistance to elements of the Marine air-ground task force engaged with the enemy rendered by other firing units, including (but not limited to) artillery, mortars, naval surface fire support, and offensive air support. (MCRP 5-12C)

fuze—A device that initiates an explosive train. (MCRP 5-12A)

hide—The positioning of a vehicle, individual, or unit so that no part is exposed to observation or direct fire. (MCRP 5-12A)

hull down—The positioning of an armored vehicle so that the muzzle of the gun or launcher is the lowest part of the vehicle exposed to the front. Hull-down positions afford maximum protection for vehicles that are engaging targets with direct fire. (MCRP 5-12A)

identification—The process of determining the friendly or hostile character of an unknown detected contact. (JP 1-02, part 1 of a 3 part definition)

incendiary—A compound that generates sufficient heat to cause the target to catch fire or causes melting or burning of equipment. (MCRP 5-12A)

indirect fire—Fire delivered on a target that is not itself used as a point of aim for the weapons or the director. (JP 1-02)

kinetic energy ammunition—The primary armor-defeating round for the 120-mm main gun and the most accurate of all tank ammunition. Kinetic energy is a combination of mass (weight) and velocity (speed) of the projectile; no explosives are needed to penetrate the target.

laser—Any device that can produce or amplify optical radiation primarily by the process of controlled stimulated emission. A laser may emit electromagnetic radiation from the ultraviolet portion of the spectrum through the infrared portion. Also, an acronym for "light amplification by stimulated emission of radiation." (JP 1-02)

laser rangefinder—A device which uses laser energy for determining the distance from the device to a place or object. Also called **LRF**. (JP 1-02)

line of contact—A general trace delineating the location where two opposing forces are engaged. (MCRP 5-12C)

line of departure—1. In land warfare, a line designated to coordinate the departure of attack elements. 2. In amphibious warfare, a suitably marked offshore coordinating line to assist assault craft to land on designated beaches at scheduled times. (JP 1-02)

line of sight—The unobstructed path from a [Marine], weapon, weapon sight, electronic-sending and -receiving antennas, or piece of reconnaissance equipment to another point. Also called **LOS**. (MCRP 5-12A)

lot number—An identification number assigned to a particular quantity or lot of materiel, such as ammunition, from a single manufacturer.

muzzle velocity—The velocity of a projectile with respect to the muzzle at the instant the projectile leaves the weapon.

obscuration—The effects of weather, battlefield dust, and debris, or the use of smoke munitions to hamper observation and target-acquisition capability or to conceal activities or movement. (MCRP 5-12A)

obstacle—Any obstruction designed or employed to disrupt, fix, turn, or block the movement of an opposing force, and to impose additional losses in personnel, time, and equipment on the opposing force. Obstacles can be natural, manmade, or a combination of both. (JP 1-02)

phase line—A line utilized for control and coordination of military operations, usually an easily identified feature in the operational area. (JP 1-02) A line utilized for control and coordination of military operations, usually an easily identified feature in the operational area. (NATO) A line utilized for control and coordination of military operations, usually a terrain feature extending across the zone of action. Also called **PL**. (MCRP 5-12A)

point target—A target of such a small dimension that it requires the accurate placement of ordnance in order to neutralize or destroy it.

primer—The cap in the base of the cartridge case that ignites the propellant charge. It may be actuated by friction, blow, pressure, or electricity.

projectile—That part of the round that travels through the gun tube.

propellant—An explosive charge for propelling a projectile.

pyrotechnic—A mixture of chemicals which, when ignited, is capable of reacting exothermically to produce light, heat, smoke, sound, or gas and may also be used to introduce a delay into an explosive train because of its known burning time. The term excludes propellants and explosives. (MCRP 5-12A)

reconnaissance—A mission undertaken to obtain, by visual observation or other detection methods, information about the activities and resources of an enemy or potential enemy, or to secure data concerning the meteorological, hydrographic, or geographic characteristics of a particular area. Also called **RECON**. (JP 1-02)

reconnaissance by fire—A method of reconnaissance in which fire is placed on a suspected enemy position to cause the enemy to disclose a presence by movement or return of fire. (JP 1-02)

sabot—A lightweight carrier in which a subcaliber projectile is centered to permit firing the projectile in the larger caliber weapon. The carrier fills the bore of the weapon from which the projectile is fired; it is normally discarded a short distance from the muzzle.

shaped charge—An explosive charge shaped so the explosive energy is focused and concentrated to move in one direction.

shock effect—The combined destructive (physical and psychological) effect on the enemy produced by the violent impact of mounted and mobile armor protected firepower of tanks and supporting troops.

signature—The visible or audible effects, such as noise, smoke, flame, heat, or debris, produced when a weapon is fired or a piece of equipment operated; also, an electronic emission subject to detection and traceable to the equipment producing it. Also called **footprint.**

situation report—A report giving the situation in the area of a reporting unit or formation. Also called **SITREP.** (JP 1-02)

spall—Fragments torn from either the outer or inner surface of armor plate as the result of a complete or partial penetration of the armor, or by dynamic effects of an explosive charge.

spot report—A concise narrative report of essential information covering events or conditions that may have an immediate and significant effect on current planning and operations that is afforded the most expeditious means of transmission consistent with requisite security. Also called **SPOTREP.** (Note: In reconnaissance and surveillance usage, spot report is not to be used.) (JP 1-02).

suppressive fire—Fires on or about a weapons system to degrade its performance below the level needed to fulfill its mission objectives, during the conduct of the fire mission. (JP 1-02)

target acquisition—The detection, identification, and location of a target in sufficient detail to permit the effective employment of weapons. Also called **TA.** (JP 1-02)

target location—The determination of where a potential target is on the battlefield.

target reference point—An easily recognizable point on the ground (either natural or man-made) used to initiate, distribute, and control fires. Target reference points (TRPs) can also designate the center of an area where the commander plans to distribute or converge the fires of all his weapons rapidly. They are used by task force and below, and can further delineate sectors of fire within an engagement area. TRPs are designated using the standard target symbol and numbers issued by the fire support officer. Once designated, TRPs also constitute indirect fire targets. Also called **TRP.** (MCRP 5-12A)

thermal imaging system—The system that provides the Abrams fire control system with night-vision capability by presenting a thermal scene in the gunner's primary sight. It operates on emitted thermal radiation rather than visible light. Also called **TIS.**

tracer—A powder element inserted in the base of some projectiles that, when ignited, burns and allows the projectile to be observed during flight.

trajectory—The flight path of a projectile from the point of fire to impact.

white phosphorus—A yellow, waxy chemical that ignites spontaneously when exposed to air; used as a filling for various projectiles; a smoke-producing agent with an incendiary effect. Also called **WP.**

wingman—One of two tanks in a section, normally the other tank in the platoon leader's or platoon sergeant's section.

APPENDIX G
REFERENCES

Marine Corps Warfighting Publications (MCWPs)

1-0	Marine Corps Operations
3-17.1	River-Crossing Opeations
3-17.3	MAGTF Breaching Operations (currently FMFM 13-7)
3-25.2	Mountain Operations (currently FMFM 7-29)
3-33.3	Marine Corps Public Affairs
3-35.1	Cold Weather Operations (under development)
3-35.5	Jungle Operations (currently FMFM 7-28)
3-35.6	Desert Operations (currently FMFM 7-27)
3-37.1	Multiservice Tactics, Techniques, and Procedures for Nuclear, Biological, and Chemical Defense Operations
3-37.1A	Nuclear, Biological, Chemical (NBC) Vulnerability Analysis
3-37.2	Multiservice Tactics, Techniques, and Procedures for Nuclear, Biological, and Chemical (NBC) Protection
3-37.3	NBC Decontamination

Marine Corps Reference Publications (MCRPs)

3-02D	Combating Terrorism
3-02E	The Individual's Guide for Understanding and Surviving Terrorism
4-11.3F	Convoy Operations Handbook
5-12A	Operational Terms and Graphics

Army Technical Manual (TM)

08953A-10	Tank M1A1 (120mm Gun)

Army Field Manual (FM)

4-30.3	Maintenance Operations and Procedures

www.ingramcontent.com/pod-product-compliance
Lightning Source LLC
Chambersburg PA
CBHW081102290526
45795CB00006B/1957